DUNCAN
EDWARDS

DUNCAN EDWARDS

The Greatest

JAMES LEIGHTON

**SIMON &
SCHUSTER**

London · New York · Sydney · Toronto · New Delhi

A CBS COMPANY

First published in Great Britain by Simon & Schuster UK Ltd, 2012
A CBS COMPANY

The right of James Leighton
to be identified as author of this work has been asserted
by him in accordance with sections 77 and 78 of the
Copyright, Designs and Patents Act, 1988.

3 5 7 9 10 8 6 4 2

Simon & Schuster UK Ltd
1st Floor
222 Gray's Inn Road
London
WC1X 8HB

www.simonandschuster.co.uk

Simon & Schuster Australia, Sydney
Simon & Schuster India, New Delhi

Every reasonable effort has been made to contact copyright holders
of material reproduced in this book. If any have inadvertently been
overlooked, the publishers would be glad to hear from them and make
good in future editions any errors or omissions brought to their attention.

A CIP catalogue record for this book is available
from the British Library

Hardback ISBN 978-0-85720-781-4

Typeset by M Rules
Printed and bound by CPI Group (UK) Ltd, Croydon, CR0 4YY

For Mum and Dad, thanks for everything

CONTENTS

'It was in the character and spirit of Duncan Edwards that I saw the true revival of British football'

Walter Winterbottom – England manager

INTRODUCTION

From as far back as I can remember, football has always been a major part of my life. In my house I didn't have much choice. My father, the beautiful game's most ardent advocate, didn't start bedtime stories with 'Once upon a time'. Instead, they usually began with: 'Did you know Denis Law once scored six goals in a cup tie against Luton in 1961 and the game was then abandoned because of rain?' Some seven-year-olds may have found such trivia tedious, but I hung on his every word.

For hours at a time, I would be transfixed as he filled my eager young mind with tales of how a 17-year-old Pelé juggled the ball over an opponent's bemused head and scored in the 1958 World Cup final, or how George Best once beat his marker merely by taking his boot off. It's fair to say that he was, and is, a football fanatic and that fanaticism has rubbed off on me.

Along with my brother, godfather and cousin, we have both traipsed up and down the country watching games at all levels in our quest to capture a memory that will last a lifetime, a moment of unparalleled genius that is so great that it would have us looking at each other in wonder, with the unspoken question being: did that really just happen? On our travels we have been fortunate to have witnessed some of the game's greatest players in action, as well as some of the worst; but still, we were there. We had seen players do things that we could only dream of.

Together, we were at a blistering hot White Hart Lane, on 8 September 1990, when Paul Gascoigne, buoyed by his success at the World Cup that summer, sensationally scored his first and only hat-trick in English football. Throughout the 1990s we were privileged to see the enigmatic talents of Cantona, Beckham, Giggs, Ginola, Klinsmann, Bergkamp, Rivaldo and Figo conjure up moments that will forever be ingrained in our memories. In recent years, we have been treated to the sight of Henry, Ronaldinho, Ronaldo and Messi in full flight, and we were even at the 2006 FA Cup final where we witnessed Steven Gerrard deliver a complete performance, as well as two sensational goals, to win the FA Cup for Liverpool in true 'Roy of the Rovers' style.

On the way back from these football pilgrimages, we would some-times be so moved by the brilliant display that we had just witnessed that our conversation would turn to that age-old question: who was the greatest footballer of all time? Though I could never make up my mind, with my suggestions ranging from Pelé to Zidane, my godfather Barry would always give the same answer: Duncan Edwards. Usually we would scoff at this, but he was adamant: in his eyes Edwards was, and always will be, the greatest.

During the 1950s, my godfather had travelled by train, bus and foot to watch all of the top players of that era in action. Come rain or shine, every Saturday he would be at a match, crammed into a stand, twirling a rattle, with a rosette on his chest, intent on getting his football fix. The 1950s was a decade that produced some of English football's most-lauded players, and as such he was fortunate to watch the likes of Sir Stanley Matthews, Billy Wright, Sir Tom Finney and John Charles when they were at their peak. But it was Duncan Edwards of Manchester United who really caught his attention.

Big, strong, quick and fit, my godfather claimed that Manchester United's number six also had supreme ball control and skill, could spray passes to all corners of the field with both feet, was a tank in the tackle, was comfortable in any position and had the heart of a lion. Apparently, there was nothing that was beyond him.

As one of the famous Busby Babes, he was also an integral part of a team that won two league titles, played in an FA Cup final and twice reached the semi-final stages of the European Cup. He also held the record for being England's youngest post-war international and this led my godfather on to the next part of his argument: but for the Munich disaster, he was certain that Edwards, and not Bobby Moore, would have captained England to World Cup glory in 1966.

We all agreed that no doubt Duncan Edwards had been a good player, but he had played only four full seasons of professional football, hardly enough for him to warrant being called the greatest player of all time. And, even if his feats were that great, the game was different then, it was slower, less technical, less demanding. No doubt he would struggle in today's fast-paced game. Most damning of all, sometimes we claimed that the memory of those who had seen Edwards play might have become clouded by sentiment due to his tragic demise.

Ignoring our protests, my godfather always stuck to his guns and in response he would throw back a quote from Sir Bobby Charlton: 'Who is the greatest footballer ever? The best I played with? Or played against? It's the same answer, Duncan Edwards. And remember, I played with Moore, Best and Law. And I played against Pelé.' In the face of such an opinion, who were we to argue?

As the years went by, and I heard more legends from the game heap praise on Duncan Edwards, I began to wonder if my godfather might not have a point. Trying to understand this mysterious legend, I watched the few flickering black-and-white images of him in action on You Tube and read some magazine articles and books on the Busby Babes. Yet nothing I read or saw truly answered my question: was Duncan Edwards really as good as people say he was?

In an attempt to get to the bottom of Edwards' 'greatness', I decided that there was only one resource available to me that could tell his story untainted by sentiment: the newspaper reports that were written when he was still in action. Reading through hundreds of these reports was certainly an eye-opener.

Sports commentators from Edwards' time were gushing with praise after almost every game that he played. Reporters used words such as 'majestic', 'phenomenon', 'awe inspiring', 'Trojan' and 'titan' to try to describe the peerless performances of United's thoroughbred. In the end, no superlative seemed to do him justice. His feats were apparently equally heroic in defence and attack, and it is easy to see why he was so revered. While Manchester United fans were treated to the sight of their young star dominating Europe, England fans revelled in seeing him destroy Brazil and the world champions, West Germany. Gradually, I began to realise that the hype surrounding him was not unwarranted. Desperate to find out more, I set out to write a book on a life that had so much potential but was so cruelly cut short.

In my quest to get to the bottom of the legend of Duncan Edwards, I have had the honour of interviewing his team-mates from both Manchester United and England, all of whom were happy to discuss their friend in intimate detail. I've also been invited into the homes of some of Edwards' best friends away from football, so that I could understand just what sort of man he was off the pitch. Their memories and anecdotes have really helped to propel Edwards out of the staid black-and-white pictures I have seen of him and into the kind, gentle and generous man he was said to be.

Yet, during my research something else also struck me. While I had always felt that players from the 1950s would struggle in the modern game, I soon realised that in fact it would probably be the other way around. How would the likes of today's pampered, richly rewarded superstars react to two years of National Service in the middle of their careers? Would they be happy to play for just a few pounds a week? Would they look as quick and skilful after playing more than 90 matches in one season, on poor pitches, with a heavy ball and ankle-high boots? Indeed, it almost seems impossible to imagine the likes of

Cristiano Ronaldo cycling to Old Trafford on his push-bike rather than driving there in a Ferrari. But, as you will see, Duncan Edwards did all this and more.

It is my hope that at the very least this book will allow those who, like myself, never got to see Duncan Edwards play to be able finally to appreciate his incredible contribution to the game. And maybe it will even help to persuade some that Duncan Edwards was, in fact, the greatest player this world has ever seen.

PROLOGUE

'They think it's all over, it is now,' yelled an excited Kenneth Wolstenholme, as Swiss referee Gottfried Dienst put his lips to his whistle to signal the end of the 1966 World Cup final. England's exhausted and emotional captain sank to his knees on the lush Wembley turf, and put his head into his hands. He was finally a world champion.

Having defeated England's rivals West Germany in a fiercely contested game, he had delivered yet another memorable performance. As the match seemed set to go into extra-time, Bobby Charlton had galloped down the right wing before lofting a cross towards the penalty spot. Tightly marked by two defenders, the skipper muscled them both out of the way before rising powerfully to meet the ball with his forehead, straining every muscle in his neck as he did so. In a flash the ball cannoned off his head, crashed off the underside of the crossbar and into the goal. Wembley shook as pandemonium broke out in the stands. England's captain wheeled away in delight, mobbed by his delirious team-mates.

With the game at an end, Charlton, unable to contain his joy, raced towards his friend and the two embraced, their red shirts drenched in sweat and their faces lit up by smiles. Over a decade earlier the two men, both from working-class backgrounds, had started out as youth team players at Manchester United, when their only ambition had been to play in the first team. Now they stood in the middle of their national stadium, with close to 100,000 people chanting their names, and millions of viewers watching worldwide.

Charlton ruffled his hands affectionately through his captain's tousled hair and pointed him towards his proud parents, Annie and Gladstone, who were jumping up and down in the stands cheering on their son's courageous efforts. Next to them stood his friend's beaming wife, Molly, who was bouncing their five-year-old son in her arms. He waved to them and then pumped his fists triumphantly in the air. He was now where he belonged, on top of the world.

It had been a long, hard road to reach this point and he was determined to cherish every moment of his sensational triumph. In previous tournaments World Cup glory had cruelly evaded him, especially in Sweden in 1958 where England entered the competition as one of the hot favourites. Unfortunately, the lads in white shirts with the three lions emblazoned on their chests had fallen at the hands of a 17-year-old Brazilian genius by the name of Pelé.

Positioned at left-half in the final against Brazil, he had been left mesmerised; Pelé was the best player he had ever come across. His skill and technique were on a different level to anything he had witnessed in the English game, and he vowed to keep a close eye on the Brazilian so as to learn as much as he could from him.

Chile in 1962 had been a different matter altogether. On this occasion, the Brazilians spent most of the competition without their injured talisman Pelé, but a winger by the name of Garrincha took on his mantle and enjoyed an outstanding tournament. Garrincha's bandy legs lit up proceedings with lightning dribbles, tricks and flicks and impossible goals rattled in from all angles. Many felt that he could even be a rival to Pelé as the world's best footballer.

However, England's future captain, who now played in the centre of the England midfield, from where he dictated the play with his incredible range of passing, had also been in scintillating form.

Europe's finest was also now a serious contender to be considered the best player on the planet. When England and Brazil consequently clashed, in the World Cup quarter-final, excitement reverberated around the globe at the prospect of the two men coming face to face. The invigorated England star swore that he would not let this opportunity pass him by.

Come game time, the man from the streets of Dudley gave his opponent from the beaches of Brazil a torrid time. The sight of the barrel-chested Englishman teaching a Brazilian new tricks was something to behold. Garrincha couldn't get near him. The demoralised Brazilian later confided to his team-mates that he had never before come across a player who was so big yet equally quick and skilful.

Having humbled Garrincha, he had firmly established himself as the game's brightest star. Johnny Haynes and Bobby Charlton had also excelled and hope was high that, with such an abundance of talent in their ranks, England would finally be returning home as world champions. Yet in the semi-finals England came up against hosts Chile, and the South Americans, roared on by a vociferous and partisan crowd, created a sensational upset when they dumped the favourites out of the competition. After the game, he dejectedly wondered if he would ever get his hands on the prize he craved more than any other, the Jules Rimet trophy.

International honours may have remained elusive, but he found winning trophies a much easier matter with his famous Manchester United team, who swept all before them at home and in Europe. Matt Busby's confidence in his 'Babes' saw him handsomely rewarded as his team won six league titles. The unstoppable Babes also became the first British team to win the European Cup, when in 1958 they defeated Alfredo di Stefano's Real Madrid in a fascinating encounter. British football's most exciting player had been on the scoresheet that day and his performance was enough to warrant him being crowned the European Footballer of the Year at just 21 years of age.

Since that feat, United had contested another three European Cup finals and had won the trophy on two more occasions. Consequently, the Busby Babes were the toast of Europe. Their clashes with arch-rivals Real Madrid were always eagerly anticipated affairs as they guaranteed the awe-inspiring spectacle of the game's finest players going head to head. Perhaps his most cherished European Cup victory came in 1960, when United again met Real Madrid in the final, at Glasgow's Hampden Park. This high-octane tussle between the two giants of European football saw United eventually win the Cup for the second time. Most importantly, however, it saw them win it in Scotland, the birth country of his mentor, Matt Busby.

Despite such unrivalled success, Busby refused to rest on his laurels and he continued to strengthen his team with the signing of Scottish striking sensation Denis Law from the Italian side Torino. Law imme-diately fitted in alongside his team-mates and made Manchester United appear invincible. Busby, however, wasn't yet finished. In 1963 he delivered his *coup de grâce* when he gave a young Northern Irishman by the name of George Best his debut in the first team. Best's genius added yet another dimension to United and they now looked set to rule at home, and in Europe, for at least another ten years.

With newcomers Law and Best, plus Nobby Stiles, in tandem alongside those who had already cemented their legendary reputations as stars during the 1950s, United were a sensation. When the trail-blazing Red Devils bandwagon rolled into town, crowds flocked to marvel at the superstars in action. Many proclaimed them to be the best team in the history of English football.

It was certainly a golden age for the English game, and despite United's dominance both Liverpool and West Ham were also pro-ducing young players of startling quality. One such player was Bobby Moore, who slotted in alongside his national team captain at the heart of England's defence for the opening stages of the 1966 World Cup.

However, their partnership proved to be shortlived. When England's star striker, Jimmy Greaves, was injured in the early rounds against France, many clamoured for Moore's team-mate, Geoff Hurst, to replace the Spurs player in attack. Alf Ramsey had other plans. Instead, he decided to place Jack Charlton alongside Moore in defence, and he then moved his captain up in attack along with Liverpool's Roger Hunt. This move electrified the England team, with Moore and Charlton looking composed and assured at the back, and the new strike partnership terrorising defences at the other end of the field.

No finer example of this could be seen than when England faced Eusebio's much-fancied Portugal in the semi-finals. Eusebio had been heralded as the heir to the England captain's throne, but he hardly got a kick as Moore came of age with a monumental display. England's forward line also frightened the Portuguese defence with their power and movement, and this created space for Bobby Charlton to capitalise, as he scored a screamer to ease England into the World Cup final.

After near misses in Sweden and Chile, it was definitely a case of third time lucky for the England team as their victory over West Germany finally saw them capture their holy grail, the World Cup. The proud captain had dreamed of this moment for years and he couldn't wait finally to get his hands on the glistening Jules Rimet trophy. After his sturdy frame had clambered up the famous 39 Wembley steps, and he had received the greatest prize in football from Her Majesty the Queen, he paused for a moment to take in the tremendous scenes surrounding him. There was not a cloud in the sky. Everywhere he looked people were smiling joyously, waving Union Jack flags high and chanting his name. This was it. The moment he had worked so hard for. Savouring the feeling, he brought the small golden trophy to his lips, kissed it, and then lifted it above his head. The ground roared their approval. England were world champions. Duncan Edwards' destiny had been fulfilled and now, without a shadow of a doubt, he was the greatest.

If only it were all true . . .

1

A HUMBLE START

Right from the start, Duncan Edwards was renowned for his prodigious size. When, on 1 October 1936, his mother Sarah Ann (universally known as Annie) gave birth to him, he weighed a hefty 9lb 8oz. Even by today's standards that is big, but in the 1930s it was considered monstrous. His hearty weight was in fact a godsend, as this was an age when small and weak babies frequently died from illnesses such as pneumonia, tuberculosis and typhoid fever.

Edwards was brought into a world facing uncertain times. In Germany, Nazi leader Adolf Hitler had risen to power, and his regime was taking an aggressive stance towards neighbouring countries, while all the time rebuilding their armed forces. That year's Olympic Games, held in Berlin, had been used as a massive propaganda exercise, and many were worried that this was just a small taste of things to come.

Things weren't much better in the UK. In an act that sparked a constitutional crisis, King Edward VIII abdicated the throne on 11 December 1936 in order to marry American socialite and divorcée Wallis Simpson. While King George VI eventually succeeded his brother, ordinary Britons had more pressing concerns on their mind than the fate of the monarchy.

Throughout the 1930s, the UK had been recovering from the shocks of the 1929–32 Great Depression, which had been triggered by the Wall Street Crash in New York. The UK government, like those in many other European countries, was still struggling with the massive debts they had incurred during the First World War and therefore events in New York served to intensify the financial crisis. With the world's economy grinding to a halt, demand for the UK's major industrial exports (such as coal, steel and textiles) fell rapidly. Unemployment rates subsequently shot up, and even as the economy gradually improved, the numbers without work remained very high. Inevitably, because benefits were so low, this led to widespread poverty and misery, particularly in those areas that relied on traditional industries. Sometimes whole communities could face unemployment when their local mine or factory was forced to close.

Dudley, the industrial West Midlands town where Edwards was born, had once been renowned for its thriving coal and iron industry, but it had also been hit hard by the deep depression. Although conditions had improved since 1841, when Charles Dickens wrote in his novel *The Old Curiosity Shop* that the local factory chimneys 'poured out their plague of smoke, obscured the light, and made foul the melancholy air', it was still grim. Even those inhabitants of Dudley who were lucky enough to have a job were usually in very low-paid work at one of the factories or mines which dominated the landscape. Rarely had the area's nickname, 'the Black Country', seemed so appropriate.

Living conditions in the area were particularly desperate as many of the houses in the region were basic, with little thought given to space, comfort or design. Whole families were crammed into small, rotting buildings, not all of which would have running water, electricity or inside toilets. Unsurprisingly, these conditions meant that people's health, as well as morale, would often suffer.

Morale was also not helped by the fact that there were also precious few places for the workers to escape to after a hard day's toil in front of a furnace or down a mine, as the town was not renowned for its varied entertainment options. Although Dudley Zoo would open in 1937, as would the long-awaited Hippodrome cinema, there was little else to distract the workers from their lot, so many turned to the town's pubs for solace. Consequently, the drinking establishments of Dudley were among the few businesses that continued to be highly profitable during the depression.

These bleak conditions were hardly ideal for a man to bring up a family, but Gladstone Edwards had little choice. He had received a basic education and had no discernible special talents. With his options limited, he had to get by on the little money that he earned as a metal polisher in Joseph Sankey and Sons, an ironworks factory based in Bilston.

Gladstone, a quiet but kind man, enjoyed the simple things in life. His favourite meal was said to be home-made faggots and peas, and he would always have by his side an old pasteurised milk bottle filled with tea, so he could have swigs of his favourite brew while he sweated at the factory furnace.

Thankfully, living conditions for the Edwards family did improve once Duncan was born. Their application to be relocated from their dismal house at 23 Malvern Crescent, Holly Hall, was accepted, and they were re-housed on the other side of town in a new estate called the 'Priory' (this was a period when the government was encouraging a massive housebuilding programme). Enormous excitement surrounded the new estate, which looked set to provide its inhabitants with a much-improved environment, due to its spacious houses, clean roads and working sewers. Even the names of the new streets, such as Bluebell, Cedar, Hazel and Laurel, were designed to appear fresh and to create optimism.

When the time came for the Edwards family to move into 31 Elm Road, they were delighted to find that their new home was drastically different to the horrors of their last council house. It not only boasted a neat front and back garden, where Duncan could spend hours kicking a ball, but it also had large windows, making the small house appear less claustrophobic. Perhaps best of all, it had a bath and an inside toilet. There would now be no need for midnight dashes in the rain to the outhouse, or laborious efforts to fill a steel bathtub with hot water boiled from a saucepan on the stove. Despite these modern additions, the house still didn't have modern luxuries such as central heating or double glazing. On freezing winter's nights ice would gather on the inside of the windows, and the rooms would be so cold that when a person exhaled they could see their breath.

While the Priory estate was intended to help lift its residents from the squalid housing they had been accustomed to, it was still a hard place to live. Families bred bull terriers and game cocks for illegal fighting contests, the new streets soon became littered with waste and scrap, and the pubs still attracted their share of drunkards and other undesirables. Contrary to popular perceptions of the time, there was plenty of crime, muggings and assaults.

Gladstone and the bubbly Annie didn't let these problems affect their personalities. Typical of the Black Country's unique brand of people, they met adversity with humour, determination and hard work. For example, a diminutive Annie once emphatically displayed her resolute personality when she found a burglar in her home. Instead of fleeing, she was so incensed that she physically confronted the intruder and chased him out of the house.

But as the baby Edwards grew into a toddler, the threat of a conflict with Germany loomed increasingly large. Eventually, on 3 September 1939, Prime Minister Neville Chamberlain declared war. As the mobilisation of millions of men got under way, Gladstone found that his job at the factory was a reserved occupation. Rather than put his life on the line, he was able to spend the entirety of the conflict in the relative safety of Dudley, where he churned out items for the war effort.

Life as everyone knew it changed dramatically during these tough times. As the West Midlands was an industrial area, which produced weapons and machinery for the military, the Germans targeted it in

1940 with a series of air raids. While Dudley did not suffer as badly as some places, it was bombed on several occasions and the raids undoubtedly terrified the young Edwards.

Because of the threat from air raids, the residents of the town, like those across the country, were ordered to carry a gas mask with them at all times and people were obliged to cover their windows with black sheets at night, so as to hide the lights from the German bombers. In further attempts to confuse the bombers, buildings of importance were painted to look like fields, barrage balloons sailed high in the sky and smokescreen equipment was set up so that the whole area could be enveloped in a more than usually dense cloud.

Adequate protection from the bombs was a necessity, so like many others Gladstone was provided with an Anderson shelter made out of galvanised steel panels in the back garden. As soon as one of the factory sirens wailed the warning of the enemy approaching, Gladstone, Annie and Duncan stopped whatever they were doing and retreated there to safety. In the dark they would lie on mattresses on the cold floor, listening to the sound of the German planes overhead, and pray that their house would not be bombed. Duncan would be so scared that he would cling to his mother, who, while petrified herself, would make up stories to occupy her young son's mind.

Rationing of basic food items, such as bacon, butter, sugar, meat, cheese, eggs and milk, also had an enormous effect on every Briton's life. Families were now forced to make the most of whatever produce they could get their hands on. Like countless others, Gladstone began growing vegetables in the back garden, and he also kept a few chickens in a wire pen where they could produce eggs. Duncan loved animals and this was therefore one aspect of the war he did enjoy. 'He had pigeons and rabbits and would have turned our place into a farmyard if we'd let him,' remembered Annie Edwards. 'He had a black and white collie dog, too. If there was a circus anywhere near, he'd want to go to see the animals.'

Due to rationing, Annie had to learn how to make new dishes with the sparse ingredients available to her. One of Duncan's favourites was her 'meat pie', which she made with potatoes, onions and marmite. One food that wasn't rationed was Spam, and though Duncan hated the taste he had to eat it, as there was often no alternative. Despite this, he was continuing to grow rapidly, and was therefore frequently hungry, which meant that at times Gladstone and Annie would go without so that they could give their young son a proper meal.

All of this was just a way of life for Duncan; he was so young he didn't know of a world without rations, bombs, air raids and war. Instead of being concerned with such matters, his young mind became occupied with something far more exciting: football. 'He was kicking a ball before he could walk,' said Annie Edwards of her football-mad son. 'His father would hold him up by baby reins so he could stand upright and kick a ball.'

His talent with a ball, for such a young boy, appeared to be a god-given gift. 'I never had to teach my boy to play football the way Bobby Charlton's mother did,' Annie recalled. 'He was just born with the ability. It was natural. He kicked a ball without anyone ever show-ing him how.'

Football seemed to run deep throughout the Edwards family's blood. Gladstone Edwards played as a full-back with his brother, George, for a local side in the Cradley Heath league, while Duncan's grandfather had also played at an amateur level, until his tragic pre-mature death, in his early 30s. However, Duncan's uncle, Ray Westwood, was the real success story in the family, as he had played professionally for Bolton Wanderers and England during the 1930s.

As well as being avid participants in the game, the Edwards family were also fanatical supporters of their local team, Wolverhampton Wanderers. Gladstone was eager to encourage his young son also to support the mighty Wolves, and as he grew older he bombarded him with stories regarding the brilliance of their star player, Stan Cullis. However, even Gladstone had to admit that although Wolves had been one of the top sides in the country before the war, they had often flattered to deceive, having narrowly finished runners-up in the league in 1938 and 1939, before losing the last pre-war FA Cup final 4-1 to Portsmouth. When the war was drawing to a close, Gladstone hoped that Wolves could regroup and finally achieve their potential. For him, it would be all the more special as his son would now be old enough to accompany him to the games.

Gladstone was far from the only one in the Edwards household to indulge his young son's passion for the game, his wife was equally as enthusiastic. Having seen how happy Duncan was when he had a ball at his feet, Annie was determined to encourage him as much as possible. As such she made him a football kit and bought him some boots. 'I got him some little football boots,' she remembered, 'which were continually having to be replaced because of wear and tear or because his feet were getting bigger.' Duncan went everywhere in his baggy shorts, cotton shirt and hobnailed boots. Frequently Annie would have to undress him while he slept, so that she could have the rare opportunity to wash his favourite outfit.

From an early age, Duncan played football wherever he could find a game. The obsessed youngster could usually be found playing either in the courtyard of nearby Dudley Castle or at Priory Park, for hours on end in all conditions. Impromptu street games were also played in Stourbridge Street, which Duncan once recalled was 'transformed into palatial Wembley'. With jumpers for goalposts, and no one keeping score, the street was always full of the riotous sound of football-mad kids pretending they were the likes of national football hero Stanley Matthews. When it began to go dark, the street would then become dominated by the cries of mothers urging their sons to get inside.

At this time, most British households could not afford a television and therefore children had nothing better to do than to play outside together. As few could afford to own a car, with most relying on buses, trains and bicycles for their transport needs, street games were rarely interrupted by passing vehicles. In fact, almost the only time a game would come to a stop would be when the rag-and-bone man in his horse-drawn cart would clip-clop down the street shouting: 'Rag and bone! Any old rags? Any old rags?'

Ken Finch, the former mayor of Dudley, grew up on the same streets as Duncan and recalls that he was always out playing. 'Duncan would play with anyone at any time. Wherever there was a ball, Duncan Edwards was there.' Not only would he be there, but he would be organising the teams, and cajoling other watching children to take part. 'You play up-front. You in defence. You go in goals,' he would order and to a man they did just as they were told.

As leather balls were so expensive, Duncan and the boys would usually have to make do with anything that they could muster, be it a tennis ball, rags bound tightly together or even a stone. Duncan's fascination with the game was so great that he rarely went anywhere without dribbling something that had been transformed into a ball. 'He was a devil for the football. You couldn't take the football away from him,' Annie Edwards remembered. 'As a lad he went out with a ball, and came back with a ball, and would spend hours heading and kicking a ball against a wall. Even if he was dressed up on Sunday, he couldn't help kicking stones, and when we went on holiday we always had to buy him a ball.'

Most mothers today would be delighted if their young son was frequently taking part in a physical activity, but Annie Edwards wasn't always so pleased. 'For most of the games I would play in my ordinary walking shoes, a fact that caused friction at home,' Duncan once recalled. 'On one occasion my mother bought me a new pair of shoes and within a couple of hours of putting them on I arrived home with them invisible beneath great cakes of mud. My popularity was at a low ebb that night.'

Annie was very house-proud and always tried her best to ensure that Duncan looked immaculate. Trying to keep up with washing and darning his clothes was, however, a thankless task, especially when he would cover them in mud and sweat after playing football every day –

and remember, these were the days before the introduction of washing machines into British households. For hours on end, she would have to wash all of the family's clothes by hand, using a scrubbing brush, washboard and a hand-operated mangle. What made matters worse was the fact that not only were clothes rationed, but she could hardly afford to buy him new ones in any event. To avoid her young son embarrassing her by going out in threadbare, dirty rags, she would have to spend many nights sewing and washing the few clothes that Duncan had so he always looked presentable. Despite repeatedly pleading with him to be more careful, she knew she was fighting a losing battle.

As Duncan was so big and talented for his age, he was never short of offers to play, even from the older boys on the estate. On one occasion, Annie remembered passing one of the local parks where she saw a group of teenagers immersed in a game. When she got closer she heard one of them cry, 'Go on Duncan,' as a smaller boy received the ball. To her amazement, it was her young son, playing with boys twice his age. Worried for the youngster's safety, she went over to check that Duncan was all right, but the older boys reassured her that it was them she should be worried about because Duncan tackled harder than anyone they knew.

Over the years, Annie would enjoy watching her son play with the boys and can remember just how popular he was. 'They loved Duncan. I can hear them now saying, "Come on, Dunc, we're picking sides." They would pick sides and then argue which one would get Duncan.'

Throughout his childhood, Duncan could be found most evenings and Sunday mornings playing with the older boys, 'getting used to the hurly-burly of the game, and giving, I hoped, as good as I took'. These contests no doubt ingrained in him a belief that he could always hold his own against bigger and stronger opposition, and as a result he never appeared intimidated during his career.

Although Duncan was naturally gifted, he was always determined to improve himself. This desire to progress was partly inspired by an embarrassing incident that he would never forget. While playing with the older boys, a penalty was awarded and the responsibility fell on Duncan to take the kick. Eager to impress, he sprinted up to the ball with the intention of kicking it harder than anyone had ever done before. Unfortunately, the ground was wet, and as he placed his standing foot down he slipped and fell backwards, just as he made contact with the ball. Skying the ball over the crossbar, a muddy and soaking Duncan was met by howls of laughter. As he subsequently confessed, it was 'at that moment I solemnly decided that I would learn from my mistakes'.

Following this embarrassment, Duncan started to practise religiously on improving his passing and shooting technique. He was also determined to become two-footed after he realised that 'my own weakness was my left foot'. For hours at a time he would play by himself, relentlessly banging a ball with his left foot against a rough brick wall.

The evening games against the older lads were also used by Duncan as a 'testing ground for my left foot'. At first he would use his left foot only in situations where he was under little pressure, but as he improved and his confidence grew he started to play whole matches where he would limit himself to his weaker foot. Occasionally, some of his efforts were met with derision, but he learned to ignore the sneers and as time went by no one could tell which foot was stronger.

In an effort to help young players to improve, Edwards later advised them to 'watch every first-class game you can'. Sadly for Duncan, the war years had resulted in the cancellation of the Football League and while friendly games and wartime league matches were played locally by the likes of Wolves, West Bromwich Albion, Birmingham City and Aston Villa, the standard was not on a par with a competitive league contest.

In any case, it is ironic that Duncan was to issue such advice as he couldn't stand watching games when he was a child. As his interest in football had grown, Gladstone felt that it was time for a rite of passage: a trip to Molineux with his young son to watch his beloved Wolves play. Gladstone was perhaps more excited than Duncan, as he believed it would turn out to be one of the most memorable days in his lad's life. He could hardly wait to see his face when he heard the crowd roar for the first time and saw the genius of his Wolves team in full flight. But Duncan didn't appear to be enthralled with the game at all. Fidgeting throughout, he kept pulling on Gladstone's sleeve and asking when they could go home. With 20 minutes remaining, an exasperated Gladstone gave up and left so that his restless son could get back to the streets and play football with his mates.

While the kickabouts in the parks and the streets had allowed Duncan to pick up the basics of the game, it was at Priory Road Junior School, just a few hundred yards from his home, where he really began his football education. It was there where Duncan first began to play organised games, and his large frame and dominant personality saw him not only represent the school team at a young age but also captain it.

Before Duncan's arrival, the school team had enjoyed little success, but he dramatically transformed their fortunes as he made them one of the best sides in the Midlands. His football talent, coupled with his loud and exuberant demeanour on the pitch, also saw Duncan become one of the most popular boys in school, which even had the older children wanting to be his friend. 'There were lads at school you could call bullies,' said fellow pupil Ken Smith, 'but no one ever bothered Duncan. He was always left alone. I can't remember anyone picking a fight with him.'

Classmate Dorothy Hayden has recalled her schoolmate's obsession with the game and how it made him popular. 'The only thing he was ever interested in was football and if you were ever wanting him, he was usually to be found on the waste ground at the back of the school, playing football with anyone and everyone. In those days I wasn't particularly interested in football, but I used to hear the lads in my class who played in the school team alongside Duncan talk about him with something like hero-worship. Perhaps this was brought about mainly because he was instrumental in the Priory Road School achieving success in local competitions.'

Duncan's feats on the football pitch didn't, however, always endear him to other pupils at his school, or help him to avoid trouble. Joan Davies, a former classmate, remembers a time when her 'friend' was too boisterous for his own good. 'We were sitting next to each other in class one afternoon, when for some reason that Duncan knew best, he gave me an almighty thump on the nose with a large text book. This had a rather instant effect on my nose and it began to bleed rather badly. Sadly for Duncan, the teacher spotted his action and he was immediately sent to the headmaster's study where he received his punishment in the form of a few strokes of the cane. Some years later, I met him at a bus stop in Dudley while he was home on holiday, and during the casual conversation Duncan brought the incident up and we had a good laugh about it.'

It was no doubt difficult for one so young and talented to keep his feet on the ground, and sometimes his confident and almost cocky manner rubbed up his peers the wrong way. On one occasion he was said to have signed several pieces of paper in an exercise book and handed them out to all of his friends proclaiming, 'You ought to keep that. One day that name will be famous.'

However, it was not entirely unexpected that Duncan should occasionally act in this way, as everyone who saw him play football would shower him with praise. Even Dudley's mayor, George Marlow, said when presenting Duncan with a pen, 'This is for all of those autographs you're going to be signing.'

Yet if Duncan ever needed bringing back down to earth, the poor grades he achieved in school would do the trick. It wasn't because he lacked intelligence that he failed to excel academically, but merely because he didn't put the same effort into his schoolwork as he did to perfect his football skills. Consequently, Duncan was quite happy to coast along and wait impatiently until break time, or after school, so that he could get back to playing football. 'He didn't mind going to school,' Annie Edwards remembered. 'He always enjoyed drawing and history, but he always preferred to be out of doors playing football.'

Annie and Gladstone soon realised that it was a thankless task trying to get Duncan to concentrate on his schoolwork. Whether they gave him a smack, confiscated his football kit, or even locked him in his room, his thoughts would still be dominated by the game that he worshipped. If truth be told, Gladstone was secretly happy that his son loved the game as much as he did. He revelled in the fact that Duncan was scorching a blaze through Dudley junior football, and although he tried to put on a stern face, he loved watching his son singlehandedly destroy teams. Annie was not much better. Trying in vain to instil some discipline, she loved Duncan so devoutly that she could not bear to see him upset.

His academic grades may have left a lot to be desired, but such was the brilliance of the youngster's stellar performances on the football field that he made an impression on everyone who saw him play. During a game against local rivals St John's, the opposition manager Gordon Meddings was mesmerised by the sight of the broad man-child who dominated proceedings. 'It was obvious that he was something special, even though he was only ten years old,' Meddings fondly remembered. 'He covered every inch of the field, taking goal kicks, throw-ins, corners and free kicks and also managing to halt every attack made by my very useful side. Three times during the game he made solo runs, similar to the one he made against West Germany nine years later [in an England B international]. His play inspired the Priory Road boys to a 3-0 victory.'

Football may have dominated most of Duncan's time, but if his friends were participating in other sports, such as cricket, tennis or swimming, he would reluctantly join in. Though he said, 'I have taken part in these sports more to keep fit for football than anything else,' he was a natural at them all. If there was no competitive sport to be played, then rather than mope around the house, he explored the ruins of the local bombsites or set off to do some hop picking in the Worcestershire countryside, with his faithful black and white collie dog, Jimmy, for company.

One hobby that did surprisingly come close to rivalling Duncan's affections for football was Morris and Sword dancing. In fact, he was such a keen dancer that when his time at Priory Road Junior School was at an end, he chose to attend Wolverhampton Street Secondary School, rather than Park Secondary School, where many of his friends went, on the basis that Wolverhampton had a very successful Morris and Sword dancing team.

Shortly before Duncan was due to attend Wolverhampton Street, Annie gave birth to her first daughter, Carol Anne. Duncan was thrilled. Every day after school he raced back home and marvelled at his younger sister sleeping peacefully in her crib. But then one day he found she was gone. Annie had to break the devastating news that little Carol Anne had contracted meningitis and had died. For once, Duncan did not race back out to play football with his friends. Instead, he sat on the doorstep and sobbed, while his mother and father did the same inside.

Though it would take time for the wounds to heal, Duncan's good health was in direct contrast to his tragic younger sister, as he was one of the fittest, tallest and strongest boys for his age. The move to Wolverhampton Street would not only help him get over his loss, but in time would also see his football dreams flourish.

2

SCHOOLBOY PRODIGY

In September 1948, with the country now under the control of Clement Attlee's Labour government and the war an increasingly distant memory, Edwards moved to Wolverhampton Street Secondary School where he made an immediate impression on both a sporting and social level. Upon arriving, he tried out for the senior Morris and Sword dancing team and quickly became an integral member. Arts and folk teacher Mrs Cook remembered that, despite his enormous size, Edwards was still 'so light on those feet with bells at the ankles; so beautifully balanced, so dainty'.

This ability was also one of the key reasons why Edwards made such an impact on the football field. School headmaster Mr Groves would never forget seeing him play for the first time: 'He dominated the whole match. He told all the other twenty-one players what to do, and the referee and both the linesmen.' His excitement at seeing a young boy so talented saw Mr Groves make a prediction, which at the time must have seemed ridiculous to some: 'When I got home that evening I wrote to a friend and said I'd just seen a boy of eleven who would play for England one day.'

Mr Groves kept a close eye on Edwards whenever he had the opportunity to see him play, and while his juggernaut performances caught the eye, so did his confidence, leadership and size. 'The young Edwards was never afraid to go in and tackle,' he remembered. 'He had legs and thighs already like oak trees, and yet was so amazingly light on his feet. He could almost have played blindfolded. Admittedly, he had a big mouth, coming from a rough tough background, but I do not think anyone ever took exception as his advice, like his play, was so impressive. He had quietened down considerably by the time he reached fourteen.'

Although Edwards was loud-mouthed on the pitch, off it he grew into a very shy and modest young man. 'He was quiet in class and got on with his job with no star tantrums,' said Mrs Cook. 'He never bragged about football. If we wanted to know where he was playing next, one had to ask him and got the bare bones for an answer as if it was almost a casual happening.'

Loud-mouth or not, Mr Groves could not fail to be struck by the maturity of Edwards on the football field and how he seemed to dominate every game in which he played. 'He was playing in the style of a man, with wonderful balance and colossal power in his shot. Already he was showing the intelligence in his game, which became central to all he did. He already understood all about distribution of the ball. And he was such a dominating player that the ball seemed to come to him wherever he was.'

Edwards' form wasn't just being heralded by those at his school; it had also been noted by Eric Booth, the secretary of the Dudley Schools Football Association. 'He was eleven at the time, captain and centre-half of his school junior side, and we knew right away that we had something special,' he said of the first time he spotted the precocious youngster. 'In his first year at Wolverhampton Street School, he was chosen to play for the Dudley Schoolboys side, where he came up against boys of fifteen. For once in his life he looked a comparative midget alongside them, but he was still a wonderful player for his age.'

In order to protect his young star from the physicality of the older boys, Booth felt that it would be in Edwards' best interests to change positions. For his school, Edwards had lined up at centre-half, but for Dudley Schoolboys it was decided that his development would be best served if he played at outside-left, a sign that his work on his weaker left foot had paid off handsomely. Booth had hoped that this change of position would stop him getting clobbered by the older boys in the middle of the park, but he soon learned that Edwards revelled in getting involved in the rough stuff, in fact sometimes he even went looking for it.

Eric Booth would play a vital part in Edwards' embryonic football career. Rather than bore his star player with tactics, as many other coaches did, Booth spent hours working with him on his technique. He was fanatical about teaching Edwards the basic fundamental skills, such as how to strike a ball and how to control it. Above all, he urged him to pass the ball at every opportunity, as possession was the key to winning games. These were all lessons that Edwards took to instantly.

On the training field, Booth found that Edwards was a joy to coach. Not only was he very quick at picking up new skills but he was also a great help. 'Coaching sessions were such that he could pick up in an instant a new skill – trapping with the outside of the foot, or with the chest – etc,' Booth said of his gifted pupil. 'I would then send him across to half of the team and let him coach them, while I took the other half.'

A key factor that helped the youngest member of the Dudley Schoolboys team settle was that his older cousin, Dennis Stevens, was captain. Stevens and his team-mates knew what a rare talent Edwards was before many of them had seen him play, as he was the talk of the town. This didn't, however, prevent some from holding the opinion that he would be too young to make an impression, but as the old adage goes: if you're good enough then you're old enough, and Edwards was certainly good enough. 'When we met up in that schoolboy team, I was some three years older than Duncan,' Stevens remembered. 'His age did not come into it, though; all that mattered was that he could play. He had beautiful balance, could turn on a sixpence, and was very strong in the tackle. I played for Holly Hall School on the other side of Dudley from Duncan, but we still heard about how promising a player he was. You could see even then he was going to make it to the top.'

Following his eye-catching exploits for Wolverhampton Street School and the Dudley Schoolboys side, Edwards was soon being asked to represent other teams. In his second school year, he was called up to play for Worcester County, where former St John's and now Wolverhampton Street School coach Gordon Meddings was heavily involved. Edwards worshipped Meddings, and in turn his amiable coach was in awe of his pupil's astounding talent.

Meddings has never forgotten one county game that not only summed up the fact that at times Edwards could be a one-man team, but also emphasised just how hard he could hit a ball, even when it was bogged down with water and mud. The match in question was against Evesham, in the Worcester County Trophy, and conditions were so horrendous that at half time Meddings told his star player that the only way they would score was if he went for goal by himself as they were playing into the teeth of a gale.

During the second half, Edwards received the ball in his own penalty area and, with his coach's instructions still ringing in his ears, he set off on a run which saw him beat virtually the entire Evesham side. After an 80-yard slalom dribble, he suddenly found himself with just the goalkeeper to beat, but at the vital moment he opted for power rather than placement, and smashed the ball at the goalkeeper's outstretched legs. The power of the shot was so fierce, and the wind so strong, that the ball cannoned off the keeper, flew the length of the pitch, and went out for a goal kick at the opposite end of the field.

Fred Brooks, a County team-mate, recalls that these solo runs were regular occurrences. 'I remember we were playing Redditch in Dudley and the only time we could get out of our half was when we gave the ball to Duncan. I can see him now, rampaging down the left wing with one of their players looking like a young boy trying in vain to keep up with him. He was colossal.'

One of the schoolboy goalkeepers who was unlucky enough to get in the way of one of Edwards' fierce shots has never forgotten the feeling. 'Playing against him was an experience in itself,' recalls Terry Jones. 'I was a goalkeeper and in my mind I can still feel the sting of his shot to this day. If Duncan had the ball and you caught it, your hands were warmed, especially as in those days the balls were heavy leather.'

The strength and power in Edwards' legs, which created such ferocious force in his shooting, was also a factor in the bone-crunching tackles he was renowned for throughout his career. Though he played the game fairly, and did not seek to injure an opponent, at times his sheer size, commitment and momentum when flying into a tackle saw him take no prisoners.

A trial match for the Birmingham and District representative team highlighted this aspect of his game, as Edwards' enthusiasm to win the ball, and the ferocity of his tackling, ended in a nasty incident. Eager to make an impression, he had launched himself into a tackle, which ended with his opposite number shrieking in pain. It was entirely accidental – Edwards had won the ball – but his follow-through had left the boy writhing in agony. As the boy was stretchered off the field, the effect on Edwards was noticeable; he was close to tears and for the rest of the game his mind was obviously elsewhere. The following week, as Edwards played for Dudley Schoolboys, he saw that the boy he had injured was on the sideline with his leg in plaster. Despite the boy placing no blame on Edwards, he was still upset and with this playing on his conscience he initially jumped out of a few tackles, afraid that he would again hurt someone. While he would soon be back in the thick of the action, it would take a few weeks before he would steam into tackles without this incident in the back of his mind.

However, his combative style certainly didn't deter the selectors, if anything it attracted them, as Edwards was subsequently picked for the Birmingham and District side. Gordon Clayton, the goalkeeper for the team, hailed from nearby Cannock and he immediately developed a close rapport with Edwards. Clayton matched Edwards for size, but was a louder, more extroverted character, who helped to bring his friend out of his shell. Over time the two friends would not only play for the district together, but would also become team-mates at a much higher level.

Both Eric Booth and Gordon Meddings were so enthused by Edwards' ability they decided that they wanted him to play more centrally for their teams so that he could dictate games. Yet it didn't matter what position Edwards was selected to play, as in most games he would still get on the ball more than any other player. He had the ability to make things happen out of nowhere. His dynamic runs and wonderful range of passing, which would see him unerringly launch the ball to all corners of the pitch, would cause havoc in the opposition ranks. No one was left in any doubt: if you needed to win the game, give the ball to Edwards.

Booth was so impressed with Edwards' progress that he had no hesitation in putting forward the 13-year-old for the best team in the country at that age group. 'I recommended Duncan for an England Under-14 international at Oldham,' Booth recalls, 'and we were actually surprised when he was selected to take part, because you have to remember that he was still only twelve [sic] years old. We were even more surprised when he was selected to play in the match at centre-forward! However, he had such a good game that he was chosen to play against Northern Ireland.'

Before the big game, Booth tried to prepare Edwards with a blackboard tactics session where he went through the key elements of playing as an attacker. He soon gave up when he realised that his star pupil 'was one move ahead of me all the time'. It was clear that the prodigy couldn't just play the game; he could read it as well.

Most lads of Edwards' age would have jumped at the chance to play for England, but the game against Northern Ireland clashed with an event that he had been eagerly anticipating for months: the Morris and Sword dancing championships at the National Festival in Derby. Reluctantly, Edwards opted to play for England, but he was bitterly disappointed to miss out on the event.

When the local newspaper printed a story on his selection for the England team, he was just as pleased that they mentioned his dancing prowess as well his football ability. The article read, 'At school Duncan is also a star member of the Morris, sword and folk dancing teams and last year competed at the Leamington and Birmingham festivals.'

Annie Edwards was the proudest mother on the Priory estate the day the story was published in the paper. She carried a copy of it in her bag and would show it to all and sundry, telling them, 'That's my Duncan!' Gladstone was equally as pleased, as were his mates at the ironworks, who all followed Edwards' progress. The shy boy was fast becoming a local celebrity.

On 6 May 1950, Duncan Edwards made his international debut at Oldham's Boundary Park, where he played in attack. Also playing for England that day were two young players who Edwards would spend plenty of time with over the next few years, Ray Parry and David Pegg.

A fiercely proud Gladstone and Annie watched in the stands as their son, England's youngest player, took to the field. Although money was tight, Edwards' parents rarely missed a game when he played. They didn't have anything else that gave them as much joy in their lives, and they channelled all of their hopes and dreams into their only child. His exploits added a touch of excitement to their existence.

Reading the match programme, Gladstone was thrilled to see his son feature in an article titled 'These Boys Are The Stars Of Today – Keep An Eye On Them, They Will Be The Stars Of Tomorrow'. Prophesying which of the young stars had the talent to make it in the game, the article revealed that Edwards' practice with both of his feet had paid off handsomely and that he had an extraordinary range of passing for one so young. It read, 'Worcester County player. Strong and two footed. Splendid distributor, especially with long cross passes to the wing.'

The trip to Oldham was evidently worthwhile, as Edwards delivered a display that belied his tender years as he helped England thrash Northern Ireland 5-2. Standing head and shoulders above everyone else on the field, it was amazing to think that he was still so young. Launching himself at the Irish defenders, Edwards had them quaking in their boots every time he set off on a run. It was certainly a debut to remember.

During the summer of 1950, Gordon Meddings attended an FA coaching course in Blackpool and, as luck would have it, the England Under-14 and Under-15 teams were invited to help the coaches practise their drills. Meddings gave Edwards a lift to Blackpool and on arrival they checked into Stanley Matthews' hotel on the South Shore of the Lancashire resort, where the other players and coaches were also staying.

The trip to one of the UK's glamour resorts was certainly one that Edwards looked forward to. Blackpool was an oasis of excitement, colour and adventure, in direct contrast to the grey and dour industrial wasteland of the West Midlands. During the 1950s, Blackpool was the destination most young boys wanted to visit, especially as holidays abroad were virtually unheard of. Boasting a beach where holidaymakers would ride donkeys, build sandcastles and enjoy a stick of rock, and a renowned fun-fair full of the latest rides from America, there was no better place for a youngster to enjoy himself.

Amid all of the excitement, it was hard sometimes for a few of the boys to remember that they were there to work. Edwards, however, always prepared for football like a professional and he threw himself into the drills as if he were preparing for the biggest game of his life. Joe Mercer, the future Manchester City manager, who was also enrolled on the course, was taken aback by Edwards' ability.

Throughout his time in Blackpool, Mercer raved about Meddings' protégé and predicted that he had a big future ahead of him in the game.

Once the daily coaching sessions were over, the players and coaches set off into the centre of Blackpool in search of excitement. For the boys this meant a visit to the Pleasure Beach fun-fair and for the coaches it was an opportunity to spend the night in a smoky bar, enjoy a few drinks and talk football.

Though most people who visited the fair headed straight to the main attraction, the 'Big Dipper', the boys spent much of their time at the 'Beat the Goalkeeper' stall. Happy at first to take the school-boys' money, the owner of the stall proceeded to lose a fortune as they continued to smash the ball past the bewildered goalkeeper.

When the owner found out that the boys were all England Schoolboy internationals, he banned them from playing, but on reflection he soon changed his mind. Having hatched a plan, he sur-prisingly allowed the confused boys to shoot for free. With them scoring time and time again, the owner shouted to the passing pun-ters: 'Roll up! Roll up! Beat the goalkeeper and win a prize. If these young lads can do it so easily, then surely you can as well.' The boys were happy to play along, as it was an opportunity to play football, and the stall owner made a small fortune as customers kept rolling up eager to try their luck. The only person who wasn't too pleased was the goalkeeper, who repeatedly stung his hands when trying to keep out Edwards' heat-seekers!

Over the course of the next year, Edwards continued to progress rapidly and he became one of only four boys (David Pegg and Ray Parry included) from the England Under-14 team to move up to the Under-15s. A lifetime wish was fulfilled on 7 April 1951 when Edwards made his Wembley debut in an international against Wales. Wembley was packed with 53,400 as, due to the limited opportunity to watch football on TV, the schoolboy internationals always attracted large crowds. It was without a doubt the biggest crowd that Edwards had played in front of, but he went about his business as though he was back playing at the 'palatial Wembley' of Stourbridge Street. Nothing seemed to faze him and his herculean efforts saw England chalk up another victory.

The match programme not only revealed Edwards' football pedigree but also his impressive size for a 14-year-old, 'Captain of Worcester County SFA. Selected to represent Birmingham and District SFA. 14 years 6 months. Height 5ft 8in. Weight 10st 12lb.' Compared to today's teenagers, this may not seem out of the ordinary, but in the 1940s and 1950s this was considered well above average. Rationing had a profound effect on the growth of 'war babies', and subsequently few grew to be over 6ft tall due to the lack of meat and milk in their diets.

Shortly after his Wembley debut, Edwards wrote an essay entitled 'A True Wish' where he talked about how his dream of playing at the national stadium had been fulfilled. Though the essay betrays his poor grammar and spelling, it does highlight just how much playing at Wembley meant to him:

Well it all began when I was a little boy of about seven years of age. I had heard my father talkeing about a place by the name of Wembly Stadium. It was a wet day in april and my uncle Gorge and dad were sitting round the fire where my uncle Gorge said to my father, 'I see England are playing Scottland at Wembly next saterday,' 'Are they,' my father replied.

'I thought to myself 'now's my chance to ask them where this Wembly Stadium is while there on the subject.' So I turned to my uncle and asked him where the Stadium was, and he replied, 'Duncan, this Stadium as you call it is the third biggest football stadium in the world and situated in London.' I told my uncle I wish I could go there and he said I would before long. I was thirteen and I still wanted to go to Wembly and on 7th april I was picked to play for england against wales (at Wembly Stadium).

My uncle was right when he said I would some day go to Wembly Stadium.

Opportunities to play at Wembley continued to come thick and fast, as in his time as an England Schoolboy Edwards won nine caps, a record at the time. He was also the first Dudley schoolboy to play for the junior national team in over 40 years. The boy wonder was already setting records that would remain for decades to come. Yet to Edwards, setting records meant very little; he just wanted to play football.

As awards started to mount up, Edwards kept his feet on the ground and remained incredibly modest. 'He'd go and play and I wouldn't know until I cleaned out his bag later what medals or plaques he had won,' said Annie Edwards. 'He was never a show-off. He just played because he loved football.'

A further honour came Edwards' way when he was told that he would captain the England Schoolboys team in games against Scotland (twice), Wales and the Republic of Ireland. The Wales game excited him the most as the fixture was to be played at Birmingham City's St Andrews stadium, just a few miles from his Dudley home. This meant that his extended family and friends had only a short trip to see him bursting with pride as he led his team out of the tunnel. Gladstone and all of his pals from the ironworks watched on proudly and gave Edwards a loud cheer as he bounded onto the pitch. Usually, when he played he was deadly serious, but on this occasion he stood in the line-up before the match smiling from ear to ear.

Scouts from most major clubs were sat in the stands in order to eye up the genius who was causing such a stir. Edwards lived up to his reputation as he delivered an outstanding display that saw him drag England back from going a goal down to eventually beat the Welsh 2-1. Regrettably, Edwards' next, and last, game as an England Schoolboy didn't go to plan, as the team lost to Ireland by a solitary goal in Dublin.

With Edwards' England Schoolboy days at an end, scouts from all of the country's leading clubs, such as Wolves, Bolton, Everton, Blackpool and Aston Villa, chased his signature. Soon he would have to make a decision over where he would start a career that sparkled with prodigious potential. However, there was one club that was creating a sensation and Duncan was praying that they would be among his suitors.

3

THE NEW DAWN OF MANCHESTER UNITED

Although the Second World War finally came to an end in 1945, fixtures in the Football League did not resume until August the following year. Manchester United, who had not won a major trophy since 1911 and had been promoted back to the first division as recently as 1938, were at this stage an unremarkable top-flight club in dire straits.

Teetering close to bankruptcy, the war years had seen the club make virtually no income. Money was therefore extremely tight, and with an enormous overdraft of £15,000 to pay off, this meant that very limited funds were available for the incoming manager to sign new players. Matters weren't helped by the fact that Old Trafford had been badly bombed during the war, and as a result the stadium was not in a fit state to host league games until 1949.

The outlook was so bleak that it would have been of little surprise if the club had folded, but salvation came from an unlikely source. Neighbours Manchester City agreed to allow their fierce rivals the use of their stadium, Maine Road, until Old Trafford had been rebuilt. But this was not an act of charity; certain conditions were attached. City charged their rivals the hefty sum of £5000 a year for the privilege of playing at Maine Road and also demanded that their reserve team be allowed to use Old Trafford for free. United had little choice but to agree, as without this arrangement the club would surely have struggled to survive.

A huge slice of good fortune did come United's way when the club decided to appoint ex-Manchester City player Matt Busby as its new manager. Busby, an ardent Catholic from the mining community of Lanarkshire, had enjoyed a distinguished playing career where he had represented Scotland, picked up an FA Cup winner's medal with City, before then joining Liverpool, where he was made captain. His arrival would in time transform the fortunes of the struggling club beyond the wildest dreams of its directors and its fans.

Busby actually had the war to thank for leading him down this path. When the conflict had broken out, he had enlisted as a football coach for the Army Physical Training Corps. All of the players he coached were well-known professionals, such as Joe Mercer, Tommy Lawton, Cliff Britton and Frank Swift. After progressing to take charge of an army representative side, Busby thoroughly enjoyed the experience of moulding such exalted players into a team, and he began to consider a career in management. As soon as the war was over, he vowed that he would look for a suitable club where he could put his attacking football philosophy into action.

During a tour of Italy, Busby stumbled across someone he thought could be a great addition to his future plans. While he was putting his team through their paces, he was struck by another training session being given by former Welsh international and West Bromwich Albion player Jimmy Murphy. With a face like a bulldog, Murphy ripped into his players with relish. Displaying language that would make a sailor blush, perhaps the cleanest phrase he growled in his gravelly Rhondda Valleys accent was, 'Don't pussyfoot around him man, get stuck in! Hurt the bugger if you fucking have to. Make your tackles count or don't fucking bother!'

Busby was impressed. He remembered that he had come face-to-face with Murphy in his playing days and, as he recalled, he had been a hard and fiercely competitive player who didn't shirk a tackle. This playing style was evidently echoed by his high-intensity coaching sessions, where he not only preached the importance of endeavour but also of treating the ball as a prize. It was not to be given away lightly. If it was then you had better win it back instantly, or else.

On the face of it, Murphy and Busby were polar opposites. Busby was calm and conservative, while Murphy was excitable and ebullient, but Busby recognised that they could complement each other well. One would play good cop, the other bad cop. Together they had the perfect ingredients that could make a team tick. Busby decided that should he get a managerial position in football then Murphy, the 'chirpy, chunky, cheery, soft-hearted, hard-boiled Welsh piano player with an Irish name and a Satchmo voice like a cement mixer in full throttle', would join him.

Towards the end of the war, Busby was offered an assistant coaching job at his old club Liverpool, but when he realised that his ideas on the game differed to those of the board and that he would not be in charge, he decided not to pursue the opportunity. Manchester United had by this stage also been alerted to Busby's coaching potential by their chief scout, Louis Rocca, who had known Busby for a number of years due to their membership of the Manchester Catholic Sportsman's Club.

Rocca realised that a club in United's precarious position needed a strong-minded manager who was also an excellent coach, so as to get the best out of the players already at the cash-strapped outfit. In turn, Busby recognised that Manchester United had the makings of a big club but had underachieved in recent years. He was certain that, even with little money, he could improve on United's 14th-place finish, which they had achieved when they had last completed a league season in 1939. In effect, the pressure was off. All things considered it was a perfect match, but there was one thing Busby insisted on before signing on the dotted line: control. Total control.

After Busby had issued the board with an ultimatum that he would accept the position only if they would 'let me have all my own way', he was appointed as the manager of Manchester United, at the age of 36, in 1945. His contract was initially to last for five years and he would be paid the princely sum of £750 per annum.

As promised, as soon as Murphy was released from the services, Busby recruited his old army pal to act as his assistant. Together, the two of them set about rebuilding the club from top to bottom. Busby said that Murphy's appointment was a necessity as he 'was the man who would help me create a pattern that would run right through the several teams of players from fifteen years of age upwards to the first team'.

Murphy was certainly kept busy by Busby's demands. On top of managing the reserve team, he also coached the youngsters on Tuesday and Thursday nights as well as helping Busby take the first-team training sessions every morning. He was never home. Manchester United was his family. His day was consumed by football and he wouldn't have had it any other way.

With little money to spend, Murphy and Busby had to make do with the players already on the club's books, if they had not already retired due to age or because of injuries sustained in the war. To get the most out of them, they realised that training and creating the right atmosphere would be vitally important.

Unlike most managers during this era, Busby did not keep the ball away from his players during the week, a misguided notion which some felt would make them hungrier for it come Saturday. Busby's sessions nearly always involved the ball. While Busby preached the importance of passing the ball, Murphy would echo behind him, 'The ball is round to go round. Give it to a red shirt. Get it and give it.' Effectively their message was that football is a simple game. As they saw it, as long as you had the right attitude, and were fit, organised and kept possession, then you would do well.

If anyone ever stepped out of line, Murphy would rip strips from them, but Busby was careful to ensure that every player also felt as though they were part of a family. Whatever problems any of his players had, they knew that Busby would be on hand to offer them some helpful advice. Drink problem, gambling debts, marital issues, it didn't matter, Busby would do his best to help. He knew that as long as his players were settled off the pitch, then they would devote everything that they had to football, and to him.

Busby's players also came to appreciate the perks he helped to arrange for them. These included membership at the prestigious Davyhulme golf club, free cinema passes, tickets to the best shows, good food, nice hotels and smart club blazers, which were embroidered with the club crest. Busby wanted his players to have the best so that they felt pride in playing for his club. It was a masterstroke in psychology. With Busby doing all that he could to look after his boys, how could they disappoint him?

Although many had expected the destitute club to struggle under an inexperienced manager, Busby's work on the training ground paid dividends. Confounding the sceptics, United finished runners-up in the league in Busby's first season in charge. Over the next couple of years, Manchester United surprisingly emerged as a force in English football, with them again finishing runners-up in 1948, 1949 and 1951 before finally winning the championship in 1952. The club also excelled in the FA Cup, and in 1948 they reached their first final in 39 years. Waiting for them at Wembley was glamour team Blackpool, who boasted England internationals Stan Mortensen and Stanley Matthews in their ranks.

It has been said that the interest, hype and quality of the game, which saw United overturn a 2-1 deficit to win 4-2, resulted in Duncan Edwards and Bobby Charlton becoming lifelong Manchester United fans. For weeks afterwards, everyone talked about United's thrilling comeback and it certainly helped cement their position as one of the most entertaining teams in the country. Edwards couldn't help but be mesmerised by the reputation of Busby's dream team.

Players such as Johnny Carey, Jack Rowley, Johnny Morris, Charlie

Mitten, Jimmy Delaney and Stan Pearson had been primarily responsible for putting United back on the map, and in later years, Busby spoke in glowing terms about all of them.

Carey captained the side, and during his time with United he played in virtually every position, including a stint in goal. He was a particular favourite of Busby's, as he was Catholic, didn't drink or swear and most importantly of all, he was the consummate professional. Carey acted as Busby's on-field lieutenant, where he dictated the manager's philosophy on football to his team-mates as if he were Busby himself. Busby felt that this was a vital attribute, as a captain needs a 'good understanding of his manager's likes and dislikes', and Carey certainly knew what they were.

Such was Busby's loyalty to Carey that it led to a confrontation with the board. Harold Hardman, a director who would one day become chairman of the club, was heard to disagree, while sat in the stands, with his manager's continued selection of Carey, a player who Hardman did not rate very highly. Furious at Hardman undermining him in front of the fans, Busby followed him into the toilets at half time, locked the door, and said between gritted teeth, 'Never dare say anything like that to me again in front of people.' The message was received loud and clear. In future, Hardman kept his opinions to himself.

Mitten was another Busby favourite, not only for his playing ability but also for his cheeky personality. Mitten had in fact signed for United in 1936, aged 15, but due to the outbreak of the war, it took him a decade before he made his official debut. Such was Mitten's talent that Busby said he could 'land a corner kick on a six-pence at will'. And when taking penalty kicks, Busby recalled that 'he would ask the opposing goalkeeper which net stanchion he would like him to hit with as accurate a left foot as ever graced the game'. Busby lauded Mitten as 'an integral part of one of the best forward lines ever seen in these islands, or any other place for that matter'.

Mitten was also one of the big personalities in the dressing room, who would have everyone rolling with laughter at his wisecracks. 'Last-minute Charlie, we called him,' said Busby, 'because the last minute was the time this cheeky Charlie arrived, sometimes having paid a social visit to the dogs en route, greyhounds being his favourite animals at the time. Give Charlie a rollicking and you would as often as not finish up roaring your head off with laughter. Some people you can take a bit of backchat from and it does not offend. Of such was Cheeky Charlie.'

Unfortunately, Busby didn't count on just how 'cheeky' Charlie could be, as in 1950 he dramatically walked out on the club to join Independiente Santa Fé in Colombia, who offered the player vast sums to join them (this in an age when the maximum wage was £12 per week). Manchester United didn't receive a transfer fee for Mitten, as Colombia was not under the jurisdiction of FIFA at the time, but when he sheepishly returned just a year later, Busby heavily fined him, before offloading him to Fulham. Players soon learned that if you ever crossed Busby there would rarely be a second chance.

The Mitten affair left a sour taste in Busby's mouth and some predicted that he would also have problems controlling forward Rowley, who was regarded in some quarters as a troublemaker. Despite these reservations, Busby confided that Rowley never gave him 'a moment's trouble' and that 'he must rank as one of the greatest players it has been my good fortune to handle'. Rowley was nicknamed 'The Gunner' due to his lethal left foot and Busby sometimes wondered, 'Who could whack the ball harder, Jack Rowley or Bobby Charlton?'

Inside-forward Morris, on the other hand, while initially proving to be a valuable player, did cause Busby trouble when in 1948 he attempted to lead a players' rebellion regarding bonuses. Shortly after the failed plot, Busby revealed his ruthless streak by dropping him to the Reserves, but Morris's attitude became so intolerable that he had no option but to offload him to Derby County for a world record fee of £24,500. In later years, a similar situation would arise when Johnny

Giles clashed with the manager over money and he too would be unceremoniously moved on.

In Busby's autobiography, *Soccer at the Top*, he revealed why he had taken such a hard line with Morris, talented player though he was. 'I had to make my point once and for all. There could be only one boss. Otherwise we should possibly have twelve bosses and the gifted individuals I had striven to mould into a team might have disintegrated into eleven individuals again, and even eleven players who included eight internationals would be nothing playing as eleven individual entertainers. Much as I admire individual, spontaneous, extemporaneous brilliance, the greatest orchestras need a conductor.' No one was ever left in doubt who that conductor was. Busby could be the nicest man you ever met, but you crossed him at your peril.

One of the few players Busby purchased after the war was Scottish forward Delaney, from Celtic. Many felt that Delaney's best days were behind him, and questioned the signing due to an appalling injury record that saw him nicknamed 'Old Brittle Bones'. Regardless of this, Busby loved Delaney's never-say-die attitude and how 'he would chase the unlikely and sometimes impossible ball just in case'. Delaney was also a very clever player, who Busby said 'put himself into places that hurt the opposition'. As a result, he set up many vital goals during his time at United and turned out to be one of Busby's most successful signings.

Pearson was another forward who enjoyed immense success under Busby, with perhaps his finest moment in a United shirt coming when he scored in the 1948 FA Cup final. Busby felt that his predatory instincts made him 'the perfect goal-taker', who was 'absolutely devastating in the penalty box'. Pearson's partnership with Rowley was subsequently regarded as one of the most prolific and feared in English football.

Though the players, most of whom Busby had inherited and then trained and moulded into a team, had performed admirably for him, he was conscious of the fact that the majority of them had a limited shelf life, owing to their advancing years. As such, the 1952 title success proved to be the swansong for many of these United stars, as their age finally began to catch up with them. Busby himself even said that 'all teams, especially teams with players of a like age, are apt to be over the top within five years of reaching it'. With United having won the FA Cup in 1948, the end of the 1952 season would have been approaching Busby's five-year limit for many of his team.

Thankfully, Busby had planned for this scenario since he had joined the club. 'From the start of my managership, and even before, I had envisaged my own, my very own, nursery or crèche,' he stated. 'The pre-war method of team-building was to wait for a weakness to occur and try to repair it by buying a player or finding one from junior football. Teenagers were a sensation if they made a first division team. I like to think that I was the first to recognise and organise vital young talents as soon as they left school.'

From the moment that Busby had arrived at Manchester United, he set about putting in place a system that would identify and capture the best young players in the country. In order to help him do this, he assembled an outstanding backroom staff.

Joe Armstrong, a former United goalkeeper, was a vital cog in Busby's talent-spotting machine. He had been promoted to chief scout in 1950, after the death of Rocca, and Busby affectionately called him a 'little ferret', as not only did he have an eye for a player but critically he would also do whatever was necessary to sign them. Former Manchester United youth player Eamon Dunphy fondly remembers Armstrong doing just this, 'If the family was religious, Joe would add a Miraculous Medal he'd brought especially from Rome to the other gifts he bore. The medal would be for real, as were the other kindnesses ... The Armstrong approach worked in many ways, not the least of them being that the greedy, cynical and insensitive [families] would be weeded out at the wooing stage.'

Wilf McGuinness was another United player who was enticed to Old Trafford by the silver-tongued Armstrong. While Armstrong was a natural salesman, McGuinness is quick to point out that he was not by any means false, 'Though Joe was a born charmer, he was no confidence trickster, but a genuinely warm personality who looked after us all to the best of his ability and set the tone for the rest of the Old Trafford community.'

As well as bringing Armstrong to the club, Busby also hired the gentle Bert Whalley to coach the young players. Whalley had in fact been a player under Busby at United, but when he retired in 1947, Busby spotted his potential and appointed him to work as Murphy's assistant. Busby described Whalley as a 'soft spoken, studious type, a good judge and a particularly good influence on youngsters'.

Whalley's attention to detail was legendary. Every Friday night before a game, he would deliver a handwritten letter to all of the young players. In it he would outline what they had done well or poorly in the previous game, a description of the team they would be playing against the next day and also instructions for how they were to deal with their opposite number.

A stroke of good fortune, which provided Busby with another invaluable member of staff, was that trainer Tom 'Tosher' Curry had been at United since 1934 and Busby found that he fitted in perfectly with his plans. Curry had played for Newcastle United during his playing career and when he retired he then built a reputation, at both Newcastle and then Carlisle, as being able to bring the best out of young players. Curry was very popular at United and acted as a surrogate father to many of the youth team, who were away from home for the first time. It seems that Curry also loved being at the club and he kept morale high with his quips, as Busby explained:

'Tom Curry was so fond of Old Trafford that he used to bring his open razor to the ground so that he would not waste time shaving at home. If the team played badly he would leave his open razor on the dressing-room table and say: "Help yourself, lads."'

'Tom Curry was our trainer. He was an uncanny genius who would treat each one of us as his son,' remembered United star Jackie

Blanchflower, when talking about his favourite coach. 'He would build up our confidence and each of us would think that what Tom was saying was unique to us, though he would be saying the same to everyone else. He really kept us fit. Tom had a theory that a racehorse should be trained to be fit for the day of the race, not like other trainers who trained them to be fit for the day before.'

With Busby, Murphy, Armstrong, Whalley and Curry in place, Manchester United had perhaps assembled the finest talent-spotters and coaches in the history of the game. In their time together, they would create a dynasty, attracting to the club and nurturing the likes of Bobby Charlton, David Pegg, Billy Whelan, Bill Foulkes, Jackie Blanchflower, Mark Jones, Eddie Colman and, as we shall see a little later, Duncan Edwards.

This finely honed talent-spotting routine would see Armstrong, Whalley and their team of regional scouts scour the British Isles for potential stars. If they saw a young player of promise, they would send a report to Murphy, who would then discuss it with Busby. If both were keen on what they had read, they would then check out the player for themselves, as Busby recalled, 'In our relentless search for the best of the boys there are Busby-and-Murphy adventures in the James Bond class (without the ladies, of course). We have travelled tens of thousands of miles together.'

This quest to uncover the best young players in the UK provided Busby with an unparalleled reservoir of talent. The word on the football grapevine was that although Manchester United had just won the title, their next crop of players could prove to be their best yet. With so much hype building, Duncan Edwards was desperate to be a part of what promised to be the most outstanding young team in the history of the game.

4

BECOMING A BABE

Wolverhampton Wanderers were regarded by many as the most glamorous team in the country during the early 1950s. The all-star team, in their iconic gold and black shirts, boasted the likes of renowned players such as England captain Billy Wright and fellow internationals Johnny Hancocks and Jimmy Mullen. Playing an attacking and exciting brand of football under the watchful eye of manager Stan Cullis, they racked up three league titles and two FA Cups between 1949 and 1960. But rather than the trophies that Wolves accumulated, it was a series of high-profile friendlies against top foreign teams that captured the public's imagination.

During the early 1950s, club games against foreign opposition were few and far between, as the European Cup did not come into existence until 1955. Even then, the short-sighted secretary of the Football League, Alan Hardaker, who reportedly referred to foreigners as 'wops' and 'dagos', banned champions Chelsea from participating. When the continent's crack teams did then play against an English side, it was a real rarity that created enormous excitement.

Wolves' clashes against the likes of Spartak Moscow, Racing Club of Buenos Aires and Honved of Budapest electrified British football and were among the first to be staged under floodlights. Football under the lights attracted fans to Molineux like moths to a flame, while the TV coverage that broadcast these alluring fixtures into living rooms throughout the country had youngsters such as George Best idolising the team from the West Midlands.

Wolves' encounter with Ferenc Puskas' Honved, on 13 December 1954, was perhaps the most memorable of these exotic friendly games. Just a year earlier the Hungarian national side, containing six of Honved's players, had embarrassed England at Wembley with a scintillating display of fantasy football, which saw them cruise to a 6-3 win. This was England's first defeat on home soil by a continental team and it caused significant aftershocks throughout the football world, with many stunned to see the inventors of the game so soundly beaten. England tried to avenge this catastrophic defeat six months later in Hungary, but instead suffered one of their darkest days as they were again thrashed, this time by 7-1.

Another heavy defeat was therefore confidently predicted for English football when Wolves faced the star-studded Hungarian club side. Omens looked to be bleak when, after just 14 minutes, Honved had raced into a 2-0 lead. With their backs against the wall, Wolves dramatically fought back and against all odds won the game 3-2, which saw one newspaper declare them as 'the champions of the world'. Their remarkable performance, albeit in a friendly, had helped to restore some national pride and earned them the gratitude of the country.

Edwards couldn't help but have a soft spot for Wolves due to his father's love for them. As a player for the Birmingham and District side, he was even fortunate to be able to train at their ultra-modern stadium twice a week. Many thought that the natural transition would be for the boy from Dudley to graduate to his local team when he reached his 16th birthday. Indeed, even those at Wolves expected his signature to be a formality and therefore didn't put as much effort into chasing him as other clubs did. Despite being an ardent Wolves fan, Gladstone didn't try to influence his son's decision. As much as he wanted him to play for the club that he supported, first and foremost his priority was to ensure that Duncan was happy.

Don Howe, who would go on to play for England, as well as manage Arsenal, had felt certain that Edwards' future would be at Molineux. 'I was just a year or two older than Duncan, but I knew him quite well because he lived in Dudley and I lived in Sedgley. I'm almost certain the Wolves were trying to get Duncan to sign for them as a schoolboy. He was going to the Wolves; that's what we all thought in the Midlands.'

If Wolves' efforts were half-hearted, one club that did pull out all of the stops was Bolton Wanderers. The club's chief scout, Frank Pickford, raved about the youngster and went beyond the call of duty to try to persuade him to sign for the Trotters. 'Duncan Edwards was the boy who had the lot,' Pickford remembered fondly. 'From the first sighting, George Taylor [our chief coach at that time] and myself both realised what a grand player he was going to become. We saw him in a trial match at Dudley Port, but missed him after the game, so off we went to the local police station to enquire about the lad's address. "Thirty One Elm Road, Priory Estate, Dudley" we were told and I'll never forget it.'

In order to entice Duncan to his club, Pickford visited the Edwards household, which by this stage was receiving scouts from all over the country, and put on a charm offensive. Gladstone and Annie Edwards warmed to the Bolton scout, who was well mannered and humorous, and left them in no doubt that he would look after their only son as if he were his own. Pickford felt sure that this good rapport would lead to Edwards' signature. 'I didn't honestly feel any other club would get him,' he confided. 'I got on well with his mother and father, and in fact his dad and I enjoyed a couple of pints in the Royal Oak pub opposite their house.'

Sensing that Edwards was still unconvinced, Pickford invited him to travel to Bolton to meet star player Nat Lofthouse, and to have a look around their stadium, Burnden Park. Edwards did just this, and although he enjoyed himself, he was still reluctant to commit. The Bolton management were, however, confident that they still held an ace card: his family ties to the club. Duncan's uncle, Ray Westwood, had of course played for the Lancashire side before the war and his cousin, Dennis Stevens, had recently signed a professional contract there. Stevens had been in no doubt that he would soon be playing alongside his young cousin once again. 'From what I gathered, Bolton were very confident of signing Duncan, and naturally, being part of the family and knowing what a player he was going to develop into, I was quite looking forward to him joining me at Bolton. At least he would have had someone he knew at the club.'

Yet despite the presence of his cousin at Burnden Park, Edwards was still not keen. Ray Parry, an England team-mate of his, had also recently signed for Bolton and Pickford asked him to intervene in order to make one last desperate attempt to persuade his friend to join him. 'The Bolton Wanderers chief scout in those days was Frank Pickford,' said Parry, 'and he convinced manager Bill Ridding that as he had already signed me for inside-left, if he could get Duncan Edwards for left-half and David Pegg for outside-left we would be able to transfer our very successful results as England Schoolboy players to the hurly-burly of Division One. So one day, Frank took me down to Dudley to try and convince Duncan that Bolton Wanderers were the side for him.'

Ray Parry's plea, however, fell on deaf ears. Edwards had already decided that he wanted to join only one team. 'Our journey had been fruitless,' Parry remembered, 'as Duncan said to me, "Sorry Ray, thanks for the interest but I'm going to join Manchester United" . . . It wouldn't have mattered if he had the opportunity to join any side in the world, he only wanted to go to Old Trafford and become a Manchester United player.'

Edwards' mother would have preferred it if her son had signed for a local club, but she also knew that there was only one team on his mind. 'All the clubs were after him as a schoolboy and we would have loved him to play for the Wolves, or the Albion, or the Villa,' Annie ruefully said. 'But he said that Manchester United were the greatest club in the country and nothing would stop him from going to Old Trafford.'

His choice of Manchester United seemed a strange one to some, given his links to other clubs, but, as previously stated, Edwards was a Manchester United fan and this obviously made the club an attractive proposition. He also revealed that there were other factors behind his desire to move to Old Trafford: 'I thought my future would be better away from the Midlands, where I lived,' he confessed. 'And United had a great reputation for giving plenty of opportunities to young players and treating them in the best possible manner.'

In spite of Edwards' preference, he had still not received a concrete offer from United at this stage. Although his England team-mate David Pegg had recently signed, it appeared that they weren't pushing the boat out for him. He need not have worried. United had in fact been keeping track of him since 1948, when the club's Midlands scout, Jack O'Brien, saw Edwards play and hurriedly wrote the following telegram to Matt Busby, 'Have today seen a schoolboy who merits special watching. His name is Duncan Edwards of Dudley. Instructions please.'

Upon receiving this message, Busby put his talent-spotting machine into overdrive and arranged for his assistants, Bert Whalley and Jimmy Murphy, to immediately go and cast their eyes over the youngster from Dudley. Following a thumbs-up from Murphy and Whalley, Busby, with the help of his assistants, started to build a dossier on Edwards whereby he looked into every aspect of not only his football ability but also his character. Murphy even went so far as to speak to the teachers at Wolverhampton Street to ensure that Edwards had the right temperament to fit into an institution like Manchester United. In the meantime, Busby's Midland scouting team, Jack O'Brien and Reg Priest, watched Edwards play at every opportunity and they continued to send rave reviews back to Old Trafford.

No matter where Busby went scouting for young players, he was always asked the same question, 'Why don't you sign Duncan Edwards?' On one occasion, Busby had been particularly keen to sign Edwards' England Schoolboys team-mate Alec Farrell, but instead he found Joe Mercer urging him to sign Edwards, who had so impressed him at that FA coaching course in Blackpool. 'When we were chatting one day, Joe said that among the many promising boys one was outstanding,' Busby recalled. 'This was a boy called Duncan Edwards. Joe had heard Duncan say in the dressing room that he wanted to go to Manchester United.'

Shortly afterwards, Busby managed to meet with Edwards and explained that Manchester United were keeping a close eye on his progress. Edwards was overjoyed, and told Busby that he didn't want to play anywhere else, as Busby explained:

'What everyone said about him was correct. It was obvious he was going to be a player of exceptional talent. So easy on the ball, two-footed, perfect balance, legs like oak trees, and a temperament to match. We had to have him, but there was one thought in the back of my mind. Would Duncan want to play for his local side, which was Wolverhampton Wanderers? I had no need to worry, because as soon as we met he said that he thought Manchester United were the greatest team in the world, and as soon as he was old enough he would sign for us.'

Despite this discussion, and Edwards' promise, United appeared to have fallen behind in the race to win his signature due to Bolton and Wolves both making strong bids to sign him before his 16th birthday. Annie and Gladstone pressured their son into signing a contract with one of the clubs, so that his future would be secure, and though Edwards was worried that Manchester United had lost interest, he held firm. An exasperated Annie remembers telling him, 'Well my son, it's your life; you go where you want to go.'

When Priest heard that Edwards was possibly wavering, he panicked at the thought that United were set to lose out on the talented youngster. In a fluster, he contacted Busby and told him that if he wanted Edwards he had to move quickly.

By this stage, Busby had seen enough. He knew that he had to have Edwards at any cost. Aware that time was of the essence, on the evening of 2 June 1952 Busby instructed Whalley to drive to Dudley immediately and not to return without Duncan Edwards' signature. Unfortunately, shortly after starting off, Whalley's car broke down and he faced having to hitch-hike back to Manchester with time ticking away.

When a tired and fed-up Whalley finally arrived back in Manchester, he was met by an excitable Jimmy Murphy. Murphy was anxious that they needed to tie up the deal that night, so he hired a car and proposed driving straight to Dudley, disregarding the fact that they would arrive in the early hours of the morning. With Busby's orders ringing in his ears, and the mad, energetic Welshman ushering him into the hire car, Whalley had no choice but to continue on his mission.

At around two in the morning, an exhausted Whalley and a restless Murphy finally arrived at the Priory estate, and in the darkness they eventually located the Edwards' home. Though all the lights in the house were out, and everyone appeared to be fast asleep, this didn't deter Murphy from enthusiastically knocking on the door and waking Gladstone Edwards, as well as Jimmy the dog, who barked loudly at the intruders and woke the neighbours.

Gladstone, who was worried that something must be seriously wrong for someone to knock on his door at such a late hour, rushed down the stairs only to be met by an embarrassed Whalley. He apologetically tried to explain their predicament in getting to Dudley, but Murphy got straight down to business, and virtually invited himself into the house, while ordering Gladstone to raise his young son from his sleep.

Annie, still half asleep and in a daze, appeared at the door to see what all the commotion was about. Murphy explained that he was from Manchester United and had a dream offer for her son. Once Annie had heard that the two gentlemen were from the club that Duncan idolised, she knew that he wouldn't mind being dragged out of bed.

Subsequently, a groggy 15-year-old Duncan Edwards trudged down the stairs wondering what on earth was going on. He soon perked up when he realised that the men were from Manchester United and that they had made this special effort to sign him. While Bolton and Wolves had spent months trying to persuade him to sign, it took only ten minutes for Edwards to agree to join Busby's revolution. Once Murphy and Whalley had triumphantly left the Edwards' home, Duncan is said to have muttered, 'I don't know what all this fuss was about. I've said all along that Manchester United were the only club I wanted to join.'

In his coaching book, *Tackle Soccer This Way*, Edwards discussed the circumstances regarding his signing. Strangely, he stated that Matt Busby himself had come to his house on the day of his 16th birthday (1 October 1952) and that was when he had decided to sign for Manchester United. It can be said with some certainty that this is incorrect, as the *Manchester Evening Chronicle* announced his signing on 4 June 1952, months before his October birthday. Records from the club also show that he was already playing for the United youth team by September 1952. Indeed, the autobiographies of Jimmy Murphy and Matt Busby also both make explicitly clear that Busby was not at the Edwards' home on the night Duncan signed. Disregarding this confusion, Duncan's wish had come true: he was officially a Manchester United player.

Gladstone and Annie were thrilled that their son was so happy, but at the same time they couldn't help but feel a little sad. Annie wished that her only son wouldn't have to move away, as she knew that the house would be deathly quiet without him bounding around the place. Gladstone was also disappointed, particularly at the fact that Duncan had spurned Wolves' advances, but he couldn't deny that

Manchester United would be a great club for his son to learn his trade.

However, Annie's disappointment would in time be somewhat tempered. Clubs were not permitted to offer the parents of promising young players financial inducements to persuade their children to sign, but mysteriously, just a few days after Edwards had agreed to join Manchester United, she was proudly showing off a brand-new, top-of-the-range washing machine.

5

WELCOME TO MANCHESTER

On a searing hot summer's day in July 1952, Gladstone and a tearful Annie waved their son off as he took the next step towards realising his dream, becoming a professional footballer with Manchester United. Dressed in Gladstone's hand-me-downs and holding a packet of Spangles, his favourite sweets, Duncan Edwards boarded the train at Dudley, sat back in his seat, and focused on the challenge that lay ahead. United had recently won the first division title, with the likes of Johnny Carey, Jack Rowley and Stan Pearson starring, and for once Edwards questioned whether he was good enough to make an impression alongside such illustrious company.

Joining him on the trip north was his old Birmingham and England Schoolboys team-mate Gordon Clayton, who had also recently signed for Manchester United. Clayton recalls the excitement of their journey to Old Trafford together clearly and remembers how Edwards was always a man of his word, no matter the circumstances. 'Duncan said he'd meet me on the train. "I'll save you a seat," he promised. He got on at Dudley, I got on at Stafford. I can see it now. The train is pulling into Stafford and he is hanging out of the window waving. He'd saved me a seat. The train was empty. But he saved my seat.'

Once the two boys arrived at London Road station, which was renamed Manchester Piccadilly in 1960, they made their way to Old Trafford to report for duty. On their way through the bustling city, where horse-drawn carts were still in operation, they were no doubt struck by the similarity between the Manchester and West Midland landscapes.

Like Dudley, Manchester was also renowned for its industry, and the city was choking under a thick blanket of smog resulting from hundreds of factories (such as the MetroVicks plant, which produced industrial electrical equipment) polluting the atmosphere, particularly around the Old Trafford area. 'When we got to the ground there was this smell,' Clayton recalled. 'It was the fumes from Trafford Park. I'll never forget that Old Trafford smell. When I think of Manchester United, I always get that funny smell.'

Trafford Park was the largest industrial estate in the UK, as well as being one of the biggest in Europe. It was a major source of employment for Mancunians, with over 54,000 people working there in the early 1950s on an average wage of just £9 5s a week (or £9.25, though footballers weren't much better off as the maximum amount that they could earn had been capped at just £14 per week since 1951). Although unemployment wasn't a problem, as it had been before the war, life was still extremely tough for many. The poor living conditions many workers had to endure was a particular source of hardship. A survey conducted after the war had found that 120,000 terraced houses inhabited by workers in Manchester were sub-standard, with 69,000 of these labelled as 'unfit for human habitation'. Some areas of the city were little better than slums, but with money tight at this time the council could not afford to do much about it.

The people who lived in these areas made up a large proportion of Manchester United's fanbase. They certainly didn't come from as far afield as the south, or even America and Asia as they do today. The club's fans were mostly born-and-bred Mancunians who worked in the factories and mills that stood in the shadow of Old

Trafford. Going to a game offered them some respite from their hard lives, and thankfully they could afford to go, with the cheapest tickets being priced in the region of 1s 3d (just over six pence in today's money).

When Edwards and Clayton arrived outside Old Trafford, they were greeted by a dirty red brick stand with the words 'Manchester United' emblazoned in red lights on top of it. This was it. This was the venue that was going to make all of their dreams come true.

The stadium may have left them smiling in excitement, but the sight that greeted them was a far cry from the ultra-modern, all-seater venue that is now regarded as one of Europe's top sporting facilities. It certainly wasn't fit for the so-called 'prawn sandwich brigade', and you'd struggle to find a megastore selling Johnny Carey bedspreads and curtains.

As discussed earlier, the stadium had been bombed during the war, and although it had eventually been rebuilt, it had been done so on a very strict budget. Consequently, there were definitely no frills. Most of the stands remained uncovered and the parts that were boasted dilapidated tin roofs, which were riddled with bullet holes. Frustrated by the legion of pigeons roosting under the roof, one board member had apparently taken to shooting at them. This may have helped solve the pigeon problem, but the bullet holes in the roof now meant that the frequent Manchester drizzle dripped onto the spectators' heads, although it has to be said that this was preferable to pigeon droppings.

Seating in the stadium was also limited, as the majority of the ground was standing only, with little access to the toilets, which in fact resembled nothing more than a hole in the wall in any event. If a fan was stuck at the front of one of the crowded stands, the toilets would be almost impossible to reach, which left them with little choice but to urinate where they were standing, sometimes onto the back of the person stood in front of them.

One of the terraced areas was the so-called 'Scoreboard End', which had the red-bricked Kilvert's Pure Lard factory towering behind it. Unsurprisingly, the end gained its name because a black and yellow scoreboard was positioned on top of the open-air stand. The scoreboard had 26 boxes which were all marked with a letter of the alphabet. Corresponding with these letters would be fixtures, which were listed in the match programme. At half time, the letters on the scoreboard would open up to be replaced by a number, letting the crowd know what the other scores were from around the country. There was no such thing as portable radios or mobile phones back then, so this was the only way the crowd would know what was going on. When the result of a big game was displayed, a huge commotion would simultaneously break out around the stadium as fans discussed what consequences the results would have for United.

Similar scenes of commotion could also be heard in the small, terraced Stretford End before most games. The stand, which backed on to the Glover's Cables factory, looked over the factory's football pitch. When the factory football team took to the field on a Saturday lunchtime, fans would gather at the top of the stand to watch the game, cheering and hollering for Glovers as if it were United in action.

The surroundings for the fans were certainly far from luxurious, but it wasn't as if it was much better for the players. Unlike most top-flight stadiums, Old Trafford did not have a purpose-built medical room or gymnasium at this stage, and the changing rooms were little better than the cold, drab facilities that most park teams use today.

There was one aspect of Old Trafford, however, that did match that of even the club's most wealthy rivals: the pitch. Unlike the bowling green playing surfaces of today, the pitch looked like a poorly kept cow field, with huge areas little more than a mud bath. In the 1950s, this sort of playing surface was the norm, so it did not particularly stand out as being any worse than anywhere else.

In spite of Old Trafford's inadequacies, fans and players at the club still regarded it as their 'Theatre of Dreams'. After all, this was where once a fortnight the local community could come together, forget about their problems, and cheer on their boys in red, who they felt were one of their own.

With their stadium tour at an end, Joe Armstrong sent the two Midland boys on their way to their digs, which would be their home for the foreseeable future. Alongside other United stars, the boys were to be housed at nearby 5 Birch Avenue, which was run by a Mr and Mrs Watson.

Mrs Watson was the perfect surrogate mother for young footballers away from home for the first time. Patient, kind and understanding, she would cook all her guests breakfast and dinner, which the boys would noisily eat together on a circular mahogany table in the dining room, and she prided herself on learning all of her residents' likes and dislikes. Nothing seemed to be too much trouble for her, and this led to a relaxed and happy atmosphere in the house. Parents could certainly rest easy knowing that their son was under her watchful eye.

The location of the house was also perfect for the United players, as it was situated just a short distance from Old Trafford, which of course meant that they could leave it until the last possible moment in the mornings before getting out of bed. Homely, with its old armchairs and rugs in front of the fireplace, those that stayed at Birch Avenue remember how the dining room always smelt of beeswax polish, due to Mrs Watson continually cleaning the oak furniture, and the distinctive clanking, tick-tock sound of an old grandfather clock, situated in the corner of the room. Even though the boys would have to share rooms, and in some cases single beds, the house was in all likelihood seen as very comfortable accommodation, especially with its inside toilets and bathroom. The majority of the Manchester United youngsters were from working-class backgrounds and the houses in Birch Avenue, situated in a respectable suburban area, would have been far better than most of them were used to.

Birch Avenue wasn't, however, just the home for young

Manchester United players. It was also a place to stay for travelling salesmen and lorry drivers who were passing through Manchester. With the testosterone of young footballers, the bravado of the sales-men and the coarse, boisterous ways of the lorry drivers, this meant that the atmosphere in the house was nearly always loud and fun-filled. It was definitely not a place for the shy and retiring.

When Edwards and Clayton first arrived, they were warmly greeted by Mrs Watson and made to feel very much at home. Showing the boys to their room, she then made them a cup of tea and told them all about the other United residents, who were away at this time on a tour of America. Edwards typically said very little. He was always nervous in strangers' company and rarely made eye contact unless he knew someone well. As Mrs Watson tried to engage him in conversation, he looked at the floor and muttered one-word answers in response, letting Clayton do all of the talking.

A few days after their arrival, the other United residents returned to the house and were surprised to see that the two newcomers had made themselves comfortable. Among the returning party was Edwards' old England Schoolboys team-mate, David Pegg, as well as Mark Jones and Jackie Blanchflower. Faced with the new recruits imposing themselves on their turf, the youngsters were initially reluc-tant to include the strangers from the Midlands in their group. They even seemed to resent the fact that since they had been away, Mrs Watson appeared to be making an extra fuss over Edwards, who she could tell was shy and homesick. As Jackie Blanchflower later explained, 'We were a bit disturbed; somebody had broken into our little circle. We were a bit jealous, probably a bit too hard on them.'

Blanchflower, nicknamed 'Twiggy', had arrived at Old Trafford from Belfast in 1949 as a hard-faced 16-year-old who looked twice his age. By trade he was a centre-back but could play a variety of dif-ferent positions, if called upon, and this versatility would sometimes see him play up-front, where he scored some vital goals. He was a tough competitor, on and off the football pitch, and behind the club's back he would sometimes take part in illegal prize-fighting competitions in order to earn some extra money. At this stage, he had already made his debut in the first team but unfortunately, prior to the club's summer tour of America, a knee injury had meant he had been unable to play for nine months.

Yorkshireman Jones was regarded by the boys as a father figure and his trademark long overcoat and trilby hat certainly made him appear years older than 19. Although he was a similar age to the other boys, he seemed wise beyond his years. Bobby Charlton has said of him, 'To us he was an old man. He smoked a pipe and had a sort of presence.' Jones' presence may have had something to do with the fact that he was 6ft 2in tall and weighed almost 13st. Despite this huge physique, team-mate Albert Scanlon said that he was 'as gentle as a mouse off the field'. On the field, however, Jones was a ruthless centre-half and it was here where his personality metamorphosed, as he was said to be as hard as nails. Jones had also made his first team debut, but he was not a regular, and would have to wait until 1955 before he would become a fixture in the side.

Pegg, a fellow Yorkshireman, was regarded by many as one of the top talents in the country. Busby was in fact so sure of his potential that he had told his mother that he would gamble his life on Pegg becoming a professional. Plenty of hype had surrounded Pegg's arrival at Old Trafford, but he never got carried away with himself. He just seemed to enjoy his life on and off the pitch. Pegg loved to spend his time listening to his favourite music stars, Frank Sinatra and Nat 'King' Cole, and would also enjoy having a dance when the boys were on a night out. Though he was tipped to have a glittering career, he had to bide his time before he made his first team debut as Busby wanted him to build up his slight frame. It wouldn't, however, be too long before he made an impact in the first division – or on the pubs and clubs of Manchester.

Unlike the other boys, Berry hadn't been groomed through the United youth system. After a long chase, Busby had in fact bought him from Birmingham City. Although he was one of the smallest players in the league, whenever he had faced United Berry had tormented Busby's team. These performances had so impressed the United manager that he pulled out all the stops to secure his services. Finally, after a number of attempts, Busby got his man for the then huge sum of £25,000. Busby wasted little time in throwing the tricky winger into action, as he went straight into the United side which went on to win the title in 1952.

Among such exuberant and exalted company, Edwards was very quiet during his first few weeks in Manchester. It was not only the fact that the other boys didn't initially make much effort to welcome him, but that they also mimicked his thick Dudley accent whenever he did speak. This was also the first time that the young lad had lived away from home, and in a big city like Manchester, he seemed overwhelmed by it all.

'Duncan was a little bit introverted when he came to Manchester at first,' Clayton has revealed. 'He wouldn't go to the bank on his own, for example. He wasn't a mixer as such. He was shy with people.'

Lonely and missing home, Edwards frequently rang his mother to see how she, dad and Jimmy the dog were faring. Reading between the lines, Annie could tell that her son wasn't happy. 'Duncan was not one to push his problems on to others,' she said. 'He never told me if he had any kind of troubles. He didn't want to worry me. If I heard anything at all, it would come from someone else. I think he must have been a bit homesick when he first went to Manchester. He used to bring me down his washing. And he always had a bunch of flowers for me. But after a while he stopped bringing down his washing and instead must have taken it to a laundry. It was a sign that he was settling up there.'

As is usually the case with young men, once they got to know one another, the banter started to flow and before long Edwards and Clayton were accepted into the gang. Soon Edwards became renowned for calling everyone 'chief' and his team-mates nicknamed him 'Brush', due to his insistence on continually brushing his room. Edwards was fanatical about everything being spotless and in his book, *Tackle Soccer This Way*, he devoted several pages to issues of cleanliness with instructions such as: 'See that shirts, shorts and socks are always clean and well darned. A smart team starts off with high morale.'

Throughout the book, Edwards reveals a zealous attention to detail regarding every aspect of football life from technique and fitness to the necessity of shinguards and looking after your football boots properly. This determination to analyse all facets of the game, and then to perfect them, played a big part in him mastering so many of the requirements of a professional footballer. Like David Beckham, he may have had something of an obsessive-compulsive disorder, as he wouldn't rest until satisfied that he could complete a task as well as the best. Team-mate Albert Scanlon recalls a time when he witnessed him do just this, 'There was one time when we were doing laps before Jimmy [Murphy] and Bert [Whalley] came out and there was a lad called Alan Rhodes there. He was a full-back from Chesterfield, but he was also a gymnast, and could do double somersaults. He'd run down the track and do it. Course, Duncan has to have a go. He falls flat on his arse the first time; the second time he does it, no problem.'

After finally settling in at Birch Avenue, Edwards began to focus on proving himself on the football pitch. Usually, he was confident that he would be the best player for any team that he played for, but now he was understandably apprehensive. He may have recently captained the England Schoolboys team, but at league champions Manchester United he was just another hopeful fresh face. Here he would be playing alongside young stars such as Roger Byrne and Johnny Berry, who had already played first team football, and older established players like Jack Rowley and Johnny Aston. It must have seemed an impossible task at times to imagine not only leapfrogging all of his fellow young prospects to challenge for a first team spot, but to then also take the position of a senior pro, who had just won a league title.

A small crumb of comfort was the youth of most of the players at the club. 'The first time I entered the dressing room to meet the other players, I wondered if I was in the right place,' Edwards recalled. 'There were so many other youngsters that it seemed almost like being back at school. I found it very easy to settle down and make friends.'

Just by looking at the man-child, one would never have guessed that he was one of the youngest players at Old Trafford. At 15 years old, he was almost 6ft in height and weighed just under 12st. His frame was solid muscle, with not an inch of fat, and his massive, muscular legs were like tree trunks, which saw him have to hitch his shorts up, over at the waistband, so that they could fit over his bulging thighs.

Bill Foulkes, who had been at United since 1950, and had continued to work down a coal mine even after making his first team debut, spoke of his disbelief when he found out Edwards' age. 'When I first bumped into Duncan at the Cliff [training ground] and they told me he was only fifteen, I simply couldn't believe it. He had a man's body, a giant's really, although he had the face of a boy. He was so mature in terms of his football and his physique, with all the natural ability anyone could imagine. Every time he did something, on the training pitch or in a match, he would surprise me.'

On 12 July 1952, Edwards commenced his first Manchester United pre-season training regime and it was certainly not for the faint-hearted. The emphasis initially focused very much on building stamina through long runs and a football was rarely seen. A typical pre-season at the club was described by Jackie Blanchflower:

'Our training started five weeks before the beginning of the season; from about 12 July we would train for about two hours in the morning and two hours in the afternoon. For the first two weeks, we'd be as stiff as boards. We trained at the university ground, running lap after lap of the track. After two weeks, when we were fit, we would be given a ball for the first time. The emphasis was placed on fitness so that we had a really sound basis for the rest of the season.'

Despite this arduous regime, Edwards threw himself into the running and didn't complain. However, he did later reveal that he did not agree that training should focus so heavily on physical fitness, particularly in the case of younger boys. 'I am so strongly against running as a training method for boys … He would do far better to forget about running and concentrate on ball work and strengthening exercises.' Edwards was ahead of his time in this thinking. Unfortunately, it would take many years for British coaches to focus more heavily on technique, rather than physical fitness, and this approach ultimately hindered the progression of football in this country. In fact, some might say that even to this day this remains a problem in the British game.

Most of the club's training was conducted at the Cliff and, even though this famous training facility produced the likes of Edwards, Charlton, Best, Giggs, Beckham and many others over the years, it was far from a glamorous setting. Even just getting there could involve a major expedition. Up early in the morning, the players would have to catch a bus, change in the city centre, and then walk to the training ground, often in the pouring rain. Upon arrival, they would then have to fight over the ancient and usually dirty training gear. 'At West Ham we'd had modern training gear. But at Old Trafford it was all great big sweaters and socks full of holes,' remembered Noel Cantwell, who joined United from West Ham in 1960. 'We were given boots in training that were like cut-off wellingtons. It would remind you of being in prison.'

Another future United starlet, Wilf McGuinness, also had harsh words for the Cliff: 'The floodlights were dreadful, you could hardly see. The training kit was the worst imaginable. It was never washed ... Afterwards you'd get in the bath – forty of you – it was black within two minutes. When you got out you'd have to have a cold shower to get the muck off. Many's the time I remember standing there shivering, looking for a towel, practically in tears after a bollocking Jimmy [Murphy] had given me.'

Despite the emphasis on running, and the appalling training conditions, Edwards was in his element and loved being a Manchester United player. If he could have trained every hour of the day, there is little doubt that he would have. Unfortunately, this would not be an option until he turned 17, as only then would he be eligible to sign a professional contract. Up until that stage, Edwards had two choices: either learn a trade or become a member of the groundstaff.

If a player opted to learn a trade then they had a variety of jobs they could choose from such as engineering, building and plumbing. During the day the player would work in their chosen job and would then train twice a week at night. It was certainly hard work, but the luckier youngsters sometimes found that their boss was a United fan, who would let them take it easy, so that they could devote more of their time to football.

Rather than learn a trade, most players preferred to join the United groundstaff. Although they would still have to perform menial tasks around Old Trafford, such as cleaning the changing rooms, painting the walls and sweeping the turnstiles, they could also train most days. This of course also gave them more of an opportunity to impress in front of both Murphy and Busby, who prowled the touchline and kept everybody on their toes.

Annie Edwards, however, hammered home to her son the importance of an alternative career, 'I told Duncan that it was important to have another trade to go with his football because you never could tell how things would work out.' Eager to please, Edwards complied with his mother's wishes, as Annie recalled, 'He said he might try his hand at cabinet-making, but he was only trying to please me.'

Unsurprisingly, Edwards' heart was never really in his cabinet-making apprenticeship. In his mind he was at Manchester United to play football and his chance of making it would only be improved if he was playing regularly. After just a few weeks in the job, he packed it in to join the groundstaff, without telling his mother, for fear she would be disappointed. 'He never told us what he'd done,' remembered Annie. 'We found out ourselves.'

This change meant that while he was expected to complete his groundstaff duties, he could also train two or three times a week with the professionals. The mundane groundstaff work may not have been glamorous, but Edwards was in high spirits, as he had the opportunity to spend more time mixing with the players that he idolised. He revealed that although they would 'rib me a great deal and laugh at me', they were always happy to dispense advice and that playing alongside them saw him pick up more in a few weeks than he would have learnt in 12 months of coaching.

It was during these training sessions where the professionals at Manchester United saw first hand just why Edwards was being heralded as a future full England international. 'We used to look at players in training to see if we might have to get them to concentrate more on their kicking, perhaps, or their heading or ball control, whatever,' said Matt Busby. 'We looked at Duncan, right at the start, and gave up trying to spot flaws in his game.'

One factor which the United staff particularly liked about Edwards, apart from his talent, was that he would do exactly what he was told, even if it was to his detriment. 'After training we used to play a practice game,' recalled Albert Scanlon. 'Bill Inglis [a former United player and coach], who liked to sneak off somewhere quiet for a smoke, says to us: "Go out there and do some laps until I'm ready for you." So Duncan puts his top on, two towels round his neck, and sets off. We did a few laps and then went back to the game. That's when we realised they were one short, and, of course it's Duncan. He's still out there running. When he finally appears after about thirty minutes Bill says: "Where the hell have you been?" and Duncan says: "No one told me to stop."'

Edwards may have had few flaws in his game, but that still didn't prevent Jimmy Murphy from attempting to mould him into the best player he could be. After youth team games on a Saturday, Murphy would tell Edwards to report for training the next day. Many footballers would have moaned at the thought of extra training on a designated rest day, particularly on a Sunday morning, when some would be nursing Saturday night hangovers, but Edwards was always keen.

Murphy knew that Edwards possessed all of the technical attributes required to be a top-class footballer, so he therefore focused on making him as fit as possible. In his thick Welsh valleys accent, Murphy used to say to him, 'At the top level you have to lose your breath, and you have to keep playing. Every time it happens, it makes you a little stronger. In all my time in football I never saw a player suffer a heart attack because he worked too hard.'

Listening intently to Murphy's advice, Edwards worked as hard as possible on his stamina and as such he soon became one of the fittest players at the club. 'One of the things that stood out about him was his fitness,' recalled McGuinness. 'We used to loosen up with a lap of the ground and moves to the side and things like that. But Duncan, he'd do anything up to ten laps in his warm-up, and those thunderous thighs of his would bounce – the muscles in them! I wouldn't say we were in awe of him exactly, but we admired him for what he could do. We tried to copy him and, instead of doing just one lap, we started doing four; but he was still far ahead of us.'

Once Murphy's lung-busting cardio sessions were finished, the day would not be at an end as the Welshman would insist on taking Edwards to the pub with him. Whereas Edwards, who rarely drank, would sip a non-alcoholic drink, Murphy would usually enjoy a glass of whisky, and regale his eager protégé with tales from his time in the game.

Slowly but surely Edwards settled into life on and off the pitch in Manchester and with the season fast approaching, he was bursting to show everyone why so much praise was being heaped on his broad young shoulders.

6

THE PRODIGY BLOSSOMS

After spending his first few weeks getting settled, Edwards finally made his Manchester United debut on 16 August 1952. The game, played in sweltering conditions, was a trial match at Old Trafford that saw the youth team split into 'The Reds' and 'The Blues'.

Edwards, as he would be in the future, was a 'Red' and for the first time he wore the number six shirt, a shirt number which he would later make his own in the first team. Lining up alongside him was his good friend Gordon Clayton and his England team-mate David Pegg. On the day 'The Reds' were victorious, as they defeated 'The Blues' 5-0, with a youngster called Bradshaw helping himself to a hat-trick. At his imperious best, Edwards had also caught the eye, excelling in defence and causing mayhem when in attack.

Despite heavily beating 'The Blues', Edwards had been impressed by the display of their right-half, Eddie Colman, not only for his playing ability but also for his non-stop chatter. Small and cheeky, Colman had already earned himself quite a reputation around the club. Some classed him as a little villain, up to no good, while others, like Bobby Charlton, would later say he was 'the cheeky-faced, mischievous boy from next door'. His team-mates regarded him as the loudest and most extroverted lad at the club, as Colman was always the first to lead a sing-song on the bus, be involved in mischief, and if out with the boys, get up and dance with a pretty girl. It seems the phrase 'life and soul of the party' was made just for him.

Colman came from Salford, a tough working-class area near Manchester, which was dominated by gasworks and terraced housing. Unlike most of his team-mates, he didn't need to stay in digs as his family home, a small house on Archie Street, which most will have seen due to its cobbled streets being filmed for the opening credits of *Coronation Street*, was close to Old Trafford.

Many of his team-mates would become regular visitors to the Colman household during their time at Manchester United, as it was here where they would usually kick off Saturday nights. An off licence on the corner of Archie Street would do a roaring trade as the play-ers would stock up on jugs of beer and sherry, which they then took back to Colman's house. Dick and Liz Colman would join the lads for a drink in the parlour and, if they were lucky, his granddad would turn up and keep everyone entertained with a few songs and jokes.

Suitably merry after a few hours' drinking, the boys would then usually venture to the Plaza ballroom, where Jimmy Savile was the DJ, or the Continental, owned by the organiser of Miss World, Eric Morley. The more confident lads, such as Colman, would have a drink and a dance, while Edwards would sit awkwardly at a table, playing with the beer mats, barely speaking. 'Eddie was a great little jiver,' recalls Wilf McGuinness. 'Duncan wasn't big on dancing or on chasing girls but the rest of us definitely were. We would all wait for smooch time, when the slow music would come on, and then we'd try our luck with one of the girls.'

Even when 'smooch time' came around, it would be rare to see Edwards on the dance floor unless his more rowdy team-mates man-aged to drag him out of his chair. He clearly had no urge to show off his Morris dancing expertise in front of his friends.

Edwards may have been shy but no one mistook this as a sign of weakness. 'Although he was unassuming he was confident. He knew what he was doing and he knew what he wanted,' said Bill Foulkes. 'He was nobody's fool. We all respected him as a person and as a player.'

Indeed, McGuinness can also recall that when the quiet Edwards did speak it was usually worth listening to. 'He didn't talk a lot and was quietly spoken in that broad Black Country accent of his. But when he did say something, you'd look at him and you'd think, "Well, I'm not going to argue with him."'

Amid the shyness, Edwards certainly had a sense of humour. He may not have had much to say but if one of his friends told a joke, his face would crack into a broad grin and his shoulders would shake as he chuckled. In return he could also be counted on to join in the banter himself from time to time, as Charlton has said: 'He was always laughing. He'd have a laugh, but never at your expense.'

Saturday nights would frequently see the young players drink the bar dry and the next day they would usually be suffering from almighty hangovers. Everyone that is but Edwards, as he very rarely succumbed to the pleasures of alcohol. In his mind, alcohol could have an adverse effect on his game, and that was something he was not prepared to sacrifice for the sake of a few drinks.

Staying clear of alcohol meant that Edwards managed to avoid trouble, unlike some of his inebriated friends. 'A few of us when we went out got into scraps,' McGuinness remembers. 'I used to throw a punch every now and again, but I never saw Duncan fight. He was a sensible lad, he never did anything stupid.'

Matt Busby's son, Sandy, who also socialised with the young Manchester United players, can remember that some of his friends who did drink would go out of their way to avoid the wrath of his father the next day. 'David Pegg and Eddie and myself got home late one night after a party and we were down at Old Trafford next day. The state they were in! David and Eddie were trying to stay out of Dad's way, but Dad had a habit of going in the dressing room and going for a pee, and usually while he was there he would ask Tom Curry about any injuries from Saturday. He went in the loo on the left of the big bath and came out a couple of minutes later saying: "Tom, tell Pegg and Colman they can come out of the toilets now." They were unshaven and dying. Dad knew where they had been.'

Edwards may have been a reserved, quiet character but he was drawn in by Colman's carefree demeanour and infectious personality. He loved his strut, his banter, and his inherent coolness, but at the same time he appreciated his down-to-earth ways. During those early awkward months at Old Trafford, Colman provided Edwards with some much-needed laughter and also served to help him settle, inviting him to his home on many occasions.

Sometimes it was easy to forget, in the midst of Colman's huge personality, that he was also a very talented footballer. Even Edwards was in awe of some of the things the livewire could do on a football pitch. In particular, Edwards marvelled at Colman's famous trick where he would slowly approach his marker like a snake charmer, luring them into committing themselves, before quickly swivelling his hips, sending his opponent one way while he set off in the opposite direction with the ball. This move saw the Old Trafford faithful nickname him 'Snake hips', something he took great pride in. No matter how hard his team-mates practised, they could never quite master the swivel move as well as he could.

Colman was, however, just one of many supremely talented youngsters at the club as Busby, Murphy and Joe Armstrong had assembled one of the best youth teams in the country. Although United had recently won the title, Busby was convinced that his next great team would revolve around his young stars. 'Despite the marvellous achievement in finally lifting the league championship in 1952, after four years of disappointment as runners-up, in my opinion the young players on the United books are worth hundreds of thousands of pounds. In a couple of years' time we shall have wonderful young material when it is most needed.'

Busby's 'young material' was the result of a revolutionary system called 'The Manchester United Junior Athletic Club', commonly referred to as the MUJAC. This system had actually been put in place before the war and had seen James Gibson, the director who owned the club, announce in an AGM in 1939, 'It is from these unusually comprehensive nurseries that the club hopes an all-Manchester team at some distant period might be produced.' With Busby focusing a lot of his attention on the MUJAC, a home-grown 'all-Manchester team' was rapidly becoming a real prospect as some of the youngsters were slowly beginning to flourish and push for a first team spot.

Put simply, the MUJAC consisted of three sides: the A team, the Colts and the Juniors. If a player progressed through each of those teams they would then play in the Reserves before finally, if they were ready, gracing the first team. The standard of each of these sides was a significant level above the other, and few made it all the way, and initially it bore little fruit. Jimmy Murphy even had to inform Busby in 1948 that not one single player in the system would make the grade. Cliff Birkett, an exciting winger at youth level, was by far the hottest prospect in the MUJAC at that stage, but even his career died a death after a handful of first team appearances. But the crop of 1952-53 were different. Murphy felt that a lot of these boys had what it took to reach the very top of the game. It was truly a once-in-a-generation harvest.

Following 'The Reds' versus 'The Blues', Edwards was selected to play for the Colts, in their Manchester Amateur League match against Heywood St James at the Cliff. Starting as they meant to go on that season, the might of the United team was too strong for Heywood, as they comfortably won 6-1. Two further top-class performances saw Edwards swiftly promoted to the A team.

Ball Haye Green were the opponents when Edwards made his A team debut, alongside the likes of Bill Foulkes and Albert Scanlon. Foulkes and Scanlon had known Edwards as a mild-mannered boy off the pitch, but once the barrel-chested youngster took to the field they were shocked at the change in him. Loudly demanding the ball and screaming at those who he did not believe were putting in the required effort, he was unrecognisable from the shy boy they had previously known. Thanks to his unbridled passion and unquenchable thirst for victory, United triumphed 4–3. Over the next few weeks Edwards and the team went from strength to strength as they steam-rollered over most opponents, but they soon found that not all the games were so easy.

As the A team played in the Manchester League, they were usually up against hardened older men who would try to physically intimidate the young United players. This tactic rarely worked, particularly against the likes of Edwards, who enjoyed a tussle. Occasionally, however, the verbal and physical intimidation did unsettle a few of the boys and produced some poor results, such as when the A team lost to Adelphi Lads Club, 2–1, in the A.Pettitt Cup. Although they were out of that competition, the boys were still doing well in the league and by the end of October the A team were in second place, just behind Taylor Bros.

In any event, being out of the A.Pettitt Cup wasn't the end of the world. The 1952–53 campaign was the inaugural season of the FA Youth Cup and Busby was determined to win the competition, as vindication for assembling the best young players in the country. In his gentle yet forceful manner, Busby made both the players and the coaching staff acutely aware that this competition should resemble the pinnacle of their ambitions. Anything less than winning it would be considered a failure.

Edwards' progress had been so swift in his first few months at the club that he was named captain of the team when they kicked off the competition with a game at the Cliff against fierce rivals Leeds United. On a windswept afternoon, United were too strong for the Leeds side as they crushed them 4–0, with Leeds centre-back Jack Charlton contributing to the scoreline with an own goal. United's debut in the competition couldn't have gone any better.

An outstanding display in the next round saw the United youngsters hit top gear as they registered what remains a record FA Youth Cup scoreline. On a day to remember, United beat a sorry-looking Nantwich 23-0, with Edwards notching five goals. Although the opposition was obviously poor, this did not stop one reporter from heralding Edwards as, 'The greatest junior prospect I have ever seen. That is no exaggeration.'

Edgar Turner, another reporter, had also been blown away by his awesome display: 'He is big and almost as strong as a man and I cannot recall one pass, long or short, by Edwards that could not be described to conjure up a phrase from the past such as a daisy cutter. His delivery of the ball to his forwards, even from well back, was equal to the best I have seen anywhere, league games and internationals included, for a very long time. When I say his tackling was strong and his covering excellent it is still not the end of the story. He also scored five goals!'

On a high, United continued their good form when they saw off high-flying Bury 2-0 at Old Trafford, with Edwards grabbing the opening goal after only six minutes. Turner was once more impressed by the young prospect and wrote: 'I am sure Matt Busby could give him a game in the first team now.' This may have seemed premature to some, the youngster had after all been at the club for just a few weeks, but there was little doubt that he was really going places.

Due to Edwards' burgeoning reputation, the crowds clamoured to watch him in action. Remarkably, this saw many of the youth team games attract bigger attendances than some top-flight clubs. Whenever Edwards got on the ball, a fizz of electricity seemed to surge around the expectant 30,000 fans packed into Old Trafford. Craning their necks over the person stood in front of them, everyone hoped to witness a moment of magic, whether it be one of his surging runs, a defence-splitting pass or a net-busting shot at goal. More often than not, the fans went home happy, having seen something they could tell their mates about at the factory the next day.

Rarely did any fan go home disappointed after watching Edwards play.

Another awe-inspiring performance, this time in a friendly against Northern Nomads, saw the hype reach fever pitch as the *Manchester Guardian* lauded yet another titanic display from United's left-half: 'The encouraging thing about the game was that it showed a player of real promise in Edwards, aged 16. He is remarkably fast, and tackled well, but best of all shot with real power with either foot. Even Rowley would not have criticised several of Edwards' drives for strength and direction.' This was high praise indeed as Rowley was regarded by many, including Busby, as having the hardest shot in British football at that time.

By early December, Edwards was well and truly in his stride. Firmly established in the A team he was, however, surprised to find that when he scoured the team sheet, posted on the peeling and mouldy changing room wall, that he had been dropped. Feeling slightly dejected, he had a quick glance at the other teams only to find to his surprise and joy that he had actually been selected to play for the Reserves against Burnley. He stood rooted to the spot in shock. Playing well for the A team was one thing, but was he really ready to take such a step up?

He may have been unsure, but his composed and confident display on his debut answered any doubts, even though the Reserves actually lost the game. Edwards was certainly not blamed for the defeat and he kept his place in the side the following week, when he played in a 2-1 victory over Preston. Privately, Busby and Murphy were thrilled at their young prospect's progress. They knew he was good but they were surprised that he had taken this step up so comfortably.

For the rest of the season, Edwards played intermittently for the Reserves but he also continued to be a fixture in the youth team, who now faced their greatest test to date in the fourth round of the FA Youth Cup. Their opponents, Everton, would have always been a tough proposition, but United's task was made much harder as they had to field a weakened team, due to Eddie Lewis and David Pegg being called up to the first team. In the face of adversity, and against the run of play, Edwards won the game with a sublime piece of genius.

When a corner into the Everton penalty area took a deflection, it ricocheted high into the air towards the edge of the box. Edwards, with his back to goal, held off his marker with one hand while he delicately cushioned the falling ball with his left instep. Swivelling his body sharply, he left his opponent standing as he swiftly pulled back his right foot and struck the ball venomously on the full volley. Before his marker or the keeper could react, the ball was nestled in the top corner.

Following his FA Youth Cup heroics, Edwards was back in action for the Reserves, just three days later, in a game he couldn't wait to take part in. The match was against Wolves, at Molineux. Playing so close to home gave Edwards the opportunity to perform in front of friends and family, and he also knew that his dad would love seeing him play against his favourite team.

By this stage, Edwards was settled in Manchester but he still missed his mum terribly, so on the journey home he made sure that he took a little something with him for her. 'I didn't see much of him when he went to United as he was playing so often, but when he did come down to play he always brought with him an armful of flowers and a box of chocolates,' Annie remembered. 'He said the lads used to laugh at him on the coach for taking them with him to games.'

In fact, Annie was lucky to receive the chocolates at all, as the United lads would try to divert Edwards' attention and pinch one when he wasn't looking. Eddie Colman would usually be the chief culprit. If he wasn't mincing down the aisle, pretending to be a Hollywood starlet, with the flowers meant for Annie in his arm, then he was waiting for Edwards to fall asleep so he could swiftly gobble down a chocolate or two. When Edwards awoke he would be furious, but he couldn't stay angry with Colman for long, whose cheeky smile and relentless banter saw him talk his way out of most situations.

Raring to show his family and friends that all of the fuss surrounding him wasn't just hype, Edwards delivered a performance that must have had the Wolves management cursing the day they let this hometown boy slip through their grip. Despite falling behind to an early goal, Edwards was unperturbed as in the second half he was rewarded for his tireless work ethic. An aimless ball was pumped up the pitch in an attempt to relieve some pressure, and although it looked like a lost cause Edwards gave chase. Powering past the Wolves right-back, he reached the ball just as it stopped dead on the left-hand side of the penalty area. Almost everyone in the ground expected him to hold up the ball and wait for support, as most other players would have done. Edwards, however, wasn't most players. Without breaking his stride he struck the ball first time, from a seemingly impossible angle, and watched as it arrowed viciously past the stranded goalkeeper, clipped the inside of the far post and slammed into the net. It was his first goal for the Reserves and such was its quality that even the Wolves fans applauded.

Although United were unable to mark the occasion with a win, as Wolves went on to score again, Edwards was not too disappointed. He had emphatically shown all those that had turned up to watch him that he was indeed the real deal. Gladstone was probably the happiest man in the stadium. His son had been the star of the show, but his beloved Wolves had triumphed. The day couldn't have gone any better.

A few weeks later, Edwards won his first piece of silverware as a Manchester United player when he played for the A team in their victory over Ashton United in the Gylcriss Cup final. With the game being played at the Cliff, Busby and Murphy stood on the touchline, casting their eyes over the boy everyone was calling 'Big Dunc'. They were not disappointed. Under his breath, Murphy muttered to the boss that perhaps the swashbuckling left-half was ready for the first team. Busby nodded his trilby-covered head in satisfaction. He had seen enough. The boy from Dudley was as good a player as he had ever seen.

It is no wonder that Busby was tempted to throw Edwards into the first team at this stage as the seniors were struggling. Almost a year on from winning the title, they had now failed to live up to their own high standards. Knocked out of the FA Cup by Everton, and well off the pace in the league, the season had been a mediocre one to say the least. The team needed fresh blood, and fast.

In an attempt to shake up the team, Busby went out and signed 21-year-old centre-forward Tommy Taylor from Barnsley for the sum of £29,999. The fee made Taylor Britain's most expensive footballer, but Busby spared him the additional psychological pressure of a £30,000 transfer fee. Taylor's signing turned out to be a very astute piece of business and he soon proved that he was worth every penny as he flourished into a giant of a target man who was priceless for both United and England. Far from being just a big lump, Taylor was also a great athlete who was very comfortable with the ball on the deck, a fact that is often overlooked when discussing his considerable merits.

Taylor's signing not only shook up the team on the pitch but off it as well. A ball of energy, he lit up the Old Trafford dressing room with tales of his drunken escapades, which often saw him end up in some sort of trouble or in the bed of a willing young lady. Taylor truly was a man who men wanted to be and women wanted to be with. Yet, as with most of Busby's signings, he didn't rock the boat, he slotted straight into the team and when it came to game time he was a deadly serious professional who gave his all whenever he pulled on the red shirt.

Coincidentally, Taylor's old club, Barnsley, were the youth team's next opponents in the quarter-final of the FA Youth Cup, but United's youngsters made short work of their challengers as they eased their way to the semi-finals with a 3-1 victory, thanks to goals by Edwards, Noel McFarlane and Scanlon. A crowd of 12,400 watched the game, easily eclipsing the 7,406 who had watched Barnsley's first team play on the same day. The youngsters from Manchester were obviously seen to be a bigger draw.

Since he had joined Manchester United, some six months previously, Edwards had risen through the ranks, playing and excelling for almost every side at the club, bar the firsts. Although Edwards had made a rapid ascent, players such as David Pegg, John Scott, Eddie Lewis and John Doherty had been promoted to the first team ahead of him, though they were all at least a year older. Yet far from being discouraged, Edwards put faith in Busby to know when the time was right to play him. 'The manager has to know precisely the right moment,' he said. 'He knows how delicate is the balance between success and failure with a youngster ... Probably most young professionals feel they are ready for a first team chance long before they are.'

Those who had witnessed Edwards' mesmeric displays for the Reserves were, however, now getting very impatient to see him blooded into the first team. This can clearly be seen in a report written in the *News Chronicle* on 1 April 1953 when the reporter, George Follows, who was also from the Black Country, wrote what must be considered one of the most enthusiastic appraisals of any player yet to appear in the Football League:

Like the father of the first atom bomb, Manchester United are waiting for something tremendous to happen. This tremendous football force they have discovered is Duncan Edwards, who is exactly sixteen and a half this morning.

Though nobody can tell exactly what will happen when Edwards explodes into first division football, one thing is certain, it will be spectacular.

Take these two testimonials from chief coaches of other clubs after a recent Youth Cup game, 'Don't say I told you so, but this boy Edwards is the finest thing on two legs.' 'Don't say I said so, but this boy Edwards has got the lot.'

What can you expect to see in Edwards?

Well, the first important thing is that this boy Edwards is a man of 12st and 5ft 10in in height. That gives him his first great asset of power.

When he heads the ball, it is not a flabby flirtation with fortune, it is bold and decisive. When he tackles, it is with a mantrap bite, and when he shoots with either foot, not even Jack Rowley – the pride of Old Trafford – is shooting harder.

Add to this, body swerve and bravery and the sixth sense in a tight corner that distinguishes the truly great player and you have 'the boy who has the lot'.

If you think this is a lot to write about a lad of sixteen, I can only say you obviously haven't seen this boy Edwards.'

The avalanche of praise and hype earned Edwards a bit of mickey-taking in the dressing room, but the only thing that mattered to him was playing in the first team. Everyone else could do the talking, he just wanted to play.

Busby knew that he couldn't hold back his boy wonder any longer. The prodigy from Dudley was, in Murphy's words, 'ripe'. On Friday, 3 April 1953, as Edwards swept the stands at Old Trafford, he was summoned to the manager's office. Sheepishly he knocked on the boss's door, and was told to enter and take a seat. As Edwards squirmed, and wondered what on earth he had done wrong, Busby finally put him at ease. 'Go and get your boots, son,' he told him. 'You're playing in the first team tomorrow against Cardiff City.'

Less than a year after joining one of the greatest teams in the country, Duncan Edwards was now set to become one of the youngest players ever to have played in the Football League. He was just 16 years and 185 days old.

For one so young, and for a boy whose lifelong ambition had been to play in the Manchester United first team, Edwards was remarkably calm before his debut. After his chat with Busby, he raced back to his digs so that he could phone his parents to tell them the good news. In those days, the call to Dudley was considered a long-distance one, as it was over 15 miles away from Manchester. Having picked up the phone, he had to wait for over a minute while the operator tried to connect him to the distant Midlands. When his father finally answered, Edwards informed him in a matter-of-fact manner, 'Oh, by the way, Mr Busby has selected me to play for the firsts tomorrow.'

Once Gladstone and Annie had heard that their son would be playing for the first team, they dropped whatever plans they had for that Saturday afternoon and made arrangements to travel to Old Trafford. Trying in vain to contain his emotions, Gladstone told one reporter, 'We are as excited as a couple of kids. In fact, Duncan is the calmest member of the family just now. He is used to playing before big crowds.'

Gladstone was correct. The prospect of playing in front of a packed stadium was certainly not one that daunted his young son. After all, not only had he recently played in youth team games that attracted over 30,000 spectators, but he had also played in front of huge crowds at Wembley in his England Schoolboy days.

Something which also no doubt helped to ease Duncan's nerves was that Busby had demanded that his Reserves play the exact same tactics and formation as the first team. Edwards already knew that Busby liked his teams to play as a unit. When the five forward players moved up the pitch, so did the wing-halves, and conversely when the forward players dropped back the wing-halves did likewise. They were a well-drilled machine. Everyone knew their jobs. Jimmy Murphy saw to that.

United's tactics were in contrast to most other teams in this era who stayed true to the old fashioned WM formation, which had been in existence since long before the war. This formation saw both inside-forwards position themselves slightly behind the centre-forward and the two wingers when in attack. The inside-forwards would then link closely with the flying wing-halves, behind whom was a back defensive wall of three – the centre-half flanked by two full-backs in what became known as the 'third back game'.

This formation would soon fall from grace when England, who lined up in the WM formation, were thrashed at Wembley by Hungary in November 1953. On that historic day, the Hungarians had deployed a revolutionary tactic that saw them play their centre-forward, Hidegkuti, in a more withdrawn role where he had positioned himself between the midfield and the wing-halves. England's centre-back Harry Johnston, who had been tasked with marking Hidegkuti, was frequently left in no-man's land as he was not sure whether to follow him or to keep his position. Taking full advantage of this defensive shambles, Hidegkuti scored a hat-trick and had a part in setting up the other three goals that the Hungarians rattled past a static England back-line. Johnston, who had played for England since 1946, never kicked a ball for the national team again and the WM formation, long favoured by British teams, was soon consigned to history.

Before his league debut, Edwards was not only very familiar with the tactics the first team played but he was also very aware of what was expected of him. He was playing at left-half, a position which meant that he had to stop the opposition inside-forwards from being able to play, but at the same time he had to ensure that his own inside-forwards saw as much of the ball as possible. It was a role that demanded a high level of stamina. If the wing-half wasn't bombing forward in attack, then he was rushing back to cover the full-backs in defence. Perhaps more than any other position on the field, it demanded the most from a player. You needed to be quick, strong, fit and skilful, and as Edwards himself said, the biggest asset of all was being two-footed as you needed to be able to 'switch the direction of play suddenly'. It was a daunting position for the most seasoned of professionals, let alone a raw 16-year-old on his league debut.

As Edwards mentally prepared himself for the game ahead, he barely noticed that in the cramped changing room alongside him were heralded internationals such as Roger Byrne and Jack Rowley. Names and reputations didn't daunt him though; he knew he could more than hold his own among such company. As the time neared 3.00pm, he tried to focus on the game and not on the smell of liniment oil, which was wafting through the air. His red V-necked number six jersey hung on the hook beside him and he was determined that, from this day onwards, it would be his to keep.

Busby came into the room just before kick-off and as usual he gave out some last-minute instructions before Murphy geed up the team in his usual tub-thumping manner. Ripping the opposition teamsheet from the wall, he scrunched it into a ball, threw it to the floor in disgust, and said: 'Forget about them. They can't play. Fucking useless, the lot of them. That red shirt you're wearing is the best in the world, when you pull that on nothing can beat you, and always remember, your best friends out there are your six studs.' With the players suitably pumped up, the buzzer sounded as the signal for them to make their way to the tunnel. Just before Edwards walked out of the changing room, Murphy grabbed him by the collar and told him, 'Don't worry about a thing, son, you're going to do fine. Best of luck.'

Although Edwards' name was not included in the match programme, the local newspapers had reported that the boy wonder would be playing. This news had seen many fans turn up with the sole intention of witnessing the debut of the most talked-about youngster in the country and as a result there was a good crowd at Old Trafford.

Striding out of the tunnel, Edwards felt a shiver go down his spine when he heard the roar of 37,163 spectators filling the air. He had never felt anything like it. The smell of tobacco, fried onions and Bovril filled his nostrils as he took in the sight of thousands of fans fervently whirring their rattles and waving their scarves. 'UNITED, UNITED, UNITED' came the chant emanating from the Stretford End. He looked at his surroundings in awe. Surely it didn't get any better than this.

Once the game was under way, it was impossible to tell that this was Edwards' debut, let alone that he was only 16. At times he played with all the assurance and confidence of an old pro. He torpedoed passes across the field with uncanny accuracy, tackled with intent, and at one stage came close to scoring with a dipping volley. Unfortunately, many of his team-mates did not perform to such a high standard, and this meant that they crashed to a 4-1 defeat. Though the press were highly critical of the attitude of some of the United players, they were full of praise for Edwards' efforts, as Alf Clarke of the *Manchester Evening Chronicle* wrote in his match report:

'The only ray of sunshine that filtered through the United gloom was the display of the boy debutante Duncan Edwards, who did all that was asked of him, including taking a shot from 30 yards that was only just wide. He's a good 'un, the best I've seen for his age.'

Frank Taylor, a highly regarded reporter from the *News Chronicle*, also felt that Edwards had played well, but did comment that he 'looked a bit thick around the hips'. Edwards' size was deceptive. He was so broad and solidly built that many found it hard to believe that he was sheer muscle. Busby and Murphy had no problem with his bulk as it was this physique that allowed him to bulldoze his way over his opponents. In any case, he was among the quickest and fittest players at the club.

Many felt that Busby would choose to keep Edwards with the first team following such an assured debut, but that was not how he operated with youngsters. His way was to introduce his young stars gradually, just to give them a taste of the big time, without throwing them into the deep end. Wilf McGuinness can recall how the boss did something similar to Colman and himself:

We made our debuts for the Reserves together at West Bromwich Albion and we both had blinders against two international inside-forwards, Johnny Nicholls and Reg 'Paddy' Ryan. Afterwards everyone was telling us how marvellously we'd done and we were on top of the world, but we were about to learn a lesson. As the following week wore on we couldn't stop talking about our next Reserve game, but then Bert Whalley burst our bubble by sticking his head round the dressing-room door and saying: 'You two boys, Burnage on Saturday in the "B" team. All right?' Although I was shocked, I would have accepted the decision, but Eddie was having none of it. He piped up: 'No, it's not all right. It's a disgrace.' Poor Bert, a real gentleman, looked uncomfortable and asked if we wanted to see the boss. Eddie said: 'Yes, of course we want to see the boss, don't we Wilf?' What could I say? I had to agree.

So we waited a bit and then went up to Matt Busby's office. Eddie, never shy about saying his piece, plunged straight in. He blurted: 'We had blinders last week, even the West Brom players said we did. We deserve better than this. 'It's not fair.' Matt let him blather on for a while. Then he replied calmly: 'I know, you were magnificent. And both of you play an important part in my plans for the future of Manchester United. But the way I do it with young players is to give them a taste. I don't over-play them in these games, and I want to keep the youth [B] team together as much as possible. So I'm playing you in that team tomorrow. That's my decision.' Our reaction? 'Oh, thanks very much.' And we left feeling ten feet tall, rather than dejected.

Colman and McGuinness would not be the first players during Busby's reign at Old Trafford who would walk into his office seeking a confrontation, only to emerge minutes later in full agreement with his decision. Busby had a gift. He made disgruntled players into disciples. It was a mark of a brilliant man-manager.

While Edwards had been making his first team debut, the youth team had floundered in the first leg of the semi-final of the FA Youth Cup, where they had lost 2-1 to Brentford. As the first team were out of contention for any major honours, and their next game clashed with the second leg of the semi-final, Busby felt that if his ambition to win the trophy was to be realised it was imperative that Edwards played.

With the talismanic presence of their captain restored to the team,

United looked a different prospect as they blew Brentford away with a resounding 6-0 win. If anyone had ever doubted Edwards' abilities, not only as a player but also as a leader, this was a firm reminder that he was indispensable.

Busby's dream was now almost complete; only the might of Wolverhampton Wanderers stood in the way of his team achieving their potential. Wolves were, however, formidable opposition and it was a clash that many found too hard to call. But as long as Edwards was in their line-up, then United were confident that they held the upper hand.

The side may have boasted star players such as Pegg and Colman, but if Edwards was lining up alongside them he seemed to raise his team-mates' games to new levels. McGuinness has said of this, 'When Duncan was playing alongside you it felt as if you could beat the world. I'd look across at that huge frame of his, eager to get stuck in, and think "We'll be all right today". If, however, he wasn't playing then sometimes you'd wonder who was going to be the match winner in his absence. It just seemed that anything was possible when "Big Dunc" was in the team and it made you play even better as you felt so confident.'

On 4 May 1953, 20,934 people flocked to Old Trafford to watch the first leg of the final. They would witness a display of unparalleled excellence. In what must be regarded as one of the greatest-ever per-formances in the FA Youth Cup, United were irresistible. Led by their inspirational captain, they crushed Wolves 7-1, which all but won the cup for United before the second leg at Molineux. Noel McFarlane, Eddie Lewis, Pegg and Albert Scanlon all got on the scoresheet, as well as young Irishman Billy Whelan, who had signed just days before the game.

Unbelievably, Manchester United were the only club who had approached Whelan with an offer to join their groundstaff. The youngster had been one of the best young players in Ireland, but no one had seemed ready to offer him an opportunity to show his worth in the professional game. At United he would prove himself as he emerged to become a key first-team player. Painfully quiet, and fiercely religious, Whelan settled in at Birch Avenue with Edwards and co. and did all that he could to spread the word of the Lord. At one point he had even tinkered with the idea of becoming a priest, such was his devotion to Christianity. Yet Whelan's interest in religion did not stop him from being one of the lads. They were free to curse and tell risqué jokes in front of him and sometimes these gags would even bring a smile to his face. Only if someone were to use coarse language, or take the Lord's name in vain, would Whelan gently ask his friends to tone it down. No one ever took any offence, they all admired Whelan for his beliefs and his gentle, easygoing manner.

Though Edwards had not managed to get on the scoresheet against Wolves, there was no doubt that he had delivered a memorable performance. The *Wolverhampton Express and Star* reported the game under the headline 'Dudley Boy the Inspiration in Manchester United's Youth Cup Lead'. The report then explained to its readers just why there was so much talk about the young star, 'If I thought I was certain of seeing Duncan Edwards give another such polished display as he gave last night, wild horses would not keep me from Molineux. Edwards was to all intents and purposes the complete wing half-back. Strong man in a strong side, he failed only once in the whole game to make good use of the ball and if for nothing else, I would remember him for the uncanny accuracy of a series of long, raking passes across the field to the inside of the full-back, not to mention the urgency with which he played throughout.'

Following such an emphatic display of superiority, the second leg at Molineux was a damp squib with the trophy already all but won. The game finished 2-2, but United won the tie with a resounding aggregate score of 9-3. Busby's vision had been emphatically realised and his captain had been an integral part of his team's march to glory. For once Gladstone Edwards was glad that Wolves had lost as he filled up with pride when watching his son lift a trophy at Molineux.

There was no doubt about it; Edwards' first year at Manchester United could only be described as a huge success. He had captained the youth team, won two pieces of silverware, and had also risen through the ranks to play for the first team. But all this was just an appetiser. The following year would really see him make his mark on the football world with devastating effect.

7

BREAKTHROUGH

On 2 June 1953 the United Kingdom came to a standstill for the occasion of Queen Elizabeth II's coronation. At 11 o'clock, millions of people gathered in front of a radio, in the cinema, or at the home of a neighbour who was lucky enough to own a television, to watch the live broadcast of the extravagant ceremony. While the footage was in black-and-white, shown on a TV screen no bigger than 12 inches, it still managed to give ordinary people a peek into the land of plenty. Glued to their screens, ordinary Britons looked on with a mixture of pride and envy as they saw the Queen's ornate gold coronation coach pull up at Westminster Abbey where she was cheered on by thousands of well-wishers and fawned over by dignitaries in fine robes and jewels.

Once the fairytale ceremony was at an end, the celebrations truly began. In almost every street, in every town and city, people brought out tables from their houses and placed them down the middle of the road where they were filled with home-made treats. Union Jack flags, balloons and bunting were already festooned wherever they could be hung; even the flowers in the gardens were red, white and blue. After the misery of the war years, and the end of some rationing, everyone was determined to use the coronation as an excuse to have a good time.

Back home in Dudley, Edwards was happy to join in the festivities with his mother and father at the local street party. While he drank ginger beer and helped himself to cake, he shyly batted away any questions regarding his time in Manchester. As Don Howe remembers, 'He was very down to earth. He didn't get carried away with himself. He wasn't going around, like, saying, "Look at me – I'm in the first team."'

Far from living the high life that summer, jetting off to exotic destinations, or visiting VIP nightclubs, Edwards was quite happy to spend his time off playing football in the street with the local kids. As far as he was concerned, if he couldn't play football what else was there to do?

Annie loved having her son back at home with her, but the summer sped by and before she knew it he was on his way back to Manchester, on the train with Gordon Clayton. As always, Annie shed a tear on the platform, while Gladstone put on a brave face, and called her 'a silly sod'. Yet Gladstone's act was all for show; he missed Duncan as much as anyone.

A year earlier, Edwards and Clayton had been the new boys at Birch Avenue, but this time around they were among the elder statesmen. Mindful of just how hard it had been for them to settle, they vowed to ensure that they would take the newcomers under their wing. On their return they found that one of the new lads in the house was very quiet, just as Edwards had been a year before. The boy in question had travelled down from Ashington, a mining village in the North East, and seemed to be embarrassed by his Geordie accent. His name was Bobby Charlton. Edwards liked him immediately.

Like Edwards, Charlton was being heralded as a real find. Now one of the stars of the England Schoolboys team, scout Joe Armstrong had done everything in his power to persuade him to sign even before he won national honours. Again, just like Edwards, Charlton was a fanatical United fan, despite living in Newcastle United-supporting territory. He was even related to Newcastle's star player, England international Jackie Milburn, but even that wasn't enough to tempt him away from Manchester's grasp. He worshipped United and he didn't need much persuasion to become a Red.

On Charlton's arrival in Manchester, he was met at the train station by Jimmy Murphy. On their way to Birch Avenue, the ever-excitable Murphy proceeded to bombard the startled youngster with just what he could expect under his regime. One subject that Murphy was particularly keen on discussing was the brilliance of Duncan Edwards, as Charlton recalls:

'On that journey, Jimmy had said with shining eyes, "Bobby, I've got a player you will find hard to believe, he is so good. He has everything. He is tall and powerful, but he also has a wonderful touch. Right foot, left foot, it doesn't matter. I'm going to make him such a player. Just look at him – and then remember I haven't knocked the rough edges off him yet!" I had bitten my tongue on the first thought that came into my head, which was, "Well, nobody can be that good."'

Conscious of the fact that the previous year they had been a little harsh on Edwards, the likes of Jackie Blanchflower, Mark Jones, Tommy Taylor, David Pegg, Billy Whelan, Alan Rhodes and Tony Hawksworth all went out of their way to include the quiet Charlton in everything that they did. In contrast to Edwards' first few weeks at the club, Charlton was immediately considered one of the boys.

Another new recruit that summer was the smiling, banter-filled figure of Wilf McGuinness. In his autobiography, *Manchester United: Man and Babe*, he also discussed the remarkable closeness he found within the group: 'That word "family" keeps cropping up and I make no apology for that because it reflects more accurately than any other exactly what it felt like to be part of Manchester United in the 1950s.'

McGuinness was a local lad, and a hot prospect, who like Edwards before him had also captained the England Schoolboys team. With his quick wit, and bubbly personality, he easily fitted in alongside his team-mates and became one of the most popular players at the club.

Shortly after McGuinness had signed, Murphy invited Edwards and him to join him in Ireland, while he did a spot of scouting. This was a trip that the two lads eagerly anticipated, as McGuinness recalls:

Shortly after I signed for the club as a 15-year-old, Jimmy Murphy took myself and Duncan Edwards, who was a year older, to the small town of Bray, just south of Dublin on the east coast of the Irish Republic. Jimmy had some scouting to do and he thought it would be an ideal opportunity for the two of us to get to know each other off the pitch, because he surmised we would be spend- ing a lot of time together in action for United in the not-too-distant future. He spent some time with us, but mostly we were left to our own devices and we enjoyed what amounted to a carefree holiday, further cementing that family ethos.

We made a visit or two to the Arcadia dancehall and met two lovely young colleens. After more than 55 years I can't remember their names, though maybe one was called Eileen. Of course, we weren't exactly ladykillers but, like true gentlemen, we did walk the girls home, some three miles into the deep countryside. Still, it was all very polite and proper, right down to the handshakes with which we left them at their doors. Oh that Duncan, he was a modest, unassuming fellow, much quieter than me. Perhaps I should have gone with the effervescent Eddie [Colman]! Not that Duncan was a stick in the mud. Far from it, he was great fun. But he wasn't particularly assertive in a social group, especially among strangers, and sometimes I wondered if he didn't say too much at first because he was conscious of his strong Black Country inflec- tion, much the same, maybe, as the similarly reserved Bobby Charlton with his pronounced north-eastern accent.

Although football dominated their lives, the boys were still keen to taste the other entertainment options that Manchester had to offer. Just a few miles down the road from Birch Avenue there was the speedway stadium and the Old Trafford bowling club, which were both very popular, but not quite as alluring as the White City greyhound track. Initially, the players would flock to the greyhounds in order to try to supplement their meagre income by putting a few bets on the dogs. They soon learned, however, that the racetrack was one of Matt Busby's favourite haunts and that he frowned on his young players being in such establishments. Even if Busby didn't see his players there himself, he had spies all over Manchester, who would tell him where they had been spotted and what mischief they were up to. In the end, the players realised it wasn't worth the trouble, and instead spent their time keeping a low profile at the bowling club.

Snooker was another favourite pastime for the United players, and every Friday afternoon Edwards and the rest of the gang would go to Davyhulme golf club to play a few frames. Although Busby had managed to get all of his players membership at the exclusive club, in a bid to keep them away from trouble, it was all in vain as money was invariably riding on a lot of the games and the losers of such contests usually ended up upsetting the other members with their cries of anguish. As with most sports, Edwards was usually the victor. He was a natural.

Another favourite venue for the players after training was the News Theatre in Oxford Road, where they would make use of their free cinema passes. There they would enjoy a movie double bill, cartoons, the Pathé news and, if they had enough money, a packet of Butterkist popcorn. Self-appointed elder statesman Mark Jones would make the players walk the five miles to the cinema, and then the five miles back afterwards, so as to stretch their legs. After a hard morning's training, cries from players falling victim to cramp in the darkened movie theatre were not uncommon.

The trip to the cinema, and then some fish and chips for the journey home, was a favourite excursion for both Edwards and Charlton. If there was a film that they both liked, such as *On the Waterfront*, starring Marlon Brando, it was not unusual for them to watch it three times in one week. They both especially looked forward to the Pathé news segment, which was shown before the film, as sometimes it screened highlights of first division football matches, a rare sight indeed. If they were especially lucky, the sports round-up would even have some clips of Manchester United in action, an event which would have the audience hollering and cheering in appreciation.

Edwards and Charlton were inseparable at this time and the two developed a very close bond. Charlton was in awe of his friend and listened intently to his advice on how to break into the first team. 'Your chance will come, Bobby,' Edwards would tell him on their walks home. 'Just listen to what Mr Busby tells you, work hard, and you'll be fine.' Whenever Charlton needed a kind word, Edwards would be the first to give it. 'Off the field, he was soft – a real soft thing, you know,' Charlton recalled. 'In those days I never thought of him as being hard and businesslike or anything like that. If you asked him to do anything, he would have said, "Yes, I'll do it." There was nothing to dislike about him at all.'

While movies were an enjoyable pastime, football was an obsession for them both. Everything else faded into the background. Around the dinner table they would bore the others senseless talking about the game. 'As long as he had his talent and he had his football, that was all he ever talked about,' Charlton remembered. Exasperated by hearing them discuss the same subject all day long, Jackie Blanchflower would tire of telling them both, 'Will you two change the record? All I hear from you is football, football, football!'

Charlton didn't, however, get to play football as much as he would have liked during his first year. Much to his displeasure, having listened to his mother's advice, he had started an apprenticeship at an engineering firm that took up a lot of his time. Every morning he would have to get up at the crack of dawn to make his way to work, while the United groundstaff youngsters slept soundly. Edwards was particularly fond of his sleep and, as Charlton would leave the room at daybreak, his comatose team-mate would murmur to him from under the covers, 'On your way out don't slam the door.'

The atmosphere at Birch Avenue, and at the club, in 1953 was electric. Gradually, the youngsters were becoming a force, as Busby released older legends, such as Johnny Carey, to make room for his emerging stars. Edwards was particularly fond of this period of his life and felt that the incredible bond and spirit between the boys would be 'the primary reason for success'.

Training sessions became a lot less serious with the addition of so many young faces, although Murphy was always on hand to offer a stern rebuke if the high jinks meant the players weren't putting in the work. Practice games now frequently saw the married men take on the single lads and the games would only come to an end when the taken players had to get back home to their wives.

Once the games had finished, the fun didn't stop there. 'We played silly games, like hide and seek,' revealed Albert Scanlon. 'Tommy Taylor – they could never find him; he was the world champion. No one knew where he was. Someone else once shinned up a flagpole. Another hid in a wheelbarrow. Here I was, little more than a school-boy, hiding in a training ground lavatory cubicle while some of football's biggest names tried to find me.'

Unfortunately, in an effort to find Scanlon, Edwards once peered over the lavatory cubicle wall only to be met by the sight of Jimmy Murphy on the toilet. 'All right, Dunc,' winked Murphy. 'If you wanted to look at me have a crap you only had to ask!'

Everything seemed to be shaping up nicely, especially for Edwards, who started the season in top form. Playing up-front for the Reserves, in the Central League, he scored a hatful of goals as the team won their first four games and shot to the top of the table. Still in demand for the youth team, he was also picked to play at left-half in a game against a Sheffield and Hallamshire representative side.

Once again the youth team was in devastating form, much to the approval of Busby. 'I can only say how happy I am that our young players continue to make good progress,' he proudly revealed. 'Recently, our youngsters secured a 7-0 success over Sheffield, with football of high skill. The wing half-backs – the men who mean so much to any side – were at their best. I refer, of course, to Duncan Edwards and Eddie Colman.'

As a reward for his early-season form, Edwards was included in the first team match-day squad when they travelled to play Tottenham Hotspur at White Hart Lane. Named as the twelfth man, Edwards would, however, get on the field only if someone picked up an illness or an injury before the game. Frustratingly, he spent the match sat up in the stands, wishing instead that he had been playing for the Reserves or the youth team. He later revealed just how annoying he found this experience: 'Nothing is worse for a player who is eating his heart out to be on the field to have to spend a couple of Saturdays watching from the touch-line and hoping someone will not turn up.'

Although he was upset not to have played any football, his mood turned to one of jubilation just a few days later. On 1 October 1953, the day of his 17th birthday, Busby offered Edwards his first professional contract. It was perhaps not a great surprise that he would be offered professional terms, but it still came as a great relief to him and his parents that his future was now secure. For now, at least, he was saved from a life of working in the mines and factories of Dudley.

Shortly after Edwards' birthday, the United youth team were handed a tough assignment in the first round of the FA Youth Cup, a trip to Goodison Park to face Everton. The game was a tight affair, and Everton pushed the holders close, but a towering display from Edwards, and a flash of inspiration from Colman, saw United prevail 1-0.

Initially disregarding much of Murphy's enthusiasm for Edwards as hyperbole, Charlton now appreciated that this was far from the case. 'Murphy had been right, utterly right, when he first spoke to

me of the meanings and possibilities of Duncan Edwards,' he
admitted. 'Every move the big lad made ridiculed the scepticism I
had felt.'

On the same day that the youth team were victorious at Goodison
Park, United's first team had also won by the same scoreline against
Aston Villa. But the difference in the reception between the two performances was marked. While the youth team was praised, the first
team was lambasted for an inept, uninspiring display, which saw some
boo them off the field. One reporter was so disappointed with the
fare United had served up that he wrote, 'How can football sink so
low as in this game? You expect £15 a week players to serve up
something better than this, which was the season's worst performance.' The mind boggles at how this reporter would view a mediocre
performance by today's United team, who are all earning at least a
thousand times more.

The old guard's time in the first team was now inevitably nearing
the end. Busby knew that they were no longer delivering the first-
rate performances they had once guaranteed on a regular basis and he
could no longer hold his young guns back; they were ready to take
over. Following the Villa aberration, United travelled to Kilmarnock
for a midweek friendly, with several youngsters, including Edwards,
named in the squad.

United's team to face Kilmarnock was a talented one and contained many players who in time would make a big impression at Old
Trafford. One such player was Dennis Viollet, who would become
one of United's greatest-ever goalscorers with 179 goals in just 293
games. Combining with Tommy Taylor, the two were to strike up a
fearsome partnership, thanks to Taylor's prowess in the air and
Viollet's predatory instinct and burst of pace over ten yards. Viollet
had that rare knack of being in the right place at the right time and
would eagerly snap up any balls that Taylor would knock down to
him in the six-yard box.

The new-look United team flew into an early lead when Henry

Cockburn, England's international left-half, scored after only three minutes. But Cockburn's afternoon would soon come to a premature end as, shortly after scoring, he picked up an injury and had to leave the field. Looking at his bench, Busby had no hesitation in ordering a pumped-up Edwards to enter the fray (substitutes being permitted in friendlies). 'All the starry-eyed youngster can do is grab every chance that comes his way, no matter how slight, and make the most of it,' he said of his opportunity to impress the boss. Emphatically taking his chance, United went on to win 3–0 and Edwards left the field to slaps on the back from his team-mates, all of whom had been impressed with his performance. This praise filled him with pride and he confided that 'moments like that make all the months of gruelling work worth while'.

Over the course of the next few days, Busby and Murphy had a decision to make. Was it finally the right time to start playing the youngsters on a regular basis? United had started the season in miserable form having won only four of their first 15 games. As Busby saw it, he had given his older players the last 18 months to prove that they still had it and they had failed him. Surely the youngsters could not do any worse? Murphy was for once cautious. He argued that United's next match, Huddersfield away, may not be the ideal place to introduce a vastly changed team. But Busby wouldn't hear any of it. He was sure that the time was now right to finally unleash his youth revolution onto the first division.

Naming Jackie Blanchflower, Viollet and Edwards in his starting XI (with Cockburn, Stan Pearson and Harry McShane left out), the youngsters did not let him down as they emerged with a highly creditable 0–0 draw. Edwards even had a late chance to win it, after Taylor had put him through on goal, but on this occasion his shot was fired straight at the keeper. In spite of that missed opportunity, Edwards had done himself proud. Raiding up and down the left flank, he had been a constant threat and his opposite number had struggled to cope with his virtuoso performance.

On leaving the dugout at the final whistle, Busby raised his eyebrow and gave Murphy an 'I told you so' look, trying hard to keep his excitement to himself. The word was however out; United's youthful team were a sensation. The headline in the *Manchester Evening Chronicle* the next day saw a nickname born as it proclaimed, 'Busby's Bouncing Babes Keep All Town Awake'. From that point onwards, this crop of youngsters would forever be immortalised as the 'Busby Babes'.

In an interview, Busby explained just why he had put his faith in so many of his younger players for the game, 'On the Saturday we had a hard match in prospect at Huddersfield, then lying third in division one. None of the youngsters in the side had let me down at Kilmarnock, so I decided to back them, come what may. Six of the side I selected were under twenty-one years, but I knew that they would go on developing, with experience, into just as big star performers as the Johnny Carey era, which was now coming to an end of six glorious years for Manchester United.'

There was no question of Busby altering his team for the next match against Arsenal, and therefore Edwards lined up to make his third first-team appearance. During the game, Edwards came close to breaking his first-team goalscoring duck as he made a powerful break, leaving several defenders in his wake, before letting fly from 25 yards out. For a moment the shot appeared destined for the top corner, but at the last second it swerved in the air and thumped the top of the crossbar. There were to be no wonder-goal heroics on this occasion, as the match ended in another draw, but Busby was thrilled – his Babes had played with a scarcely imaginable maturity.

Having had an opportunity to settle into the side, the Babes began to hit top gear. On 14 November 1953, they travelled to a wet South Wales where they gave Cardiff City a torrid time, winning 6-1, before then meeting Stanley Matthews' Blackpool at Old Trafford, where they recorded a resounding 4-1 win. Matthews sat out the game, due to injury, but the highest home crowd of the season hadn't turned up to watch him in any event. They were there to witness why Edwards, and the rest of the youngsters, were causing such a stir in the football world.

Showing the crowd just why he was so highly rated, Edwards snuffed Blackpool's Ernie Taylor, who was regarded as one of the best players in the country, out of the game. Don Davies of the *Manchester Guardian* said of this: 'To get into the picture at all, Ernie Taylor had to wander far away from his youthful opponent Duncan Edwards. This 17-year-old left-half gives the lie direct to the adage that old heads do not grow on young shoulders. There seems little that time and experience can add to his present store of shrewdness and judgement, unless it be the reminder that there is such a thing as beginner's luck. Some of Edwards' passing on Saturday recalled the work of his more famous namesake of Leeds United fame [Willis Edwards]; a player whose outlook and culture, this Manchester colt would do well to emulate.'

The Babes continued to belie their young age with a series of awe-inspiring performances. Over the Christmas period, United thrashed their fierce rivals Liverpool 5-1 and hammered Sheffield Wednesday 5-2. Although Edwards' FA Cup debut provided United with little cheer, as they went down 5-3 to Burnley, he was named as man of the match. George Follows, of the *Daily Herald*, was particularly impressed with Edwards' efforts, 'But for me, the final memory will be of the boy Edwards striding through the mud in hopeless battle, the bravest man on the field.'

By the turn of the year, Edwards had well and truly settled into life as a first-team player and had racked up ten consecutive appearances. This was no mean feat considering that he was keeping Henry Cockburn, an England international, out of the side. Cockburn knew that there was no way that he could hope to dislodge Edwards when he was in such mesmerising form, so he therefore made a transfer request in order to get regular football elsewhere.

While many players may hold a grudge against the man keeping them out of the side, that could not be further from the truth where

Cockburn was concerned. He knew that he was in the presence of a rare talent and he therefore spent hours helping Edwards to improve his game by discussing with him opposing players' strengths and weaknesses. Cockburn's advice was gratefully received and Edwards was always happy to acknowledge his help and good nature.

On 16 January 1954, Edwards took part in his first Manchester derby at Old Trafford. Revelling in the intense atmosphere, he was again named man of the match, although he was said to be at fault for City's goal in a 1-1 draw. This performance saw the clamour grow for him to be included in the next England squad, particularly after their dismal defeat to Hungary in November.

Former United player Walter Winterbottom had been appointed as the national team's manager in 1946, but he was not solely responsible for picking the England squad. The FA Senior International Committee, made up of chairmen and directors of Football League clubs, also insisted on having their say. Notoriously conservative, the committee shied away from controversial selections and usually opted for tried and tested older players, a stance which frustrated Winterbottom, who was keen to follow the new, free-flowing style of football he had witnessed on the continent.

Players and critics alike all put forward Edwards' case that he was now ready for the international stage, although the next game wasn't due to take place until April. One of England's star players, Tom Finney, even went so far as to say that Edwards was 'one of the finest future England prospects that this country has ever had'. Alf Clarke of the *Manchester Evening Chronicle* went even further. Clarke was adamant that Edwards would be captain of the England team in five years' time, when he would still be only 22 years of age. This was of course all being said before Edwards had even earned his first senior international cap.

For now, the selectors decided to pick him for the England Under-23 team for their game against Italy. This was still a cause for celebration for Edwards, as after all, he was still only 17.

The flight to Bologna was to be Edwards' first time on an airplane and he had looked forward to the experience. Flying during this era was meant to epitomise the height of glamour and was usually only the preserve of the wealthy. From the beautiful, well-spoken air-hostesses who served freshly prepared food on china plates to the immaculate pilots who exuded confidence and charm, it was all meant to resemble one of the more civilised ways a person could spend their time. The image was certainly a far cry from today's budget airlines. Yet Edwards found that the experience did not agree with him, as he spent most of the bumpy flight rushing back and forth to the toilet, struggling to overcome airsickness. From then on, on flights for United and England, passengers were treated to the regular sight of Edwards holding a sickbag to his face as he turned a shade of green.

Expectation for England's great hope to deliver in Italy was massive, but for once Edwards failed to shine. The time he spent recovering from airsickness had undoubtedly taken its toll. Italy's youngsters popped the ball around at speed, which bewildered the heavy-footed boys from England, who at times seemed half a yard too slow. No longer could English footballers pretend that they were far superior to their foreign counterparts. After the 3-0 defeat, Edwards admiringly said of the Italians, 'They put one over on us and were a very much faster, better-thinking side on the day.' As always, in the face of defeat, he analysed his own play, as well as the opposition's, and vowed to learn from his mistakes.

On his return home, his fortunes failed to improve. His next game for United saw Edwards part of a team that crashed 5-1 at home to Bolton. Ray Parry, Edwards' old England Schoolboys team-mate, scored two of the goals and was heralded as the best player on the field. After the game Parry took the opportunity to remind his friend that he could have been playing alongside him that day rather than against him. 'Don't you worry, chief,' Edwards told Parry, 'you lot may have won the battle today but rest assured you won't win the war!'

United's youngsters did, however, seem to be tiring and Edwards in particular looked in desperate need of a rest. In his absence, the United youth team, led by an effervescent Bobby Charlton, had continued to excel in the FA Youth Cup. A 5–0 victory over Wrexham in the second round had then been followed by a 6–0 demolition of Bradford in the third. Goals had been scored freely against weaker opposition, but in the next round they drew a blank against a particularly stubborn Rotherham defence in a 0–0 draw.

The replay against Rotherham was to be played at the Cliff on 27 January 1954, and Edwards was still eligible to play. Busby felt that it would do his young star some good to play a bit of youth football in order to rebuild his confidence. No doubt he also felt that his presence would inspire his team-mates to victory. He was to be proved right on both counts.

In scintillating form, Edwards played up-front and grabbed a hat-trick, with United going through to the next round courtesy of a 3–1 win. After the game, Rotherham manager Andy Smailes was so enamoured with Edwards' display that he said, 'When I see a player like that, it makes you think footballers should be handicapped like racehorses.'

Such was his dominance that some newspapers felt that it was unfair that a player from the United first team should still be allowed to play in the Youth Cup, particularly the *South Yorkshire and Rotherham Advertiser*, who complained bitterly, while also acknowledging Edwards' match-winning prowess:

'I think it was a pity that Manchester, in their eagerness to make sure of retaining this cup, which they won last season, found it necessary to bring into the side Duncan Edwards, who played in the England Under-23 side against Italy last week and has made 14 first division appearances. I know Edwards is only 17, but I think it is against the basics of the Youth Cup to introduce professional players ... It was my first glimpse of Duncan Edwards and indeed he is an amazing player, almost of the John Charles stamp already. He was almost the entire reason for Manchester's supremacy, for not only did he score all their goals, but he also dominated the play throughout.'

This was not the first time that Edwards had been compared to John Charles, the great Welsh player, who became known as 'the Gentle Giant'. At this time Charles was plying his trade for Leeds United before moving to Juventus in 1957 for a then British record fee of £65,000. In Italy, Charles would cement his reputation as one of the finest footballers in the world by leading his team to three Serie A titles, scoring 93 goals in 150 matches in the process.

It was a huge compliment to compare Edwards to Charles, but the comparison was certainly justified. Both players could play in any position comfortably and were big, strong, quick, skilful and had no fear of putting their head in where it hurt. In later years, when Jimmy Murphy attended a sportsman's charity dinner, he chose both Charles and Edwards in an all-time World XI. When he was told that he had actually selected only ten players he replied, 'Why do you need eleven players when Edwards and Charles are in the team?'

While debate has raged as to who was the better player, Busby had this to say on the subject: 'John Charles was a giant of a player, a giant with great, great skill. But as a player, even John didn't have as much as Duncan.' Journalist Frank Taylor also felt that Edwards compared favourably to the Welsh legend, 'He was stronger than Charles in the tackle; more powerful going through for goal. It was sometimes possible to shut John Charles out of a game; Duncan Edwards never. He never held back from a tackle; he never gave up trying; he was always in the game, always looking for the ball. Charles often played in spasms. Edwards had only one style – 100 per cent go all the time.' Debate will always rage on this subject, but what nobody can deny is that both Charles and Edwards were world-class players who were critical factors in the success of their club and country.

By selecting Edwards for the youth team against Rotherham, Busby had proven to be a supreme judge of how to look after a player. Edwards' confidence was now not only sky-high, but the youth team's adventures in the cup were also set to continue. Having watched Edwards brimming with swagger and endeavour in training, Busby felt that his young star was suitably reinvigorated and could continue in the first team.

Soon after, Edwards faced Spurs at Old Trafford. Spurs were one of the great teams of the 1950s, heralded for their 'push and run' style of play, but on this occasion they were second best. Strolling powerfully across the pitch like a champion gladiator in the coliseum, Edwards had set up the first of United's two goals with a defence-splitting pass and then had a shot cleared off the line amid another all-action display in the mud. Bobby Charlton has recalled that although the poor conditions were a hindrance to some players, the muddy pitches and heavy ball never had an adverse affect on his team-mate. 'Muddy pitches meant nothing to him. You've got to remember that the old leather ball in those days got very heavy in the wet. But he would still hit 60- or 70-yard passes with his right foot or his left. On the floor or in the air – it didn't matter.'

With so much praise coming his way, after wins against Preston and Sunderland, Edwards gradually started to note a change in the way his team-mates, and those in the street, acted around him. At Birch Avenue he was now regarded as a first teamer and the younger lads looked up at him in awe. On nights out at Eddie Colman's, and then in Manchester, he found that he now had senior status and that people were always keen to ask his opinion or wanted to buy him a drink. It was something that would take him some time to get used to and the many fans that did try to stop him for a chat were taken aback at just how shy their big, bustling, brute of a player was away from the football pitch. 'He's polite,' said Gordon Clayton, of his friend's attitude to fans, 'but he rarely stops to talk.'

Some may have mistaken his reluctance to talk as arrogance, but that was far from the case. Still just a teenager, British football's most promising player didn't yet quite carry the confidence of a man. On the football pitch he was a phenomenon, but off it he would take some time to feel comfortable in his own skin.

After playing in some of the biggest stadiums in the country, Edwards' next game saw him play at one of the smallest. Despite having excelled in recent first team games, Busby opted to play him in the quarter-final of the Youth Cup at Bexley Heath and Welling in Kent. Bexley's minute ground had never before been paid a visit by a team boasting such an array of talent and this helped to swell the crowd to well over 8,000. The ground's small wooden stand looked close to bursting, with so many bodies crushed together, and at times the ropes surrounding the pitch struggled to keep the spectators back.

Most attended the game to witness the United team's brand of fantasy football, but an uncharacteristic slow start saw some of the crowd grow restless. With Edwards for once failing to exert his authority on the game, a fan seated behind Murphy shouted, 'Murphy, where's this great Edwards of yours? We ain't seen him yet!'

Just at this precise moment, Edwards picked up the ball in the centre circle. Striding forward purposefully, he held off a challenge as he approached another player at speed. Sharply dropping his shoulder, he left the player for dead before detonating the ball with a wallop of his right boot 30 yards from goal. Piercing the cold air like an exocet missile, the ball still seemed to be gathering pace as it exploded into the top corner. Immediately Jimmy Murphy turned to the crowd, who had just been muttering that his star player was overrated, and said with a smug smile on his face, 'That, ladies and gentlemen, is Duncan Edwards.'

That wonder goal may have put United one up, but Bexley Heath scrambled an equaliser in the second half and it took a late David Pegg strike to seal a hard-fought victory. United's reward for a gritty performance would be a two-legged semi-final tie against West Bromwich Albion.

After yet another heroic youth team display, Edwards was back with the first team shortly afterwards, helping them to defeat

Huddersfield Town 3-1. His performance saw him book a place on the plane with the England B side as they travelled to West Germany for the first post-war international at any level between the two countries. The newspapers were filled with stories about the significance of this event, but in the end Edwards stole the headlines. His magnificent, all-action exhibition of footballing artistry saw the *Daily Express* report that he had added 'the most colourful chapter yet in his exciting and romantic story'.

Dominating the game with an astounding display of fire and fantasy, Edwards was in his element. Motoring up and down the field, with a seemingly inexhaustible engine, he was constantly involved in the play and all that England did well seemed to go through him. The papers had a field day as they somehow tried to convey in words just how dominant he had been. Desmond Hackett of the *Daily Express* wrote, 'Already man-sized and carrying a football brain to match, this Edwards is going to become the terror of the continent before he has even got down to serious shaving. He was certainly the despair of the Germans.'

Some of Hackett's colleagues in the press box, such as John Graydon of the *Evening Chronicle*, even felt that Edwards must now have caught the eye of the England selectors. 'In Germany, his tackling put the continentals completely off their game and when he cleared the ball, he hit it really hard and accurately to his colleagues. If he gives a good game against Arsenal, he is favourite to be England's left-half in the forthcoming match against Scotland.'

Walter Winterbottom was desperate to call upon Edwards' services, so before his squad was announced he arranged for the selectors to watch him play at Arsenal. It seemed that the bandwagon towards full international honours was building an unstoppable momentum and a good performance against Arsenal would all but guarantee him a call-up in his first full season as a professional.

Proving, however, that he was human after all, Edwards for once let nerves get the better of him as he delivered perhaps his worst performance in a Manchester United shirt. With the game passing him by, he became frustrated by his inability to get on the ball and he began to wander from his position, which opened up a gaping hole on the left side of United's defence. When he finally did receive the ball, he snatched at shots and scuffed a few of his trademark cross-field passes. At the end of the game, which United lost 3-1, Edwards sat dejectedly in the Highbury dressing room, assessing not only his culpability in two of Arsenal's goals, but also how he had blown his chance of making the England squad.

Things then went from bad to worse as the next game, against Cardiff City, saw United squander a 2-0 lead. Inexplicably capitulating, the team had conceded three goals in the last 15 minutes. Confidence is a valuable commodity and United were obviously now in short supply of it, as they then lost 2-0 to a Stanley Matthews-inspired Blackpool at Bloomfield Road. Just a few years earlier, Edwards had been emulating the silky-skilled Matthews on the streets of Dudley, now here he was, coming up against his idol in the flesh. In the circumstances, Edwards had a decent game, and kept Matthews relatively quiet, but this defeat effectively ended any aspirations United may have had of a title challenge.

Results were mixed as the season petered out and although Edwards continued to keep up his prodigious work-rate his overall game was below par. His display against Portsmouth was particularly off-colour and George Follows subsequently wrote that he was 'distressingly inaccurate in his passing'. With two meaningless games remaining of the season, Busby felt that Edwards' development would be best served if he played in the FA Youth Cup final, something he was more than happy to do. After all, he would be back among friends and he would have the chance to add more silverware to his already jam-packed trophy cabinet.

In Edwards' absence, the youth team had comprehensively brushed aside West Bromwich Albion 7-1 in the semi-finals. Managers are usually reluctant to change a winning side, but a talent such as

Edwards' demanded to be included. Eagerly awaiting United in the final would again be Wolverhampton Wanderers, who sought revenge for their humiliating 9-3 hammering a year earlier. An expectant Old Trafford played host to the first leg on 23 April 1954, with a crowd of 18,246 turning up to cheer United on.

United were clear favourites to win the trophy and everything seemed to be going to plan when Edwards scored in the opening minutes. Far from being discouraged, Wolves then shocked the defending champions by striking back with three goals. At times they threatened to run away with the game and United were just hanging on, leaving Murphy apoplectic on the touchline.

During the break, Edwards was moved from left-half to centre-forward and this changed the game. Early into the second half he scored his second goal, a towering header, to make the score 3-2. Wave after wave of attacks besieged the Wolves goal and eventually they cracked as David Pegg levelled the scores. Wolves were now on the rack and it looked to all and sundry as if United would go on to win comfortably. However, a rare Wolves break saw them score an improbable goal and United were again behind with just minutes remaining. With an unheard-of home defeat staring them in the face, the fighting spirit of the Babes again shone through as Pegg dramatically scored a late equaliser. It had certainly been a game fit for a final and the players walked off the field congratulating one another on a pulsating encounter.

Just three days later the youth team, containing the likes of Edwards, Charlton, Colman and Pegg, made their way to the West Midlands for the second leg. Among the 28,651 spectators was Edwards' ever-loyal fan club, which included his parents, his friends from the streets of Dudley, his school teachers, as well as Gordon Meddings and Eric Booth. His two former coaches swelled with pride as they watched their protégé blossom from a raw but talented youngster into a fully fledged first division player.

In the first leg, Edwards had caused the Wolves defence all manner of problems at centre-forward, and therefore it was no surprise to see him again selected in this position. In an attempt to negate his influence, the Wolves defenders were told to man-mark him out of the game, but even when he was surrounded by gold shirts, he still managed to have a big impact on proceedings.

A vociferous crowd roared on the Wolves team, but they were silenced in the 33rd minute when Edwards rose in the penalty box to meet an inch-perfect Charlton cross. But just as he was about to make contact with the ball a Wolves player, who had sensed the danger, hauled him down. Without hesitating, the referee pointed to the penalty spot. Pegg was the designated penalty-taker and he dispatched his effort with the minimum of fuss. United had a vital one-goal lead and try as they might Wolves could not level the scores. The Youth Cup was again on its way back to Old Trafford. On the way back up to Manchester, the players celebrated with a few bottles of lemonade while Colman led a sing-song. Life was good!

Once the boys had arrived in Manchester, they decided to continue the celebrations. 'To celebrate we went into a pub in town called Willoughbys,' recalls Wilf McGuinness, who had also played his part in the final. 'It just shows we weren't that into the nightlife because it was a gay bar! It was quite amusing when we found out. "Oh," said Duncan. "Oh dear!"'

For many the season was now over, but for Edwards there still remained unfinished business. That summer the England senior team were due in Switzerland to take part in the 1954 World Cup. Against the odds, Edwards still hoped that he could gatecrash the party. If his dream was to become a reality, however, he would have to put in a good performance on 30 April, when he was selected to play in a trial match for Young England against Old England at Highbury.

Edwards was not the only United youngster who was hoping that they could make the breakthrough. Also featuring for the Young England team were the likes of Roger Byrne, Tommy Taylor and Dennis Viollet. In opposition was, however, a fearsome front line who were universally regarded as not only being the best in England but among the best in the world. The likes of Stanley Matthews, Wilf Mannion, Tommy Lawton and Len Shackleton were the great entertainers of British football and together they comprised one of the most thrilling attacking line-ups in England's history. Edwards knew he would have his work cut out if he was going to keep that stellar quartet quiet.

On the day, Edwards performed adequately, and was not at fault for the two goals Young England conceded in a 2-1 defeat. Frustratingly though, he had not done enough to force his way into the selectors' thinking. His time would no doubt surely come. Despite this disappointment, he had thoroughly enjoyed testing his wits against the senior stars. 'The opposing forward line of Matthews, Mannion, Lawton, Shackleton and Langton certainly gave us the run-around, but I really enjoyed playing against such great players,' Edwards recalled. 'They set out to play exhibition football, while beating us – and managed to do both.'

Although Edwards did not travel to Switzerland for the World Cup, he did play for the England B team in Basel on 22 May, losing 2–0 to their hosts, before joining the United youth team, who were playing in the Blue Star youth tournament in Zurich. The tournament was regarded as the most prestigious youth competition in Europe, and as a result all of the top clubs fielded teams. Busby and Murphy travelled with their United colts so that they could personally witness how their home-grown stars fared against the best in the business.

Upon reaching Zurich, the team checked in to the Stoller Hotel, which was located in the centre of the bustling city. For some this was the first time that they had stayed in a hotel and at times they struggled to grasp just how they were expected to behave. 'None of us was used to hotel life and our etiquette at mealtimes might have left a bit to be desired,' McGuinness recalls. 'Occasionally it was downright embarrassing, for instance when the waitresses brought us salad we had no idea whether to eat it before or after our main course! It seems daft now, but we were only young lads out in the big, wide world for the first time.'

Busby and Murphy had no such problems settling in. Upon arrival they spotted the nearest bar, just across the street, and for the duration of the tournament they made it their unofficial headquarters. It was in that smoke-filled cellar where they cooked up their tactical master plan. Using pint glasses to experiment with formations, they discussed how to get the best out of their fledgling team. If anyone from the United party needed to locate Murphy or Busby, they knew that they could find them in the bar, cigarette and whisky in hand, meticulously going over their plans.

This zealous approach saw United make easy work of their group as they comprehensively won their opening four games. Their play had been so mesmerising at times that they soon grabbed the attention of some of the world's greatest players, with the Brazilian World Cup squad turning up to watch them play. In the presence of such illustrious spectators, the United boys somehow found an extra gear and delivered their most exhilarating display of the tournament as they won 9-1. On this occasion, Billy Whelan was the star of the show. After scoring a particularly memorable solo goal, he even had the Brazilian players standing to applaud. Whelan's performance was in fact so impressive that the Brazilians tried to get him to go back to Brazil with them.

Edwards had played all of the group games at left-half, but for the final against Red Star of Zurich, Busby opted to play him up-front. It was an inspired move as Edwards hit a hat-trick, which saw United win the game 4-0. Sepp Blatter, now president of football's governing body FIFA, played for Zurich in the final and to this day he ranks Edwards' display as up there with the best he has ever seen.

United's reward for winning the trophy was an exhibition match against a Swiss Youth select side. Thrillingly, the game was to be played in the Swiss national stadium before the senior Swiss team played the Netherlands. Once again, United and Edwards were irresistible as they destroyed their opponents in a 4–0 rout, with the boy wonder again on the scoresheet. There was now little doubt, United's youngsters were the best Europe had to offer and Edwards was the team's crown jewel.

8

THE SUPERSTAR EMERGES

Recently, the superstar footballer has become a symbol of our celebrity-obsessed age. In years gone by, most fans were merely interested in what a player did on the pitch, but no more. Now we need to know everything about them. Who are they dating? What clothes do they wear? What nightclubs do they frequent? Where do they go on holiday? The 'Beckham Effect' has well and truly erupted.

Such is the intense spotlight on footballers that it is almost impossible to go a day without a picture of a player doing a mundane everyday act being splashed across the pages of one of the tabloids. Even if a player is minded to keep a low profile, there is virtually no escape from the media machine. With numerous TV channels completely devoted to sport, including Sky Sports News (a station which announces 'breaking news' from the football world as if it is an event of international importance), as well as countless newspapers, magazines, websites, radio stations and chatrooms, all broadcasting all things football-related, then a player would have to be a monk to avoid the glare.

Yet it wasn't always like this. Although football was still enormously popular during the 1950s, the coverage was far from what it is today. Apart from the brief, grainy, black-and-white highlights of a handful of games shown in the Pathé news round-up at the cinema, the only chance supporters got to watch a game, unless they actually went to the stadium, came when the FA Cup final and England internationals were shown on TV. Even then, most people didn't own a television so viewing figures would be low. To emphasise this, coverage of the first broadcast FA Cup final, between Sunderland and Preston North End in 1937, was officially watched by only 10,000 people. In contrast, the worldwide viewing figures for the 2005 final topped 484 million.

One of the few dedicated football publications for sale at this time was *Charles Buchan's Football Monthly*, which was established in 1951. The publication quickly became very popular, especially with schoolboys, as it carried full-page spreads on football stars, sometimes with colour pictures. Occasionally, an interview would reveal some tantalising detail about the players' personal lives, such as the fact that John Sellars, the Stoke City right-half, enjoyed designing ladies' shoes in his spare time, but mostly it stuck to football. There was no widespread interest in what a player did off the pitch and there were certainly no celebrity magazines, such as *Heat* or *Hello!*, filling their pages with the life and times of a footballer or of their 'WAGs'.

Although Edwards' Aunt Marjorie has said that 'he was as famous as Beckham at one time. It was Duncan Edwards this, Duncan Edwards that', he was not hounded like today's stars. A footballer's every move was not considered newsworthy. In any case, Edwards very rarely did anything off the pitch that would attract the attention of the press. However, the same could not be said for some of his team-mates. If they had been playing today, then some of their off-the-field exploits would have kept the gossip columnists very busy. Very busy indeed.

Dennis Viollet is certainly one 'Babe' who would have made quite a name for himself. His roving eye and extra-curricular activities were the things that modern newspaper editors dream of. It has been said that Viollet was so keen on the ladies that, rather than join his team-mates on social trips to the cinema, he would put on his best suit, slick back his hair, add a spray of cologne, and head off into the centre of Manchester, alone, where he would use his charm to try to woo anyone that crossed his path in a skirt. Of course, footballers have been, and always will be, partial to using their fame to attract the opposite sex, but even by these standards Viollet was said to be insatiable. No doubt his exploits could have kept the *News of the World* in business for years.

Indeed, the press would also have enjoyed writing about the likes of Jackie Blanchflower and Tommy Taylor, who sometimes got so bladdered on Saturday nights that they would virtually crawl home on their hands and knees and could be seen singing loudly on the top deck of the bus. Taylor was of course Britain's most expensive footballer as well as an England centre-forward. If a player in a similar position was to act this way in public today then he would be vilified.

The 'Babes' weren't angels, but neither were they devils. Like most footballers of this era, they lived their lives just like everyone else did. After all, most of the players lived among the fans and earned a salary that was not far above the average. None of them could be accused of being big-time Charlies when they were earning a maximum of £15 per week (the level that applied between 1953 and 1957) and could be seen travelling on the bus to Old Trafford on match days.

Edwards was certainly no big-time Charlie; he hated being the centre of attention away from football. However, when he returned to Dudley in the summer of 1954, he began to realise that things had irrevocably changed. In the past, although everyone knew who he was, he had been treated no differently to anyone else, just as he liked it. But now, after a season that had propelled him into the consciousness of all football supporters, he was no longer Duncan of Elm Road but Duncan Edwards, Manchester United superstar. It seemed that almost everywhere he went, football fans wanted to stop him for a chat, shake his hand or ask for an autograph. He was always happy to oblige, but the intense interest made him feel uneasy, especially due to his shy nature.

In contrast to the previous summer, where he had been happy to take part in the street games with his friends, he now wanted a few weeks away from football and the talk surrounding him. 'I can remember that as a boy the only relaxation I wanted from football was to play more football,' Edwards reminisced. 'As with any sport that is your life, you can live too close to it. Not only are you training and playing all the time, but the talk wherever you go is of football.'

Subsequently, Edwards picked up a new hobby that allowed him to have some peace from the mayhem. 'My main relaxation is fishing,' he confided. 'Quietly I collect my sandwiches and Thermos flask and sneak off to a river to sit there in peace and quiet with never a thought for the bustling world of professional football.' In the quiet solitude of the riverbanks, Edwards could relax in peace, without a soul to bother him, and without any mention of football.

Another source of relaxation that summer, which would also have a profound impact on his life, was a holiday with Gordon Clayton. A five-star VIP trip to an exotic destination was, however, out of the question. Instead, the boys treated themselves to a week at Butlin's in Pwllheli, where they stayed in a chalet and lapped up the nightly performances of the Redcoats.

Much to the amazement of fellow holidaymakers, Clayton and Edwards took part in a camp football match during their stay, which was organised by Newcastle defender Jimmy Scoular, who worked at the resort during the off-season to make some extra money on the side. One of Edwards' team-mates in the game was a lad from Manchester called Dave Sharrock, who was on holiday with his girl-friend, Pat. 'At that time he'd just turned seventeen and was in United's first team,' Sharrock remembers. 'I couldn't believe I was playing on the same team as him. He wasn't going around telling everyone who he was though, he just enjoyed the game. He was a lovely person.'

Striking up a close bond, Edwards and Sharrock became good friends beyond their time at Butlin's. Back in Manchester they would regularly meet up, especially for games of tennis. 'In those days I was a good tennis player and Duncan was pretty good as well,' says Sharrock. 'We used to have some good matches together and he was very competitive but it was always fun.'

However, when a refreshed Edwards returned to Manchester, he found that his living arrangements at Birch Avenue had become complicated. The house was shrouded with scandal as Mrs Watson had discovered that her husband was having an affair with one of the maids. This unfortunate situation meant that all of the Manchester United residents were hastily moved out.

Hard though it was to leave the motherly figure of Mrs Watson behind, Edwards went to live at 19 Gorse Avenue, in Stretford, located just the other side of Old Trafford cricket ground from his old digs. Having initially felt a little nervous, Edwards settled in very quickly and was doted on by the Dorman family who did every-thing that they could to make him feel comfortable in his new surroundings.

Something which also helped him to settle was the fact that Edwards and his team-mates Tommy Taylor and Kenny Morgans, who lived nearby, were rapturously received by the young children in the area. Richard Foulser, a huge United fan, was only nine years old at the time and could scarcely believe that Duncan Edwards, his idol, not only lived next door but also treated all the local kids as his friends. If the Manchester United superstar wasn't out building snow-men with them, then he would be taking part in their football matches in the street, sometimes even providing them with a ball that he had liberated from Old Trafford.

On one occasion, Edwards was so immersed in a game that he forgot his surroundings and smashed a rocket past a helpless ten-year-old goalkeeper. As he celebrated his goal, with his young team-mates mobbing him, he failed to notice that his shot had flown into a neighbour's garden and had destroyed some flowers. When the irate owner came charging out of his house, he was expecting to berate some children but he was taken aback when he realised that it was Manchester United's finest who was at fault. 'Sorry chief, I'm really sorry. I got carried away with the nippers,' Duncan hastily apologised. 'Don't worry, Dunc,' came the man's reply. 'Just make sure you do the same on Saturday!'

Edwards certainly enjoyed his young friends' company as it kept his feet on the ground, away from the relentless glare and hype of Old Trafford. Every Sunday morning, Foulser can remember that he and his friends would knock on the United star's door and would be invited into the lounge, where Edwards would sit in his pyjamas, drinking a cup of tea, eager to discuss the game from the day before. To the children of Gorse Avenue, Duncan Edwards was a god.

With the new season fast approaching, Edwards came to realise that his incredible exploits from the previous season had left all Manchester United fans insatiable for more. Wherever he went, be it the post office, bus stop or newsagents, he was bombarded with questions: How are you feeling about the season then, Dunc? Up-front or left-half this year? Do you think we have a chance for the league? It was clear that everyone was fully expecting another year of heroics. He did not intend to disappoint them.

United kicked off the season with a home game against Portsmouth and were clear favourites to start the campaign with an easy win. However, the South Coast team ripped up the script as they stunned Old Trafford with a shock 3-1 victory. This was not the start that Edwards had envisaged. Matters thankfully improved as the team went the next eight games undefeated, a run that saw them march towards the top of the table.

Edwards' captivating performance against Spurs in this spell saw the *Daily Herald*'s headline exclaim, 'Edwards Out On His Own'.

Reporter George Follows, finding it hard to keep his enthusiasm in check, wrote, 'The youngest player on view, 17-year-old Duncan Edwards, was the star of the match. He got through a tremendous amount of work and earned applause time and again, not only for his constructive work, but also for his defensive qualities. He gave one of the best displays of wing-half play we have seen at Old Trafford for years. Everything he did was accomplished with the ease and grace of a seasoned player.'

Fortunately, he gave this outstanding performance in front of the England selectors, who were now sitting up and taking notice of his displays, particularly after England's disappointing showing in the World Cup that summer, where the national team had crashed out at the quarter-final stage to Uruguay. Committee member Shentall, who had been sent to run the rule over Edwards, proclaimed in his match report that the youngster had been the best player on the field. In his view, the committee needed to seriously consider calling up such a talent. But would they listen?

While everything on the pitch was heading in the right direction, Edwards also found happiness off it. Despite having a handsome, friendly face, a warm, generous manner and the advantage of being a well-known football star, he had not enjoyed much success with the opposite sex. One reason for this was that when he did go out with the lads, he never approached a girl due to his shyness and chronic fear of rejection. If he did manage to speak to a young lady, he invariably ended up tongue-tied and struggled to engage in conversation. Gordon Clayton has said of this, 'He never really enjoyed a big group. He'd go to the Locarno [Dance Hall], but he wouldn't dance. He wasn't one for the "birds". He had a dabble here and there like the rest of us, but he was very shy with girls.'

This attitude was in contrast to a number of his team-mates who all eagerly pursued girls when they hit the town, *en masse*, on a Saturday night, as Sandy Busby recalls, 'There was a drink because you needed the Dutch courage to go up and ask a girl for a dance and most of the lads were quite shy. David Pegg was always well groomed, very, very smart. Dave, Tommy [Taylor] and Jackie [Blanchflower] were always big pals, they used to knock around together. They all had similar backgrounds, all working class, but always very polite, which helped with the girls. If you didn't get a girl you'd go to the Ping Hong restaurant on Oxford Street, across from the Old Gaumont picture house. The Kardomah, Espresso Bongo, Deno's, the Continental and the Whisky a Gogo were all popular as well.'

Edwards was not actively looking for a girlfriend, but fate suddenly intervened one evening when he attended a function at Ringway airport. Walking through the lobby, he saw his friend Dave Sharrock and his girlfriend Pat enjoying a cup of coffee. Sat with them was an immaculately turned-out petite brunette with tousled curls and ruby lips. As Edwards approached the table she turned to look and gave him a friendly smile. Having greeted his friends, Pat introduced Edwards to her good friend Molly Leach. Smiling in acknowledgement, he tried to think of something to say but words escaped him. She was beautiful and he was acting like a bumbling fool.

Taking a seat, he tried his best not to say anything stupid but in any event, he just wanted to listen to Molly, who merrily chatted away in a soft Manchester accent. She had a spark about her and was unlike any of the girls he usually encountered on nights out with Colman, Taylor and Pegg. Educated at a grammar school, she was well-spoken and intelligent, but also had a wicked sense of humour. Most importantly of all, she made him feel at ease.

He soon learned that she was 19, and worked as a secretary at Cooks, a textile machine manufacturer in Altrincham. She already knew who he was, as it was almost impossible to live in Manchester at this time and not be aware of Duncan Edwards. Gradually Edwards began to feel more comfortable, particularly when he realised that Molly seemed to smile at everything he said and teased him for his shyness. Sensing that their two friends were getting on famously,

Dave and Pat left them to spend the rest of the night chatting to each other.

From that day onwards, Edwards was besotted and his feelings were reciprocated by an equally love-struck Molly. Nearly every spare minute that he had away from football he tried to spend with his new girlfriend. Early dates saw them go to the cinema together, but they soon learned that they had differing tastes in films. Duncan loved watching westerns, while Molly enjoyed romantic comedies, particularly those starring Audrey Hepburn. Eager to please, he did not protest. He was just happy to spend the time with her.

One of their favourite date nights became going to watch the planes take off and land at Ringway airport. Molly would tell Edwards how one day she hoped to be on one of those planes, jetting off to an exotic destination, while he told her that flying wasn't all it was cracked up to be. On some rare occasions, Molly even persuaded him to dance in nightclubs with her, but she confided that 'he only danced to the slow ones'. If Molly wanted to dance to a more up-tempo number, Eddie Colman was more than happy to oblige. Many a time Edwards would sit at a table, sipping his lemonade, talking about football with Bobby Charlton, while Molly and Colman flew around the dance floor.

Apart from his shy nature, one of the main reasons he tried to avoid dancing with Molly was because of the interest it would create. For instance, if they went to the Locarno dance hall, where Eddie Shaw and his band used to play, Edwards would be singled out by a spotlight. Shaw would announce to the crowd, 'Ladies and gentlemen, Manchester United's Duncan Edwards is with us tonight. Let's have a round of applause!' Edwards would be mortified, as Dave Sharrock explained: 'Duncan used to cringe. You could hear people saying, "Who does that Duncan Edwards think he is?" It wasn't his fault, though. He used to plead with Eddie to stop. In the end Dunc used to get so embarrassed that he would refuse to go dancing.'

Molly's family were all ardent Manchester City fans, and from time to time she even persuaded Edwards to go to Maine Road with her to watch them play. He was quite happy to go along, but he wasn't so keen on some of the abuse that came his way from the fans. Consequently, he tried to sneak out early to avoid any confrontations. 'He hated being recognised,' Molly later revealed. 'He would do anything to avoid fuss.' The City fans' banter would, however, be the least of his worries as when his team-mates found out that he had been watching their bitter rivals they really let him have it.

Gordon Clayton was understandably a little put out that his pal had now replaced him with a girl. 'Once Duncan met Molly he disappeared off the social radar,' he said. 'Molly was a nice girl, very nice, but a bit up-market for us. Not what you would call a footballer's girl. Duncan was a famous face by then; it was difficult to go out. Now he could go round to Molly's and sit with her. That's what he loved to do.'

Such was Duncan's longing to be with Molly that he used to cycle to her office after training to have lunch with her. When she had finished for the day, he would again return so that he could chaperone her home. Seeing a Manchester United star turn up at their office, the workers at Cooks besieged Edwards with questions and autograph requests. He happily complied but was embarrassed by all of the fuss and eventually used to wait around the corner, wearing a heavy overcoat and a trilby hat, like a Cold War spy, so that he could not be recognised.

These frequent visits to see his girlfriend saw him get into trouble on one occasion. As he was cycling back from Molly's house, a policeman stopped him for having no lights on his bike. The fact that he was a Manchester United star carried no weight with the policeman, and he was made to attend Sale Magistrates, where he received a fine of 10/- (50p). This may appear to have been a trivial matter, but Matt Busby was far from impressed with such a breach of discipline, and gave his star a dressing down for embarrassing the club.

Heaven knows what Busby would have made of some of the modern footballers' indiscretions!

Head over heels in love, and with England's selectors taking a keen interest, Edwards was truly content. But his run of good fortune came to an abrupt end as he had to endure a torrid afternoon against United's fierce rivals, Manchester City.

Since the start of the season, City had been experimenting with a new formation, the so-called 'Revie Plan', which had been inspired by Hungary. This tactic saw City centre-forward Don Revie drop deeper, and play almost as an inside-forward. In the modern game, we would say that he played 'in the hole'. However, the genius of City's plan, in an era where players wore shirt numbers which corresponded with their positions, was that Revie still wore the centre-forward's number nine, rather than the inside-forward's number eight or ten. This meant that defenders and midfielders weren't sure who to mark, as the man in the number nine shirt, who was meant to stay in a central position and be the furthest forward opposition player, kept dropping deep. Although this revolutionary line-up had started in disastrous fashion, as City had lost the first game that they had experimented with it 5-0, by the time they faced their rivals it had started to prosper, as United found to their cost.

On a miserable afternoon, United played with none of their usual zip and vigour and Edwards, in particular, struggled to impose himself on the game. With the score tied at 2-2, a seemingly innocuous shot cannoned off his outstretched leg and looped into the corner of the United goal. Maine Road erupted as the fans enjoyed the sight of a demoralised Edwards, squatting in the mud, cursing his luck. This was one City goal that Molly chose not to cheer.

Usually a trip to Wolves would be the perfect tonic for Duncan to get over such a catastrophe. Not only would he get to perform for his friends and family, but more often than not, he emerged as a winner. On this occasion, however, he again performed poorly as Wolves comprehensively dismantled United with a 4-2 win. Having been clear at the top of the league, United were now looking nervously over their shoulders at the chasing pack.

Some of United's more fickle fans began to berate Edwards for his last two sub-standard performances. A few even questioned whether his love life was now interfering with his football. It didn't matter that prior to this rough patch, all and sundry had been touting him for England, all that mattered were his current lacklustre displays. On closer examination, it may well have been the case that Duncan's off-the-pitch activities had seen him momentarily take his eye off the ball, as revealed by trade union leader Lord Stan Orme:

'I was chairman of my trade union branch, the AEU, in Broadheath and we used to meet every fortnight on a Friday night. I used to catch the all-night bus coming back at about twenty to twelve from Broadheath, and I remember getting on one particular night and Duncan Edwards was sat there in the corner seat and the conductor was talking to him. Edwards was courting a girl in Timperley and he'd just taken her home. And you know Busby had them all in digs in Trafford with a landlady to look after them. I said to Edwards, "Big game tomorrow." And he said, "Don't let anybody, especially the boss, know I'm on this bloody bus at quarter to midnight. He'll go mad!"'

Just a few weeks after George Follows' glowing review of Edwards, he now began to suggest that perhaps he had been wrong and that the Manchester United left-half was over-hyped. Criticism from the crowd was one thing for Edwards to bear, but he found it difficult to take from reporters who he knew personally. He was hurt by Follows' criticism and initially went into his shell, cursing himself for falling below his own high standards. However, as the days went by the harsh words served only to fire him up and he was determined to show that Follows was wrong. Come the next game at Old Trafford, Edwards was delighted to find that his critic would be reporting on the match. 'I thought to myself: "I'll show him something,"' he remembered. 'He will never have seen the likes of this. So I went out and played probably the best game I have ever played in my life. After that I was content again.'

Over time, Edwards learned that it was best to avoid reading the criticism of him in newspapers, as all that really counted was the opinion of Busby. Journalist Frank Taylor wrote about an incident where he witnessed how Edwards dealt with such matters, after Henry Rose of the *Daily Express* had written a less than complimentary article:

After he had published the piece, Henry the peacemaker had second thoughts. Maybe he had been too tough on a young player still in the early years of his career. When next he went to Old Trafford, Henry pushed his way down to the dressing rooms under the stands, and buttonholed Duncan.

'Hope you don't mind my public censure of your play in the *Express*,' Henry began. 'Don't let it put you off your game, son. But people are talking, and I don't want to see you get a bad name in the game, as a chap who puts brawn before brains.'

Duncan beamed boyishly. 'Never even read it, Henry, so it doesn't hurt me. I don't mind what the papers say about me. After all, you have a job of work to do. You must justify your pay. That's fair enough by me. I don't really care what you write about me. It's what Mr Busby says that I take notice of . . . But it's very kind of you to think of me that way.'

This brash reply flabbergasted the usually ebullient Henry. 'Can you beat that?' he said afterwards. 'No player ever spoke that way to me before.' And in his warm-hearted way, Henry smiled: 'But you have to hand it to the kid, though. I don't believe he does care what the press says about him.'

Edwards had the critics eating their words when he found his form again in spectacular style. His exploits saw United go on the goal trail by putting five past Cardiff City before then hitting Chelsea for six (though that season's eventual champions did score five themselves). While he didn't score in these games, his range of passing and ability to change the game caught the eye. 'He always gave the right ball,' remembers Wilf McGuinness. 'If it needed a short pass he could do that or if it needed a long pass he could play it anywhere on the field. When you're watching a game and think that the play needed changing, he would do it without being told. He was a manager's dream.'

His form was in fact so good that the Football League picked him to play for their representative side against the Irish League team, at Anfield. Also joining Edwards in the team were his Manchester United team-mates Roger Byrne and Ray Wood. In a belting encounter, the Football League ran out 4-2 winners, but the real bonus for Edwards wasn't the win, but being able to line up alongside one of his heroes. Slotting in beside him in the half-back line was Wolves and England captain Billy Wright.

During the 1950s Wright was a giant in the game as he captained his country no less than 90 times. Similar in style to Rio Ferdinand, he seemed to glide through games with a wonderful appreciation for his team-mates and an unparalleled ability to read the game. Wright also wasn't afraid to get stuck in, but remarkably in his 646 professional appearances for club and country he was never cautioned. He was certainly a player, and a person, who Edwards wished to emulate.

After the prestige of playing for the Football League, Edwards was soon back to his bread and butter with Manchester United. His form, and the team's, was unfortunately inconsistent. His first game back saw him play in a 2-2 home draw with Newcastle. On the day, he was particularly sluggish and struggled to get around the pitch with his usual zest and intensity. Busby hoped that it was a one-off and kept faith with him for their next game, a trip to Everton. Yet for once Busby's instincts were wrong as this was one game that Edwards wished he could forget. Disastrously mistiming a tackle, he gave away a penalty and then scored an own goal in a 4-2 defeat.

Edwards wasn't the only United player to fall below his own high standards, as most were out of form and low on confidence. In fact the only player who was truly hitting the heights was Dennis Viollet, who had hit a purple patch, scoring 14 goals in the first 17 games of the season. Without his contribution, United could have been settled in the mediocrity of mid-table instead of still in with a shout of a title push.

Busby could find no answer to United's poor form as they crashed to a catastrophic 3-0 away defeat to Sheffield United. Again, Edwards was out of sorts, and this saw Busby decide that his jaded star was in urgent need of a rest. Struggling under the weight of expectation, Busby believed that a spell out of the limelight would serve his young star well. He therefore allowed him to miss a trip to Scotland, where United were due to play Hibs in a friendly, and then also rested him for the home game against Arsenal. Even when his form had deserted him, Edwards was still desperate to play. 'I enjoy every game,' he once said. 'Even when things are going badly.'

When Edwards was brought back into the side, for the away trip to West Bromwich Albion, he still looked to be carrying the weight of the world on his shoulders. His slack display was just one of many as United fell to another defeat and lost further ground in the title race. Frustratingly, he then missed the next game against Leicester City, as an infected boil on his ankle meant that he could not even put on his sock without grimacing. When the boil had finally healed, Busby felt that his young gun would be best served with a stint back with his mates in the youth team.

Back among the carefree spirits of Eddie Colman and Wilf McGuinness, Edwards was soon playing again with a smile on his face. Selected to play at centre-forward in the second round of the FA Youth Cup against Manchester City, he was hoping to hit the goal trail, but at half time United were 1-0 down and he had struggled to get into the game. Jimmy Murphy anxiously chain-smoked cigarettes as he delivered a furious tirade at his team. Striding down the

An early photograph of Edwards wearing an England Schoolboys cap. He made his debut for them on 6 May 1950, at the age of 13. (Getty Images)

Not yet quite 16 years old, a fresh-faced Edwards arrived at Old Trafford after a late-night dash by Jimmy Murphy and Bert Whalley to sign him up. (Mirrorpix)

Edwards (front, right) sits down for a meal in digs. For his entire career at United, he lived in similar accommodation, sharing his room and the dining table with his team-mates. (Getty Images)

The United youth team lines up outside the Hotel Pickie in Bangor during the 1953–54 season. Edwards is seated front row centre, with Eddie Colman to his right and Liam Whelan to his left; behind him is Jimmy Murphy, with Bert Whalley to his left. Edwards' close friend from the Midlands, Gordon Clayton, is standing on the back row, fourth from the left. (Getty Images)

Matt Busby, centre of the picture, instructs his players on the training ground. Edwards is fourth from right, with Mark Jones to his left. Jones and Tommy Taylor (second left) were considered giants at the time, which gives some idea of Edwards' own imposing physical presence. (Getty Images)

Duncan Edwards was never going to be a fashion icon, as this photo of him taken just before his 17th birthday shows. Even when the rock 'n' roll era began, he would still favour the styles of an older time. (Mirrorpix)

Duncan and Molly Leach, the love of his life, pose for a photograph at the wedding of the friends who had introduced them to each other, Dave and Pat Sharrock. (Courtesy of Dave and Pat Sharrock)

Edwards was ill in bed with the flu on his 21st birthday. His team-mates went out to celebrate in his absence, while Molly tended to the ailing star. (Mirrorpix)

Aged 16 years and 185 days, Edwards leaves the pitch after making his senior debut for United in a 4–1 defeat against Cardiff City, 4 April 1953. Such had been his impact at the club, that Busby felt he could not hold him back any longer. (Mirrorpix)

A family affair. Edwards gets in the block just as his cousin Dennis Stevens shoots for goal as United take on Bolton Wanderers on 22 January 1955. (Mirrorpix)

Edwards had it all as a player. He was fearless in the tackle and brilliant in the air. (Mirrorpix)

The moment United lost the Double. Ray Wood lies dazed on the floor after being caught by Aston Villa's Peter McParland in the 1957 FA Cup final. Edwards (wearing the number six shirt) stands over the fallen Villa forward. (Getty Images)

Edwards (just behind captain Billy Wright's shoulder) looks away from the camera ahead of making his England debut against Scotland on 2 April 1955. (Mirrorpix)

Edwards trains at Highbury with legend Stanley Matthews (left) and Billy Wright ahead of England's game against Scotland in April 1957. (Getty Images)

Edwards signs his autograph for a young boy at Highbury on 1 February 1958, the last game he would ever play in England. (Getty Images)

The United side prepare to fly out to Belgrade for their European Cup quarter-final tie. Edwards, always a nervous passenger, is standing between Roger Byrne (in the pale overcoat) and Albert Scanlon (holding newspaper). (Getty Images)

The famous picture of the Busby Babes lining up before their game against Red Star Belgrade on 5 February. Edwards is nearest to the camera. (Getty Images)

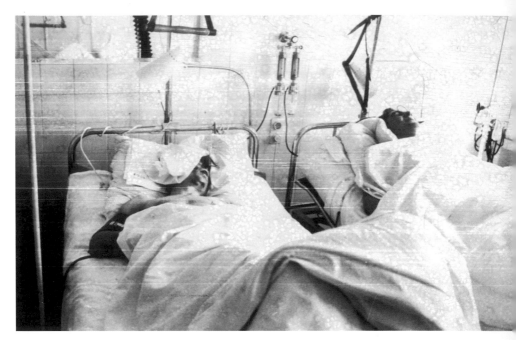

Edwards (right) fights for his life in the Rechts Der Isar Hospital in Munich alongside Johnny Berry. Sadly, after 15 days, he passed away. (Mirrorpix)

Annie and Gladstone Edwards kept all their beloved son's England caps and his medals on display in their front room in Dudley. (Getty Images)

Annie Edwards is escorted to a memorial service to mark the 40th anniversary of Munich, in 1998. (Mirrorpix)

tunnel for the second half, Edwards walked up to Murphy and told him, 'Don't you worry, chief, I'll get some goals for you!' True to his word Edwards stepped out into the thick fog enveloping Maine Road and duly struck twice to win the game.

Next up, in the third round, was a trip to Oakwell where United faced a fired-up Barnsley. No doubt relishing the prospect of a show-down with the defending champions, the Tykes raced into a two-goal lead and United's invincible aura was waning fast. At half time, Murphy again lost his rag and reminded his team that they were Manchester United players. 'We don't lose at shit holes like this with-out one hell of a fight!' he raged. Once again, as Edwards was about to leave the changing room, with the captain's armband hugging his enormous bicep, he whispered to Murphy, 'Calm down, I'll take care of this for you.' And he did. In the second 45 minutes, he set up three goals and scored the fourth as United improbably came from behind to win the game. Murphy, with a cigarette hanging out of his mouth, could only look on in wonder.

These inspirational performances for the youth team were enough to persuade Busby that Edwards was again ready for the firsts. Yet, despite the lay-off and his mesmeric displays for the youngsters, it took him some time to regain his feet as United went three games over Christmas without a win.

The New Year thankfully heralded a change in fortune, as Edwards not only inspired United to a 4–1 win over Blackpool, but he also scored his first goal for the club with a stunning effort as Don Davies of the *Manchester Guardian* reported:

By common consent, the outstanding incident of a somewhat desultory second half was the scoring of Edwards' first goal for United. Ever since he pulled a red jersey over his muscular frame, this just 18-year-old has dreamt of one thing only; namely to smite the ball so hard that it either bursts in transit or defies the effort of any goalkeeper to intercept it. On Saturday, with about 20 minutes remaining for play, Edwards at last detected his opportunity.

Darting forward, he put every ounce of his prodigious strength into the mighty, uninhibited swipe. There was a sharp crack of boot on leather – a veritable detonation, this – and a clearing of the atmosphere by a blurred object, which first soared over Farm's upraised arms then dipped suddenly and passed in under the cross-bar.

A scene of great commotion followed. Spectators hugged each other, then threw their heads back and brayed their approval. Edwards leaped and gambolled like a soul possessed, until his ador-ing colleagues fell upon him and pinned him down with their embraces. Chilton too, a smiling Caius Marcius Coriolanus, raced upfield and patted the prodigy's head: 'That's my brave boy.'

Having scored such an outstanding goal, Edwards found it hard to keep his emotions in check. Old footage from the 1950s shows that in most cases the goalscorer's celebrations usually saw them walk solemnly back to the centre circle to wait for the game to restart. Any player who went beyond this unofficial code of conduct ran the risk of a tirade of self-righteous conservative criticism from some mem-bers of the press. Times were, however, changing and the advent of rock 'n' roll soon blew away the staidness of the post-war years, with the younger generation wanting to let their emotions out, none more so than Edwards, who said:

'A great deal of fuss is made by people sniping at football about the high spirits among players when they score a goal. The fact that they might jump for joy, slap each other on the back and perhaps shake the hand of the scorer is seen as something to be sneered at.

'In reality these high jinks are just a spontaneous outburst climax-ing a game that is hard on the nerves as well as the feet. A goal brings relief to the tension and the players are human enough to show it. I can see nothing criminal in that.'

It is hard now to imagine there being such criticism over such modest celebrations. We have now become so used to players throwing off their shirts, dancing and even crying after scoring a goal that if they were to acknowledge a goal with a pat on the backside and a pump of the fists we would probably accuse them of not caring enough.

Just as Edwards was back firing on all cylinders, his progress was interrupted as he had to begin his National Service. From 1950, all healthy males between the ages of 17 and 21 were expected to serve two years in the armed forces. It didn't matter if you were a famous footballer or a movie star, no one could escape, unless they worked in certain reserved trades such as coal mining.

Fellow Babe Bill Foulkes also left Manchester to start his military duty on the same day as Edwards and he can recall just how upset his team-mate was at the prospect of leaving behind his beloved Molly. 'We turned up together at Manchester Piccadilly station but a rail strike was on, so they put us in the back of a truck and we travelled down to Birmingham in it,' Foulkes recalled. 'From Birmingham they put us in a minibus and Duncan was then practically thrown out at Woolwich Arsenal. I was going on to Aldershot. As he got off the truck to go to the barracks, he had tears rolling down his cheeks.'

Eventually settling into barracks at Nesscliffe, near Shrewsbury, an apprehensive Private Duncan Edwards, Army no. 23145376, was given a job as an ammunition storeman. Thankfully, one of his superiors was a big Manchester United fan and he gave a grateful Edwards some leeway so that he could keep fit and continue to play for his club. In return, he was expected to turn out for the various army football teams and this saw him play over 180 games in his two years in the forces. Playing so much football saw Edwards declare that army life 'wasn't too bad'.

In public, he may have put on a brave face, but in private Edwards loathed the monotony of army life. 'The only time I saw him shaken was during his National Service,' Foulkes said of Edwards' reticence about his new life. 'He didn't like the regimentation, what he saw as the petty discipline of life in the forces and, though he never made a song and dance about it, he railed against it in private. Because of who he was, there was always someone trying to bring him down, to make life difficult for him, and he told me: "I'll be bloody glad to get out of this, the sooner the better!"' However, it could have been worse; he could have been Eddie Colman, who became his barracks' designated rat catcher.

Future England captain Jimmy Armfield, who was at the time just a youngster with Blackpool, also did National Service during the mid 1950s. He has recalled that even if you were a big football star you were still treated just the same as everybody else:

'At the start it was a serious case of bullshit baffles brains. We soon had a saying – if it moves, salute it; if it doesn't, whitewash it. On the first day we were each handed a metal plate covered in gunge that had to be removed before we could put any food on it. Needless to say, we weren't given anything to remove it with.'

Every morning without fail, Edwards and his fellow recruits would rise at 6.15am, wash, shave and polish their boots with spit and shine, before going to the cookhouse for breakfast at 7.00am sharp. After wolfing down some glue-like porridge, the troops had to be on parade to report for duty at 7.55am for another day of back-breaking sweat and toil. This was to be Edwards' life for the next two years. On top of all that, there was also the worry that trouble could again erupt in the Far East, following the Korean War, or later on that the Suez Canal crisis could explode in Egypt. If such a thing did occur then Edwards knew that there was a real prospect that he would be shipped off to fight in a war. It was no wonder he couldn't wait for his time in the army to come to an end.

Something that did help improve Edwards' troubled state of mind was the presence of his friend Bobby Charlton, who joined up a few months later. As had been the case when Charlton had first arrived in Manchester, Edwards saw to it that he was well looked after. 'He took

charge of me the moment I arrived at Army Camp,' Charlton said, as
he remembered how Edwards had carried his bed out of the room,
when he had found that springs were sticking out of it, and had then
replaced it with a more suitable one. As always, Charlton could rely
on his friend to show him the ropes and make him feel at home.

Army life may have been grim, but playing for the football team
was thankfully one part of National Service that Duncan did enjoy.
The side was also a very talented one that contained seven players
who had either won, or would go on to win, England caps, such as
Alan Hodgkinson and Graham Shaw of Sheffield United, Trevor
Smith of Birmingham City, Stan Anderson of Sunderland, Jimmy
Armfield of Blackpool, Manchester United's Bill Foulkes and
Edwards himself. The team also boasted the likes of Busby Babe
Eddie Colman, Maurice Setters of West Brom and Dave Dunmore of
Spurs. It was a side that could have quite comfortably held its own in
the first division.

In order to keep fit for the army team and their clubs, the players
would frequently train together. Armfield has never forgotten the
first time he trained with Edwards. Before going out onto the field,
Armfield's lace snapped so as he went back inside to replace it
Edwards went out onto the field by himself to warm up with a ball.
Watching as he fixed his lace, Armfield couldn't take his eyes off
Edwards as he messed around. 'He was wearing a white shirt, shorts,
no socks and white pumps and performing a few tricks with the football on his own,' he recalls. 'I watched him through the army hut
window for a while and was amazed to see what a superb touch he
had on the ball. He was actually bouncing it with the sole of his foot
on the ground and must have repeated it twenty or thirty times. I
then watched him collect the ball on the instep with either foot or on
his head with no trouble at all. Many people overlooked his highly
skilled techniques.'

When they teamed up together for the army team, Armfield can
vividly remember Edwards' meticulous pre-match preparation,

which was the same for every game. First he would put on his socks, then his boots, followed by his shinguards, before then finally putting on his shorts, just moments before he was due on the pitch. 'I can still see this powerful figure stalking the dressing room,' Armfield has said, 'and at the time I would always think, "I'm glad he's playing for us."'

While games for the army came thick and fast, Edwards was also still regularly turning out for United. Soon he became accustomed to the routine that would see him travel back to Manchester via train on Friday nights, so that he could spend some time with Molly, before playing on the Saturday. It was an exhausting schedule, but the thought of seeing Molly, and playing for the club he loved, pulled him through.

One of his first games for United following conscription was in the third round of the FA Cup against third division Reading. Billed as David versus Goliath, the underdogs almost caused a sensational upset when they went 1-0 up. A late Colin Webster goal saved United's blushes and in the replay, at Old Trafford, United made quick work of their lower league opponents as they mercilessly put four past them and finally progressed to the next round.

Before Edwards could pull on the red shirt again, he was called up to represent the England Under-23 side, who were due to play Italy at Stamford Bridge. The last game against the Italians had seen England humiliated 3-0 and Edwards, still feeling the after-effects of airsickness, had been particularly out of sorts. This time around he was an inspiration as he led the team to a shock 5-1 win. *The Times* reported that he was 'the master of the midfield', while Geoffrey Green in his fascinating book, *Soccer in the Fifties*, wrote: 'Edwards, indeed – the master of the 40- or 50-yard pass – played like a tornado, attacking, defending, always wanting to be at the eye of the storm. He pounded forward on a solo run like a runaway tank to release a shell from the edge of the penalty area that would have penetrated a steel wall.'

While Edwards kept up this good form in his next two matches for United, his endeavours were not suitably rewarded. Following a 1–1 draw with Bolton, United faced their rivals Manchester City in the fourth round of the FA Cup. From the first minute, the Citizens gave United a torrid time and swiftly went into the lead. Fortunately for United, Edwards kept them in the game as he twice cleared off the line, once with an overhead kick, before then setting off on a dynamic run, which was described by John Barrie in the *Sunday Express*, 'He was strong and fearless as he bulldozed his way through, shaking off challengers as though they did not exist. But just as he brought the ball under control on the far side of the penalty area, he was tackled unceremoniously and had nothing to show for his endeavour but a free kick.'

United's task was made more difficult when Allenby Chilton was sent off, and things got worse when City duly scored again. Despite being up against it, Edwards refused to bow down as, according to Barrie, he 'took on the work of three men'. His heroic efforts were ultimately in vain as United could not get a goal back and they were out of the FA Cup, a trophy that their rivals would eventually miss out on in the field that season.

For some time, Busby and Murphy had been tinkering with the idea of utilising Edwards in a more forward position, owing to his outstanding form in the youth team when he had played there. It was only the prolific goalscoring form of Dennis Viollet and Tommy Taylor, along with Edwards' own immense contribution at left-half, that prevented them from experimenting sooner. However, for their next game against Huddersfield, Viollet was injured, so Busby elected to play Edwards at inside-left, alongside his old mate, David Pegg, who played outside-left. This change of position reaped immediate dividends, with Edwards setting up Pegg for the first goal and then proceeding to score the second himself. Johnny Berry eventually grabbed a third and United strolled to a comfortable win.

Some players moan if they are not played in their favourite position, but Busby knew that this would never be the case with Edwards. 'Unlike most youngsters he has no temperament at all about his game,' Busby said. 'So long as he is playing football he's quite happy.' This was very true, but if asked which position was his favourite Edwards would claim that it was at left-half as 'it's a position where you can't be shut out of the game'. Bobby Charlton, however, could never quite pin down where his friend was at his most effective: 'He could play in just about any position. Central defender, sweeper, right or left back, anywhere in midfield or attack, goalkeeper too – they all came alike to him. Whenever there was an emergency, they could move him to deal with it.'

His versatility was clear for all to see in his next game, an England Under-23s clash against the auld enemy, Scotland, at Clyde's Shawfield Stadium. Beginning the game at left-half, Edwards set the tone with a few early challenges of bone-crunching intensity which led to England centre-forward Bobby Ayre becoming the victim of Scottish retaliation. Forced to leave the field through injury, and with substitutes being allowed, Ayre was replaced by Stan Anderson, who came on to play left-half with Edwards moved up in attack.

After a quiet first half, the game sprang into life as the second period became the Duncan Edwards show. Early on he signalled his intent with a piledriver, which rocked the woodwork, but he was more accurate with his next attempt as it flew into the back of the net. He added his second, and England's fourth, shortly afterwards before he then completed his hat-trick with another howitzer which flashed past the startled Scotland keeper before he could move. Some of the demoralised Scottish crowd, who had been booing Edwards' every touch earlier in the game, started to applaud the young English star. Johnny Haynes added a sixth goal late on, but everyone who was at the game left talking begrudgingly of just one thing: the endless possibilities of Duncan Edwards.

Alf Clarke, in his *Manchester Evening Chronicle* column, discussed

Edwards' glittering future in the game after this peerless performance:

> I have said before and I repeat it, that Duncan Edwards is certain to be England's future captain. Chief problem is where to play him. He is a brilliant wing half-back, can also adapt himself to centre-half and now both United and England realise his possibilities in attack. That is where I think he should be played. That is why United did so well at Huddersfield last weekend and that is why England 'B' won so handsomely at Clyde.
>
> One international player told me that Edwards might get too heavy. He may be correct in his belief, but I recall that Frank Barson, a former United centre-half, was stones too heavy when he returned at the start of the season, but always succeeded in getting down to soccer weight and it never affected his play.
>
> We cannot escape from the fact that Duncan Edwards is the greatest young player of his age. I know we had our Bastins, Carters, Dohertys and others, but I rank Edwards as the best young player I have ever seen.

Following this high praise, Edwards came back down to earth with an almighty bump in his next match, against Manchester City. Wearing the number ten shirt, Edwards continued to play up-front, but he could do nothing but watch as the United defence got torn asunder. Old Trafford was humiliatingly silenced as the team from the other side of Manchester scored five without reply. This would be United's heaviest home derby defeat until 2011, when they were to lose 6-1. Edwards was the only United player who emerged with any credit that day. It was said by one newspaper that he had 'pretty well faced Manchester City by himself'.

Busby's deployment of Edwards in attack had been designed to result in an avalanche of goals. Unfortunately, Busby hadn't counted on it being at the wrong end. Removing him from left-half had significantly weakened the United defence, and as a result they had started to concede goals at a fast rate. While he continued with the experiment, Wolves struck four past United in the next game (though Edwards did score one for United), and then Cardiff City hit three without response shortly afterwards. United finally managed to get a win against Burnley (Edwards scoring the only goal with a bullet header), but Busby began to realise that until he could get a left-half to rival Edwards he could not yet afford to have his star player up-front.

Although Edwards was still receiving plenty of plaudits for the way he was playing, some opponents, fans and referees took exception to some of his wholehearted challenges. A reckless tackle in the game against Burnley saw him lucky to escape with just a stern talking-to. Shortly afterwards, in an inter-league representative match, he added to his reputation for delivering blitzkrieg challenges when he was cautioned for a wild lunge on Gordon Smith. His combative style saw some opposing fans start to heckle and boo him mercilessly. He said of this treatment, 'On several league grounds the boos start as soon as I step on to the pitch. They go in one ear and out the other.' Nothing could distract Edwards from the job at hand, he was fully focused on one thing: winning football matches.

However, such were the nature of some of Edwards' challenges that the FA felt the need to write to him to remind him of the duty of fair play. He was insulted by the notion that he did not play fairly and threw away the letter without giving it a moment's thought.

Roger Byrne defended his team-mate, as he felt that not only did Edwards never intend to harm an opponent, but that he was also the victim of wind-up merchants. 'Old opponents try to needle him to cash in on his impetuosity. Besides dishing it out, Duncan takes plenty of knocks himself.' United supporters were also quick to defend their young star. 'He doesn't throw his weight about,' one fan told author Arthur Hopcraft. 'He just distributes it where it will do the most good.'

Hopcraft himself once recalled watching Edwards in action where he witnessed an opposing player futilely attempt to rough him up. 'By the middle of the first half one of the opposition's inside-forwards – I forget, I am ashamed to say, the team involved, but perhaps this is also a kindness – was reacting furiously to the frustration of being treated like a small child by Edwards, firmly but without viciousness or much concern. The player threw himself several times at Edwards, either missing the moving body entirely or bouncing off it, and on each occasion the man beside me sucked in his breath, shook his head and said softly: "Nay, lad, not with 'im, not with 'im."'

Future United star Maurice Setters also famously tried to get under Edwards' skin when he played for West Bromwich Albion against United. As Edwards stood on the touchline, attempting to take a throw, Setters stood almost nose to nose with him. In order to make Setters move, Edwards feinted forward, as if he was going to head-butt him. Fearing for his safety, Setters was so frightened that he staggered backwards and fell over, much to the delight of the crowd.

Having been knocked out of the FA Cup, United had a free week-end with no competitive fixture. Luckily, this coincided with the youth team's game against Plymouth, in the fifth round of the FA Youth Cup. In the previous round, the team, without Edwards, had hammered Sheffield United 7-0, and as such the boys were on a high.

Feeling invincible, especially with Edwards back in the fold, they delivered an inspired performance, which resulted in a magnificent 9-0 win. Even though Edwards played at centre-back, he still managed to get on the scoresheet, and in some style. Breaking out of defence, he shimmied past two players and broke into the opposition half at pace and, still 40 yards from goal, he unleashed a daisy-cutter which saw the ball sear its way into the bottom corner. Opposing managers were soon beginning to realise that it didn't matter what position he played, they could not contain him.

Following his youth team heroics, Edwards was selected to play for the England 'B' team against West Germany. As the senior team were shortly due to play their last international of the season, he was desperate to do well against the West Germans to be in contention for a place in the squad. However, as on previous occasions, when a senior England call-up seemed within his reach, he failed to produce his best form. The game finished 1-1 and reporter George Follows was moved to say, 'A rather poor showing and did nothing to claim a place in the full England side to face Scotland in April.'

Edwards knew he had one last chance to impress the England selectors, a game against Preston North End at Deepdale. Despite psyching himself up to show the selectors that he deserved a place, he once again gave another insipid display, which included one air shot that earned the jeers of the crowd. Although United won the game 2-0, a dejected Edwards walked off the pitch feeling that another chance had slipped from his grasp.

Back at his army barracks, Edwards was unable to sleep that night. Fidgeting on his camp bed, he realised that his last few performances had not done him any favours and that his wait for a full international cap may have to continue. At times, during his fitful sleep, he sometimes even wondered whether it was just not meant to be.

His pessimism was to prove to be misguided as the next morning he awoke to sensational news. He had made the squad to face Scotland at Wembley on 2 April 1955. He was stunned. If he were to play, he would become the youngest player in the 20th century to have represented England in a full international, at just 18 years and 183 days of age. A large part of that morning was subsequently spent ringing his friends and family to make sure that they could make it to Wembley. Most importantly of all, he checked if the army would grant him leave to play.

England's team to play Scotland was a supremely talented one containing a number of names that still resonate with all football fans to this day. The line-up was as follows: Williams (Wolves); Meadows (Manchester City); Byrne (Manchester United); Armstrong (Chelsea); Wright (Wolves, captain); Edwards (Manchester United);

Matthews (Blackpool); Revie (Manchester City); Lofthouse (Bolton Wanderers); Wilshaw (Wolves); Blunstone (Chelsea).

While there was an array of stars in the squad, Edwards was particularly looking forward to linking up with Stanley Matthews. At 40 years of age, Matthews had incredibly won three England caps before Duncan had even been born, but he was still going from strength to strength. His finest moment had come in the 1953 FA Cup final when he helped to drag Blackpool back, from being 3-1 down, to beat Bolton 4-3. Such were his efforts that the game was christened 'the Matthews final'. As most players his age settled into retirement, Matthews continued to astound everyone as he was crowned the European Footballer of the Year in 1956, when he was 42 years old.

If truth be told, Matthews was also looking forward to playing and training alongside Edwards to get a first-hand look at what all the fuss was about. He was not left disappointed. 'They all said you had to be strong, with big, thick thighs, Edwards' build was no surprise,' said Matthews. 'But, he was so quick, and that was what made the difference. I can't remember any other player that size who was quick like that.'

Normally so calm and confident before a big game, many mistook this for a sign that Edwards was immune to feeling any nerves. Busby once commented, 'The bigger the occasion, the better he liked it. He had no nerves before a game. He was like George Best in that respect. While other players would have to be pacing up and down a dressing room, rubbing their legs, doing exercises and looking for ways to pass the time, Duncan, and George later, was always calm. They would glance through a programme or get changed casually and wait without a trace of tension.'

Although he may have sat quietly in the changing room, Edwards would admit that he did in fact suffer from nerves. 'If you suffer from butterflies in the stomach while you are changing, don't despair – so do I and every other player I have met. Go round the England dressing room before an international and you will find every man

suffering from nerves of some description. Even such an old cam-
paigner as Billy Wright admits to them.'

A senior international debut at Wembley, against Scotland, was a
bigger game than most, and while Duncan was understandably apprehensive, his England team-mates helped him through it. 'By
lunchtime on the Saturday, I really had "butterflies",' he confessed.
'Once I got to Wembley itself and into the dressing rooms, there
were good luck telegrams to read and I began to feel better. All the
players wished me luck before we went out and Billy Wright said
that if anyone shouted at me just to take it with a pinch of salt.'

When he had played up-front against the Scotland Under-23 side,
Edwards had torn them apart, but for this match England's manager
Walter Winterbottom decided to play him at left-half. Feeling at
ease in his favoured berth, Edwards looked immediately at home on
the international stage and showed off the full array of his talent to
the enraptured Wembley crowd. Flying into tackles, diligently keeping possession and performing flicks and tricks, he became a crowd
favourite. As if the day wasn't memorable enough, England hammered Scotland 7-2. A star had been born. Henry Rose of the *Daily
Express* proclaimed, 'Edwards was a wing-half in the true English tra-
dition. Powerful in everything he did, he was a young colossus.'

Winterbottom was thrilled, not only with his new addition's display but also with his manner among the squad, 'He was such a nice
person, he was so modest. I was pleased to see him looking so happy
as he trained and played.'

Billy Wright had also been blown away, 'Duncan was the most
exciting prospect I had ever seen,' he fondly remembered. 'He had
immense strength in the tackle, and was dynamic on the ball. Duncan
played with such assurance and confidence that you would have
thought he was a veteran rather than a young man just starting out on
his international career. Walter Winterbottom summed it up when he
said quietly to me after the match, "I think we've uncovered a gem."
As Duncan was born and raised in Dudley in the West Midlands, Stan

Cullis kept scratching his head while trying to work out how he had let him escape from on his doorstep to Old Trafford.'

His selection and subsequent performance against Scotland had ensured that Edwards would not just be a one-cap wonder. After the game he was told that he had booked a place on the plane for England's summer matches against Portugal, France and Spain. He was thrilled.

Despite the fact that Edwards was now an established first team player, and a full international, Busby had no hesitation in playing him in the FA Youth Cup semi-final clash with Chelsea. This was a decision that again earned Busby plenty of criticism, which he answered in a typically forthright manner, in an article featured in the *Manchester Evening Chronicle*.

A London friend told me that Manchester United were 'not play-ing fair' in their Youth Cup competition progress by including Duncan Edwards, the 18-year-old international. 'Oh yes,' he said. 'I know that he qualifies by age, but here is a player who has actu-ally played for England at Wembley, is included in the England touring party going to France, Spain and Portugal in the close season and has also secured other representative honours.'

He then added, 'I was addressing a meeting of soccer referees the other night and the question cropped up. The general opinion was that Manchester United should not include him in their youth team.'

So that's what some people think. It annoys me! Duncan is eli-gible to participate in the Youth Cup. And, what is more, is keen to play. He is no seeker of cups and medals, but he is just as anx-ious as any other United young player to have the United name inscribed on the Cup for the third successive season. It would be an achievement which perhaps may never be equalled.

He may be 'outsize' in juniors, but he will probably tell you that he has to work just as hard – if not harder – in the Youth Cup competition as in senior football. He is, they say, 'football daft'. He dreams football and loves to talk about it and is eager to learn everything he can from the game. Duncan Edwards has not become a great footballer by bulldozer tactics. He is undoubtedly one of the greatest examples we have ever had of a footballer maturing at an early age.

But if the rules of the competition mean that he is eligible to take part, then I see no earthly reason to quibble, I don't doubt that if other clubs had the opportunity they would willingly include him in their Youth side.

Duncan Edwards has come to the front the hard way. That is by constant training and coaching. The United youngster never needs to be told what to do – though he is not alone in that respect. He, like others, is determined to make a success of his career as a foot-baller. He is willing to listen to advice and put that advice into practice on the field. Here is an 18-year-old whose example can be a lesson to every soccer-thinking youth.

I am happy to think that Duncan is getting so many honours from the game. I am glad to know that he remains as keen a player in junior soccer circles as in representative games. But to suggest that because of his exceptional talent he should not play in Youth games is in my opinion ridiculous.

Busby's argument that Edwards should be allowed to play in youth team games faced further scrutiny after his monumental display in the semi-final. Before the first leg, at Chelsea's Stamford Bridge, Murphy was keen to emphasise to his young stars that they were not just a one-man team. He urged them to try to take on some responsibility themselves, instead of always looking to Edwards to rescue them when they were in trouble.

Listening intently, Murphy's players carried out his instructions to the letter as the first half turned into an unmitigated disaster. At the break, they were lucky to be just a goal down and Edwards, positioned at left-half, had had a marginal influence on the game. Try as they might, his illustrious team-mates just could not seem to get the better of Chelsea without their star player conducting proceedings. 'When it got desperate we all looked for Duncan,' remembers McGuinness. 'We all thought we were good players, but we looked at Duncan as the greatest.'

Marching into a demoralised dressing room at half time, a red-faced Murphy exploded at his team. 'Remember I told you not to automatically pass the ball to Duncan?' he bellowed. 'Well, forget what I said. Give him the fucking ball whenever you can!'

Murphy subsequently put Edwards at centre-forward, with the order to demand the ball at every opportunity. Bobby Charlton always enjoyed seeing the sight of 'Big Dunc' up-front, the man he referred to as 'the Busby Babes' talisman', as if you were in trouble you could hoof the ball up to the big man, who would bring it down instantly, and create something out of nothing. 'We liked him up there,' McGuinness remembers. 'If you gave him a bad pass he could turn it into a good one and he was outstanding playing with his back to goal.'

After some relentless early pressure, United won a corner. Charlton walked across to take it and knew that if he could clip a ball into the middle of the area, Edwards would make it his. As the inch-perfect cross soared towards the penalty spot, Edwards surged towards it. Leaping high above the Chelsea defence, he arched his body backwards and then snapped it forwards, meeting the ball on his forehead with a thump which sent it hurtling into the top corner. Charlton could only describe the goal in one way, 'bloody sensational'.

Ambling back to the halfway line, with his team-mates mobbing him, Edwards shouted over to Murphy, 'Will that do for you, chief?' Murphy gave him the thumbs up and laughed. Edwards was, however, far from finished. In the closing minutes, he received the ball 40 yards from goal. Conscious that time was running out, he urgently rampaged forward, striding powerfully through the mud, before igniting the ball with a thunderous strike. Zipping through the air, the ball cannoned off both posts and into the net, leaving the helpless goalkeeper stood rooted to his line, stunned. Having looked dead and buried at half time, Edwards had dragged the team to within one game of yet another FA Youth Cup final.

At Old Trafford, the second leg was balanced on a knife-edge when Chelsea scored early on to bring the aggregate scores level at 2-2. But United were unflustered. With Edwards up-front they knew that they always stood a chance. Once again, the big man delivered by scoring another two goals to put United into the final. It seemed that everything he touched was turning to goals.

On 27 April 1955 United's Cup final opponents, West Bromwich Albion, travelled to Old Trafford for a date with the most-feared youth team in Europe. Hoping that United would have a rare off day, they would be bitterly disappointed. From the first minute to the last, West Brom were totally outclassed as Edwards, Colman and Charlton tore them to shreds. At times it looked as if it could be a cricket score, but in the end United had to settle for scoring just four. Every touch was greeted by an appreciative cheer from the crowd, knowing that they were witnessing a group of players who were at the top of their game.

At the Hawthorns a shell-shocked West Brom put up little resistance as Edwards and Charlton struck to help United to a 3-0 win. For the third consecutive season, United had won the FA Youth Cup. This was to be Edwards' last game in the competition, but even without him United still went on to win the Youth Cup the following two seasons. Busby's dynasty looked set to rule English and European football for a long time to come.

9

A SEASON OF GLORY

With the 1954-55 season at an end, Edwards craved some much-needed rest but he had no such luck. In May he was granted leave from the army to join up with the United first team in Copenhagen for a series of friendlies, before then jetting off with Roger Byrne to play for England against France, Spain and Portugal.

Billy Wright continued to be a huge influence on Edwards and he listened intently to everything that the great man had to say. 'Before an international match I always have a talk with Billy Wright, the England captain, about players in the side I may not have seen,' he said. 'Wright now knows most of the continental players and he will brief me on their tricks, their strengths and oddities.'

Feeling the pace after a long season, England's performances against the best teams on the continent were unsurprisingly limp. As a result they managed only a solitary draw and two defeats. No blame was, however, attributed to Edwards. He was progressing nicely and Walter Winterbottom now counted him as one of the first names on his teamsheet. Winterbottom also knew that as his star gained more experience at international level he would continue to improve, a thought which was a frightening prospect.

Despite the poor results, Edwards did enjoy the trip abroad, particularly Spain, where he got the chance to watch the bullfighting in Madrid, although journalist Geoffrey Green may have wished that he had given it a miss. 'In the summer tour of 1955 the England team had an afternoon off to watch a bull fight in Madrid,' Green reminisced. 'Afterwards Edwards pretended to be a bull: I played the part of the matador. As I was still waving my handkerchief as if it were the cape, the "bull" struck me amidships like some tornado. Sent flying, I broke a finger and to this day the swollen joint reminds me of that splendid young-spirited man.'

Following England's tiring end-of-season tour, Edwards did not even have the luxury of spending some time with Molly as he was immediately sent back to his army depot. There was definitely no chance of a rest from football at camp either. Everywhere he turned someone was urging him to play. Whether it was an order to turn out for an army representative side or an invitation to play five-a-side, or head tennis in the gym, there was no escape.

Colonel Edward Orton has recalled one such depot game that was played just a few days after Edwards had appeared for England. Although the depot had an England international playing in their defence, they fell behind 4-2 and the game looked lost. 'We moved Edwards to centre-forward,' said Orton, of his last-ditch attempt to try to salvage a result. 'From there he shot five goals in thirteen minutes before returning to defence to help us see out a 7-4 win.'

Bobby Charlton was also in Edwards' depot team and the two of them in tandem must have been a terrifying prospect for the opposition. Charlton can remember one game in particular where the two combined to score a wonderful goal:

When we were based in Shrewsbury for our National Service we were picked for a Western Command team playing the Royal Air Force in Cosford. He was at his most masterful. His play was always filled with confidence and authority, but on this day he was particularly dominant. Jimmy Murphy had told him that he should always demand the ball as a right, and that he should do it loudly. 'Maybe there is a big crowd and a team-mate might not hear you,' Murphy said, 'so make it clear that you want it.' Against the RAF Duncan's desire for possession was insatiable. The move that I will never forget started when he shouted for the goalkeeper to give him the ball. Naturally, the goalkeeper complied. Then Duncan passed to the full-back, who promptly delivered it back after receiving the firmest order. I was next in the chain. I received the ball and duly returned it to sender. By now the RAF was in full retreat. The last act involved the centre-forward. He held the ball for a moment, then rolled it into Duncan's path. At this point he was running into the box. He shot immediately, straight at the head of the goal-keeper. The goalkeeper made no attempt to save. Instead, he ducked as the ball rocketed into the back of the net.

Although in reality the army games meant very little, Edwards would play each one with his usual full commitment. If he was going to play, he wanted to win. 'Now I am not one of those people who believe that it doesn't matter whether you win or lose,' he said. 'I believe the object in starting a game of football is to win it. That is why it is known as a competitive sport. If you are not interested in winning then don't play.'

Edwards was in fact desperate to play football at any level, as long as it meant he was getting a game. Later on in his career, when he was an established international and the bright star of British football, he was asked to present some trophies at a boys' five-a-side tournament. However, once he found out that some of United's junior players were taking part in the competition, he rushed into Matt Busby's office and asked if he could get a game, as he was still 'only 21' and therefore eligible. While Busby liked to indulge his young star's enthusiasm, on this occasion he told him that it was out of the question.

On his return to Old Trafford, Edwards received a pleasant surprise:

an improved contract in recognition of his outstanding progress. The new deal would see him paid £15 per week during the season and £12 per week during the off-season. It was hardly the mega-riches you hear of players earning today, but unfortunately for players in this age the FA imposed a maximum wage limit which meant that the game's stars earned little more than the man in the street. It would not be until 1961 that the maximum wage was abolished, following the threat of a players' strike, and stars such as Johnny Haynes could start earning £100 and upwards per week.

By the start of the 1955-56 season, Busby had completely over-hauled his squad by replacing his ageing players with the starlets from his youth system. The only regular players that now remained at United from the 1952 title triumph were Johnny Berry and club cap-tain Roger Byrne. The team was undeniably based on youth, and as such they personified a cultural revolution that would soon see the Babes turned into stars of the era.

In November 1955 rock 'n' roll fever gripped Britain for the very first time. The single 'Rock Around the Clock', by Bill Haley and his Comets, was a sensation as it shot straight to the top of the charts. Also released at this time was the rock 'n' roll-based film *Blackboard Jungle*, which saw cinemas full to the brim with those who were desperate to hear this revolutionary beat-driven sound louder than they had ever heard it before. The film also introduced the American phrase 'Daddy-O' to British audiences and soon those who wanted to be hip were heard to utter 'jive talk' such as 'crazy cat', 'square', 'dig' and 'kick'.

More than simply introducing new slang talk to British youngsters, the advent of rock 'n' roll did something far more important: it set apart teenagers from children and adults for the very first time. Previously, you had been seen as a child until you were old enough to be 'grown up' and there was nothing in between. Now, with rationing at an end, and the poverty of the Second World War years diminish-ing, the young had some money in their pockets and this was eagerly spent on all things connected to rock 'n' roll. The market duly noticed this correlation and so began a bombardment of rock 'n' roll music and films. The teenagers lapped it all up, desperate to set themselves apart from the po-faced, straitlaced lives their parents seemed to lead and the innocence of their childhood.

All things American were especially popular with British youth, who had spent their childhood in a drab world of Woodbine cigarettes, war, ration books, bomb sites, outside toilets and corporal punishment. In contrast, America had the best music, flash cars, notorious gangsters, Hollywood films, iconic stars, golden beaches, sun, exotic cities such as New York and Los Angeles, numerous TV stations, jukeboxes, burgers, comics and so on and so on. This was a message that an influx of American films and songs was happy to ram down the throats of British kids who were in thrall to it all. Before long, the youth of Britain began trying to speak, dress and act just like their US counterparts.

Fashion became one of the key differentiators during this time. Most young men had dressed like their fathers up until this point, with staid suits, shirts and hats being the predominant outfit of choice. Historian Peter Hennessy has said of this, 'If you glance at a photograph of a terrace in any football annual dealing with the first postwar decade, you are struck by the absence of banners and the homogeneity of appearances.'

But now teenagers wanted to set themselves apart from the style of their fathers. They rushed to the barbers to get their hair coiffed into a style similar to actor Tony Curtis's slicked-back pompadour, bought tight jeans and white t-shirts just like James Dean sported in *Rebel Without a Cause*, and when Elvis Presley emerged, they even tried to speak with a curled-up lip, just like he did.

The 'Teddy Boy' fashion also became very popular, particularly with United's Eddie Colman, who became known as the club's style guru. This subculture had been inspired by the styles worn by dandies in the Edwardian period and favourite items of clothing included drape jackets, usually with a velvet collar, high-waist drainpipe trousers, often exposing brightly coloured socks, which were then traditionally worn with crepe-soled shoes known as 'brothel creepers'.

Although Colman and some of the other United players jumped onto this fashion bandwagon, Edwards wasn't really interested in such things, perhaps due to the fact that he couldn't fit his huge legs into the fashionable skinny trousers anyway. With this fad passing him by, he continued to dress like someone twice his age. 'He was bulky in those ill-fitting jackets and wide trousers with broad turn-ups,' said author Arthur Hopcraft, after looking at pictures of Duncan in Annie Edwards' photo album. 'He could have been a young miner freshly scrubbed for a night at the Labour Club dance. He did not look important, in the celebrated sense; he looked as if he mattered, and belonged, to his family and his friends. The anonymity of style was true to his generation and his kind.'

The Teddy Boy style, and introduction of rock 'n' roll, may have all seemed relatively harmless, but newspapers were soon full of stories regarding the 'Teddy Boy menace'. These stories were fuelled by incidents at cinemas when *Blackboard Jungle* was playing, and later the film *Rock Around the Clock*, as while most patrons chose to sing and dance along to the music, some 'Teds' slashed the red velvet chairs and hurled lit cigarettes from balconies into the stalls. Gang fights even broke out in some establishments, which caught the attention of the media who were eager to stick the boot into a craze they felt was making some teenagers act like maniacs.

BBC Radio was one of the first to strike back, as it refused to play any records associated with this new peril and as a result banned rock 'n' roll from the airwaves. Jim Davidson, the BBC Radio Head of Light Music, proclaimed that those who played this sort of music were 'freaks' who were 'the bottom of the gimmick noise barrel'. Even *Melody Maker* magazine, which is today indelibly linked with rock 'n' roll, could also not be persuaded that this new sound was a force for good. Steve Race, one of its columnists, wrote: 'Viewed as a social phenomenon, the current craze for rock and roll is one of the most terrifying things ever to have happened to popular music. The promotion and acceptance of this cult is a monstrous threat . . . let us oppose it to the end.' Thankfully for teenagers, Radio Luxembourg answered their prayers as the station started to fill its programmes with rock 'n' roll records from America. As soon as Elvis appeared on the scene in 1956, swivelling his hips and singing like a black soul singer, the game was up: rock 'n' roll had won.

Not only had rock 'n' roll won, but there would be no halt to the youth revolution as youngsters started to dominate music, film and, thanks to the prowess of the Babes, sport. Before the Babes came onto the scene, the image of British footballers was of young men who wore sober suits, sported sensible side-parted haircuts, slicked with Brylcreem, and listened to jazz and big band music, all while smoking a pipe. To all intents and purposes, they looked, acted and spoke as if they were middle-aged. But the Babes put an end to this preconception of footballers and for the first time made them fashionable.

By 1955 many in the team, such as Eddie Colman, Colin Webster and Tommy Taylor, wore their hair in rock 'n' roll-style quiffs. Their clothes changed from sensible suits to drainpipe trousers, jeans with turn-ups, lumberjack shirts and tight t-shirts. They could have passed for extras in a Marlon Brando film. This change in style, aping the teenage fashion revolution, coupled with the fact that they were one of the youngest teams in the history of the game, saw them become pin-ups. All of a sudden football, which had once been the domain of men, began to be watched by screaming girls in voluminous skirts and bobby socks.

'There were a lot of girls, groupies if you like,' Wilf McGuinness has recalled of this period. 'We noticed them as we ran out, but our minds were focused on the game. But we used to think, there's the girls cheering us on, because they stayed there every week. It was unbelievable.'

What also made the Babes especially appealing was that they were so accessible. Tom Clare, a United fan who lived in Manchester at this time, recalls just how easy it was to have contact with the team, 'If you waited long enough after a match, you could walk with them or travel with one of them on the bus; you would meet them in the shops, and always at the local dancehalls – the Locarno in Sale, the Plaza on Oxford Street, or at Belle Vue – mostly on Saturday evenings after home games. I have a few mates in Sale who are a little older than me, but who have related to me tales of how they used to sit with them in the Locarno, and the United lads would have a lemonade on top of the table, but half a mild underneath it.'

The Babes truly were the boys next door. All of the players lived in Manchester itself, most in modest houses, alongside United fans, as their wages wouldn't stretch to anything more luxurious. There were also no foreigners in the team, unless you counted Irishmen Jackie Blanchflower and Billy Whelan. Nearly all of the players were 'local' boys from the north who understood the motivations and frustrations of the average fan. It was all a far cry from players of today who often live in a world of roped-off VIP nightclubs, remote mansions and seem to do everything that they can to keep themselves from mixing with the public.

The Busby Babes were a young, vibrant, good-looking team, who had a strong bond with their fans, and who also happened to be tremendously talented. It is little wonder they became so popular with football supporters up and down the country. With so much talk surrounding his Babes, Busby was sure that the forthcoming season would see all of his hopes and dreams for this crop of players come to fruition.

However, as the new season got under way, Edwards looked a little weary. He had been playing an average of three games a week over the course of the year, at all levels, up and down the country and across Europe. It took him a few games to freshen up, but his below-par displays were masked by the fact that his team-mates started strongly as United rocketed to the top of the league.

At the end of August, Edwards' form slowly began to pick up. In a

home game against West Bromwich Albion, he set up a goal for
Dennis Viollet in a 3-1 win and then scored both goals himself in
United's 2-1 victory over Spurs at White Hart Lane. Wilf McGuinness
believes that his second goal against Spurs summed up not only the
magic of the Busby Babes but also the majesty of Duncan Edwards:

> I always remember Bobby Smith going past a few players and just as
> he was about to put the ball into an empty net Big Dunc put his
> foot in the way and the ball stood still as Bobby went flying. Big
> Dunc looked up and passed the ball to our right-half, Eddie
> Colman. Eddie swivelled his hips, he sent their team one way and
> the crowd the other before then backheeling the ball to Duncan.
> From the edge of our penalty area Duncan drilled a fifty-yard pass
> below head height to our left-winger, David Pegg, who controlled
> the ball with one touch and then slipped it inside to Bobby
> Charlton. Bobby let the ball roll through his legs before curling it
> into the Spurs half. There to meet it was Duncan Edwards who had
> run from our penalty area into their half in a matter of seconds.
> With three Spurs players in front of him he dribbled delicately past
> the first, he smashed through the second and the third jumped out
> of the way. Thirty yards from goal he shot and the ball flew into the
> net. Everyone in the crowd stood up to cheer the great Duncan
> Edwards.

While McGuinness' memory may be at fault as regards some of the
players who were involved in the move, his description of this wonder
goal reflects the enthusiastic press accounts of Edwards' sublime goal.

So how did Edwards celebrate his moment of genius? He rushed to
his London hotel to grab some sleep, before rising at 5.00am the next
day in order to catch a train back to his army depot.

Over the previous years, Edwards had enjoyed little luck in
Manchester derby games and the next one, at Maine Road, was not to
be any different. City took the lead in the first half and Edwards, who

was deputising up-front for the injured Dennis Viollet, had a number of chances to equalise only to be thwarted time and time again by goalkeeper Bert Trautmann. Being frustrated by Trautmann was, however, no disgrace and Edwards rated him as the best in the business. 'Sometimes in our matches I have noticed that he seems to know what is going to happen before the man in possession of the ball does,' he said when discussing Trautmann's unbelievable ability to reach even the most well-placed shot. 'Some of his cat-like saves from seemingly impossible positions are uncanny.'

While Trautmann, a former German prisoner of war, who would play the last 15 minutes of the 1956 FA Cup final with a broken neck, had prevented him from scoring, Edwards' energetic display seemed to herald a return to form. Yet in early September he developed a high fever and he was immediately hospitalised. Having caught a severe bout of influenza, he spent the next few days in Park Hospital, which caused him to lose almost a stone in weight. For the next six weeks, Edwards was unable to play any football and he spent most of his days in bed recuperating and trying to recover his energy. Thankfully, he had Molly there to look after him, and when he was well enough she encouraged him to get some fresh air by joining her for walks to feed the ducks. Annie Edwards was glad that Duncan had such a devoted girlfriend taking care of her son in her absence.

With Edwards missing from the side, United's form was patchy. Out of the seven games he missed they won three, lost two and drew twice. Much to Busby's relief, Edwards finally returned in mid-October when he participated in a friendly game in Scotland. However, he was understandably rusty, and at fault for two of the opposition's goals, as United slumped to a 4-1 defeat.

His performance in Scotland may have left a lot to be desired, but Busby still had no hesitation in naming him in the team to face Huddersfield just a few days later. Belying his lack of match sharpness, Edwards turned in an enthusiastic display, resulting in United recording a 3-0 win. His trademark tenacity in the tackle had also evidently returned as the referee had to give him a long lecture after a particularly hard challenge on a Huddersfield player.

Happy to be back in action, a rejuvenated Edwards looked forward to travelling around the country to play three games in the space of seven days. A tricky trip to Wales to face Cardiff City was first up, and Tommy Taylor's solitary goal at Ninian Park saw United record an important victory, which was enough to move them back to the top of the table. Next up was a trip to Scotland with the army to face Glasgow Rangers at Ibrox. Colonel Mitchell, who was in charge of the side, selected Edwards to play up-front, which meant that he would come face-to-face with Rangers and Scotland star defender George Young. Edwards was eager to prove his superiority, but when asked by the press for his thoughts on the encounter he diplomatically replied, 'I hope we both have a good game.'

On this occasion, Young emerged victorious by delivering a fault-less performance. The Scots had devised a game-plan which saw them cut out any attempted passes to Edwards, and if any did get through Young was quick to put him under pressure. Unable to get on the ball, Edwards started to drift around the pitch in a futile attempt to shed his marker but it was to no avail; Young had won this battle. The *Glasgow Herald* said of their contest, 'The young centre-forward had an extremely poor night against George Young. Indeed, when the game was only ten minutes old, he seemed to realise that he had scant chance of doing anything in the centre of the field. From then on, he roved both right and left wings, leaving Young in complete control of the defence.'

Edwards was pleased to find that his next game for the army team saw him joined by his United team-mates Bill Foulkes, Eddie Colman and Tommy Taylor. This added quality and familiarity allowed them to pick him out with ease and as such they subsequently managed a respectable 2-2 draw against an FA XI at St James' Park.

After an absence from the national team, due to his illness, the England selectors were relieved when Edwards showed he was back to top form with an all-action display in his next game, against Arsenal. The *Manchester Evening News* headline read: 'Sparkler Edwards Gives England Selectors a Happy Day,' with the match report stating, 'Duncan Edwards was the star performer for United and Alf Clarke felt that it wouldn't be long before he was again picked for England.'

Edwards may have performed well, but United could only draw the game, and they then lost their next match to Bolton Wanderers. Despite the loss, the United fans went home talking about how Colman had sold the great Nat Lofthouse a dummy which had left him for dead. Busby said of his infamous swivel hips, 'He's the only player in the first division who can sell a dummy with his backside.' The press were also impressed and said that the young right-half had a wiggle like Marilyn Monroe. United's fans may have been entertained, but their position at the top of the table was now under threat. They needed to get back to winning ways fast.

With their form deserting them, United faced one of their toughest games of the season when they met the champions, Chelsea, at Old Trafford. Ted Drake's team contained an array of stars, such as Roy Bentley, and they had won the league at a canter the previous season. Busby and Murphy knew that this was a must-win game and in the changing room before kick-off they rallied their players with reminders of all of the hard work they had put in, and how they had a duty to perform for the fans, some of whom had spent all week working in factories, looking forward to this clash. Edwards was particularly fired up and walked onto the pitch clapping his hands and shouting, 'Come on lads, let's get stuck into this lot!' Early in the game this enthusiasm threatened to derail United, as he was so pumped up he uncharacteristically snapped when he was the victim of a strong challenge. Grabbing the offending Chelsea player, Ken Armstrong, by the throat, the two players had to be separated by the referee before being warned that if there was a repeat of this conduct they would both be given their marching orders.

Once the game had settled, United were superior in all areas and they had Chelsea on the back foot. Unable to match their opponents, Chelsea sank without a trace, losing the game 3-0. The team left the pitch to a standing ovation as Edwards pumped his fists victoriously towards Molly and his proud parents, who were watching in their seats in the Main Stand.

Back into his stride, Edwards delivered his best display of the season in the following game at Blackpool, where the *Manchester Evening News* reported that he had played like a 'Trojan'. Colman was now enjoying a prolonged run in the side at right-half, and with Edwards on the opposite flank, United looked sensational. The team now had a tremendous balance, with Duncan bombarding down the left complemented by Eddie's fleet-footed surges on the right.

As United entered the Christmas period they were still in top spot, but faced a testing and congested fixture list. Results were mixed but some respite was provided when Edwards was finally victorious in a Manchester derby, which saw United beat City 2-1 at Old Trafford. The win was sweet, but a display of petulance in the match earned him the ire of the referee and from a watching Molly. Shepherding the ball out of play for a supposed goal kick, he was enraged when the referee awarded a corner. Unable to contain his temper, he picked up the ball and slammed it to the ground, while heatedly questioning the decision. This conduct earned him a booking, and a ticking-off from Molly, who hated seeing her boyfriend act 'ungentlemanly'. Although Edwards sometimes found it hard to contain his will to win on the field, he was never one to lose his cool away from football. 'I never saw him lose his temper off the pitch,' Wilf McGuinness has said. 'He was a gentle giant.'

The start of 1956 didn't provide Edwards with much cheer. A cut on his knee, which he had picked up while on army duty, had turned septic and this meant that he would miss United's FA Cup tie against second division Bristol Rovers. For him to miss a game through injury was very rare as he usually played on through the pain. Trainer Tom Curry once revealed how Edwards had played on with a badly sprained ankle, 'He got up, stamped his foot a few times, and carried on. At the end of the match his ankle was so swollen that the boot had to be cut away.'

United had of course struggled against minnows in the FA Cup the previous year but had ultimately managed to progress to the next round at the second attempt. This time, however, they would be on the receiving end of one of the most humiliating results in the club's history. The underdogs humbled the mighty Manchester United 4-0 and for once the normally calm Matt Busby lost his cool at his play-ers for their lacklustre efforts. Whether or not Edwards' presence would have made a difference it is hard to say, but it was certainly an experience he was glad to miss.

After this shock defeat, Edwards was rushed back into the team, but United's results remained indifferent as they beat Sheffield United only to then be defeated by Preston North End. Surprisingly, Edwards had not managed to get on the scoresheet for United since September, but he had continued to score freely for the army as he was playing consistently as a forward.

At the end of January, he again travelled to Scotland with the army to play against East Fife. Once again, he was selected to play up-front and, although he scored in the 2-1 win, the game will forever be remembered by those who witnessed it for one of Edwards' shots. As the ball fell to him on the edge of the box he swivelled and caught it sweetly on the full volley, sending it charging towards the goal. Such was the velocity of the shot that the goalkeeper didn't have time to react as it caught him square in the face, knocking him unconscious. Seeing the keeper sprawled in a star shape, Edwards raced towards him and shouted in his ear, 'You all right there, chief?' Failing to get a response, he hurriedly waved for the trainers to come onto the field. Amazingly, the keeper was out cold for almost five minutes, and after finally being brought around, he was unable to continue.

February was set to be a hectic month for United, as their title chal-lenge was entering a crucial stage. If they were going to come through it unscathed, then it was vital that all of their star players were fit and playing well. Busby was, however, infuriated when he found out that Edwards, Colman and Foulkes had been selected to play for the British Army in a game against their Belgian counterparts, the same day that United were due to play Luton. No matter how much he pleaded, he could not get his players released. What really rubbed salt into the wound was that, once the players had arrived in Belgium, the army game was called off due to bad weather. Edwards was far from pleased, not only at missing United's game, but also because he was violently seasick on the ferry home.

Bad weather was also causing a problem for the Football League, due to snow and ice battering the country. Some games were called off or abandoned, with undersoil heating having not yet been invented, but United's fixtures incredibly went ahead. Adapting well to the sub-zero conditions, they still managed to beat Wolves and then Aston Villa to go six points clear at the top of the table.

Edwards and his team-mates now had the bit between their teeth. The championship was within their sights. After two successive hard-fought draws they then had a morale-boosting win against Bolton, where Edwards subdued the bustling England centre-forward Nat Lofthouse. This was followed by a hectic Easter weekend that began with a 5-2 thrashing of Newcastle, then a day later by a 2-0 win at Huddersfield and finally a 0-0 draw in the return fixture against Newcastle. All of which now set up the team nicely for their date with fate, a title-deciding game against Blackpool.

On 7 April 1956, over 62,000 fans crammed excitedly into Old Trafford to witness the clash that could decide where the title would end up. Blackpool knew that for them this game was do or die. If they did not win, United would be champions.

United's players were sure that this would be their day, but they started poorly and Blackpool capitalised by opening the scoring. A muted first-half display saw a few murmurs of discontent emanate from the stands as United could not break down the wall of tangerine shirts, who diligently defended the final third. Although United grabbed an equaliser on the stroke of half time, via a Johnny Berry penalty, a second goal seemed beyond them. Time and time again, just as it looked as though Blackpool were rocking, a United player was thwarted by a last-gasp tackle as they bore down on goal. United may have had most of the possession, but Blackpool certainly seemed to have the rub of the green.

With the game inching towards the final whistle, Berry provided some inspiration. Urged on by the crowd's desperate roar, he jinked down the wing and chipped a cross to the back post, hoping that a team-mate would get on the end of it. To all intents and purposes it looked an easy claim for the Blackpool keeper, but as he ran to pluck the ball out of the air he slipped in the mud. Suddenly the ball fell out of his hands and the goal was left gaping. Desperately trying to keep his balance, Tommy Taylor stretched out a leg and managed to poke the ball goalwards. For a second Old Trafford fell silent. Trickling its way through the muddy six-yard area, the ball was suddenly grasped at by a Blackpool defender, who made a last-ditch attempt to stop it crossing the line with his hands. Both sets of players looked on agonisingly as the ball squirmed away from his grip and span across the line. GOAL! Old Trafford exploded. Hats and scarves were liberally thrown into the air and in the terraced areas the crowd surged forward, with many struggling to remain on their feet.

Taylor, the match-winner, his red shirt covered in mud, raised his arm aloft in celebration, mobbed by some of the Babes as he did so. Edwards, turning towards the Main Stand, grabbed the ball and booted it into the crowd. Staring up at the sky he lifted both his hands above his head and shouted with joy.

Minutes later the final whistle blew. The Babes of Manchester United were champions of England. Amazingly, Roger Byrne and Johnny Berry were the only players in the team who were over 25 years old.

Ian Greaves, the Manchester United right-back, believed that Edwards' display had been key to their victory: 'Duncan Edwards was majestic, playing like three men. Mind you, it always seemed like that!' However, Taylor deserved an enormous amount of credit for bringing the title back to Old Trafford, not only for scoring the winning goal but for the 25 goals he scored in total that season. His was a significant contribution.

That night the Manchester United players celebrated their victory in style. Mrs Dorman laid on a feast for Edwards at Gorse Avenue, after which he set off to join his team-mates at Colman's house where the serious drinking got under way. Once the house had been drunk dry, the boys descended on the Plaza nightclub where bottles of champagne were provided free of charge for the champions.

While the Babes drank themselves silly, Edwards stayed away from the alcohol, as he had an England match coming up. In spite of this, he was amid all the banter and felt on top of the world. At just 19 years of age, he was a first division champion and an England international. He also counted himself lucky that he had great friends such as Bobby Charlton and Colman, as well as having met the love of his life, Molly Leach. Life couldn't get much better.

Once the partying and celebrating were over, Edwards joined up with the England squad in order to prepare for battle with the Scots. Running the gauntlet at Hampden Park, he soon learned just what these fixtures were all about. The venom and viciousness emanating from the stands momentarily caught him off guard; he had never experienced such hostility. He then did himself no favours in the eyes of the Scottish supporters when he steamed into star player Bobby Johnstone, who had to spend considerable time having treatment and spent the remainder of the match hobbling in obvious discomfort.

Bob Forsyth, a fan who had followed Edwards' career since its inception, was at the game, and he was staggered by his idol's development. 'I had seen Duncan play quite a few times,' he recalled. 'I had actually seen him come on as substitute at Kilmarnock as something of a raw youngster a couple of years previously and had followed his career from a distance ever since. Watching him against Scotland that afternoon, you could notice how much he had developed, both physically and as a player in such a short time. He almost scored, I remember, when Hewie misjudged a clearance. His first-time effort went narrowly wide. In one way, I was grateful, as I would have probably shouted my appreciation, which may not have gone down too well. Early in the second half, he upended one of the Scottish forwards, Leggat I think it was, and every time he got the ball or went near one of the Scottish players after that, he was heartily booed by sections of the crowd.'

The crowd had more reason to jeer Edwards when he played a key part in setting up England's late equaliser in a 1-1 draw. Marauding down the touchline, he held off two challenges before playing a neat one-two with Johnny Haynes. Seeing Tommy Taylor at the back post, he clipped an inch-perfect ball for his team-mate to head back across goal, where Haynes was waiting to tap it into the net. The goal was greeted by a bitter silence. All the Scots could muster was a grudging respect that Edwards had proven his world-class credentials.

A sterner test awaited Edwards in his next appearance in an England shirt, a date with the Brazilians at Wembley. Just as they are today, Brazil were then regarded as one of the best teams in the world and this contest had football fans salivating. For once the hype turned out to be well justified.

England went in front as early as the second minute when the mesmeric trio of Edwards, 41-year-old Stanley Matthews and Haynes combined brilliantly to set up Taylor. Three minutes later, England were amazingly two up when Matthews nutmegged Brazil's Canhoteiro and passed the ball to Colin Grainger, who proceeded to bury it on his England debut. For the rest of the half, England had the bemused Brazilians chasing shadows and looked to be in complete control. It was a performance that looked to have finally banished the nightmare of the 1953 Hungary defeat.

But all of England's good work was soon to be undone. Just after the break, Brazil pulled one back when Paulinho's speculative shot took a cruel deflection off Roger Byrne and looped over the helpless Reg Matthews in the England goal. Minutes later, a rare Billy Wright mistake gifted Brazil's star player, Didi, with the ball. Without hesitating, Didi struck from 20 yards to level the scores. It would have been easy for England to crumble, but to their credit they regrouped and continued with their high-tempo passing game.

Faced with the power, desire and pace of this supreme England side, Brazil were unable to cope. Despite the team missing two penalties, Taylor and Grainger both scored again to lead England to a famous victory. Edwards was ecstatic. He had played a key part against celebrated South American opposition and the team had proved that they were no longer also-rans. Once again, they were capable of being more than a match for the best teams in the world. In an emphatic fashion they had shown their critics that they had finally adapted their game to cope with the change in tactics and style of play on the international stage.

After such a monumental clash, Edwards had little time to catch his breath, as he was then whisked off on a three-match continental tour with the England team. Following a draw and a win, against Sweden and Finland, the final match of the tour, against West Germany, saw England really turn on the style.

Despite the country being decimated after the Second World War, the West Germans had managed to rebuild their football team and had improbably won the 1954 World Cup. England were playing well, and confidence was high, but the prospect of beating the world champions in Berlin was slim. Never one to care about reputations, Edwards threw himself into battle and in the process scored one of the finest goals ever seen on German soil.

Seizing the ball midway in the German half, Edwards propelled himself towards the goal, zigzagging through several desperate lunges on his way. Oblivious to the fact that the young Englishman possessed one of the hardest shots in football, the German defenders stood off, hoping that they could shepherd the youngster away from goal. This was to prove to be a huge mistake. Sensing an opportunity, Edwards unleashed a pile-driver from the edge of the box which almost demolished the German goal on impact. As the ball hit the net, the few thousand British servicemen who were in the crowd went wild with delight.

England famously went on to win the game 3-1, but the headlines belonged to Edwards. The next day the German press was full of stories regarding the brilliance of Duncan Edwards, with one publication even nicknaming him 'Boom Boom', much to the delight of the England players, who enjoyed ribbing their team-mate about his new name.

Billy Wright counted himself lucky that he had witnessed such a triumphant display from England's young star. 'The name of Duncan Edwards was on the lips of everybody who saw this match. He was phenomenal. There have been few individual performances to match what he produced in Germany that day. He tackled like a lion, attacked at every opportunity and topped it all off with a cracker of a goal. He was still only twenty [he was actually still 19 at this point] and was already a world-class player. Many of the thousands of British soldiers in the crowd surrounded him at the final whistle and carried him off. It was fantastic to be part of it. We had beaten the world champions in their own back yard.'

Following such an unforgettable evening, and with his season at an end, Edwards decided for once to let himself go at the after-match celebrations. 'After the game a few of the lads, including Duncan, had a few drinks,' remembered England forward Nat Lofthouse. 'There was plenty of strong German wine being drunk at the banquet as we all celebrated the victory. Duncan didn't normally have much to drink, and some of the lads warned him about it being stronger than what he would be used to. He assured us that he would be all right, but in the end, the German wine did a better job of stopping Duncan than its football side, and he finished up in the toilet, a bit worse for wear. Even at nineteen, Duncan was already half the England side.'

'Boom Boom' had certainly had a month to remember. He had won the title with Manchester United, destroyed the majestic Brazil at Wembley, and topped it all by scoring a wonder goal in Berlin to defeat the world champions. The future sparkled with limitless possibilities.

10

EUROPEAN PIONEERS

On 20 July 1957 Prime Minister Harold Macmillan told the nation, 'Most of our people have never had it so good.' Macmillan was of course talking about the boom in the post-war global economy that had fuelled high levels of employment combined with an unprecedented rise in consumerism. Industrial towns such as Dudley were particularly buoyant due to a huge increase in demand for steel and coal, which resulted in an increase in jobs and, for many, wages. Manchester, though its wealth had long been based on a declining cotton industry, also shared in some of this prosperity.

With more money in their pockets, people cast aside the misery of the war years and began to treat themselves to material items such as televisions, cars, fridges and washing machines. As new houses were built, fewer people had to contend with outside toilets, and double-glazing and central heating became a more common feature of many houses. It was as if the world had stepped out of what had almost amounted to a Dickensian way of life and had finally entered the 20th century.

However, while Macmillan's statement related to the newfound prosperity of the British population, it could also have applied to how Manchester United fans were feeling at the end of the 1956-57 season as this would turn out to be a campaign where they had certainly 'never had it so good'. Without a shadow of a doubt this was one of the most exciting periods in the club's history.

When United had last won the league, in 1952, that honour had been a reward in itself. This time around, as champions of England, United were now invited to take part in the fledgling European Cup which would determine who was the best team on the continent. Following the unprecedented interest in the friendly games that Wolves had played against foreign opposition, this was a competition that had created enormous excitement among fans. Sadly, the Football League did not feel the same way.

The previous season's champions, Chelsea, had applied to the Football League for permission to enter the inaugural European Cup competition a year earlier, only to be put in their place. Alan Hardaker, the secretary of the Football League, felt that English clubs already participated in enough competitions and that Europe would be a shortlived, unnecessary distraction, which could also interfere with the league fixture list. There was also an element of arrogance in Hardaker's reasoning, as he still felt that foreigners had nothing to teach a nation that had invented the game. Chairmen of several league sides amazingly agreed with this short-sighted stance and successfully encouraged Chelsea to resist. Staggeringly, in spite of Hardaker's argument that English clubs already played in enough competitions, he subsequently sanctioned the creation of the League Cup in 1960!

Matt Busby was not so easily persuaded. He was a staunch advocate of the European Cup and felt that it could propel his Babes to new levels. Eamon Dunphy, in his exceptional biography of the United manager, *A Strange Kind of Glory*, outlined what he felt were the key reasons for Busby's enthusiasm for the new competition:

His rationale for engaging in European competition was threefold. First, it would provide money to pay for the floodlights United had still to install, and for the large, ever-expanding wage bill rising in proportion to the number of first division quality players on United's books. Second, the extra competition, seen as a problem by the Football League, was a blessing to Busby – players could be kept happy and gain experience playing in the Champions Cup. His final reason was more abstract than practical. He understood how irrevocably the balance of power was shifting away from the English game, and saw that football in the future would be an international game. The world was contracting, travel was easier, people were curious about abroad. As a football man he was intrigued by the international game. Football as played by the Hungarians was his kind of game.

But these weren't the only reasons behind Busby's enthusiasm. Perhaps more than any other, there was one that lit the fire in his belly and had him dreaming at night. Glory. The glory of his cherished Manchester United team not only being the first English side to take part in the competition, but also becoming the first British side to win it. As with the FA Youth Cup, Busby always liked to be a pioneer. He didn't like merely to dip his toe into the water, he liked to be a trailblazer, enjoying new adventures and in the process writing history.

In order to strengthen his hand, Busby tried to convince FA chairman Stanley Rous, who happened to despise Hardaker, that it would be in British football's best interests if United were to play in Europe. Rous didn't take much persuading. After all, until recently England's national side had struggled against foreign opposition and by Busby's reasoning the more English teams exposed themselves to the European style of play and tactics, the more they would learn and in turn improve. Rous agreed with this line of thinking and gave Busby his blessing.

Another backer in Busby's corner was United chairman Harold Hardman, who was intrigued to hear that not only would this new competition help to improve the team but that it could also swell the Old Trafford coffers. This was music to Hardman's ears, as even though the British economy was rapidly improving, first division clubs were starting to feel the squeeze.

Although wages for players were laughably low compared to today, they had still risen considerably since the end of the war and all signs pointed to this trend continuing. In 1947, the maximum wage had been set at £12 per week, but in 1957 it would increase for the third time since then to £17 per week, and the following year it would rise again, this time to £20. As Eamon Dunphy said above, United were feeling this more than most as they had a big squad of top-quality players, with most demanding the maximum salary allowed at that time, as well as any extras they could persuade the club to part with.

Another strain on football clubs' accounts was the fact that attendance figures as a whole were starting to drop off quite dramatically. The first few years after the war had seen a huge boom in attendances, due in part to low admission prices and the fact that people were desperate to watch football having been starved of it during the war. However, since those heady days there had been a loss of over 8 million spectators through the turnstiles, despite the fact that there were now more games being played in the Football League than ever before (total league attendances fell from 41.2 million in 1948-49 to 33.1 million in 1955-56, and would fall again in the new campaign). United were luckier than most, as they frequently enjoyed a full house, but since the start of the decade they had averaged crowds of over 40,000 in only one season (1951-52). The signs were worrying and Hardman was eager to do what he could to boost revenues.

With the backing of Rous and Hardman, Busby confronted Hardaker and told him that United would be entering Europe that season, with or without his approval. Hardaker attempted to talk Busby round, but he would hear nothing of it. Eventually, Hardaker backed down when he realised Busby's determination to ensure that Manchester United took part, but to make matters difficult for the rebels he left Busby with a threat: if Europe did interfere with United's Football League fixtures, then Hardaker would hit them with a heavy fine and a points deduction.

Before thoughts turned to Europe, the champions of England

kicked off the season with a home game against Birmingham City. Surprisingly they never got into their stride and were lucky to emerge with a point after a 2–2 draw. United were in fact a goal down with just minutes remaining, but as the game seemed lost Edwards, according to the *Manchester Evening News*, set off into the opposition's half 'combining the power of a battleship with the manoeuvrability of a destroyer' to set up the equaliser.

Emphatically blowing away the early-season cobwebs, United were soon back to their show-stopping best as they went the next 11 league games without defeat. During this spell, Edwards was magnificent. After a 2–1 win at Chelsea *The Times* declared that 'Edwards is a giant both in thrusting attack after attack and in covering Byrne in any emergencies.'

One of these matches saw Edwards come face to face with Newcastle's star player, Jackie Milburn. Some critics predicted that if anyone could give the giant from Dudley the run-around, it could be the magician in the black and white shirt. Edwards admired Milburn but had heard that he was easy to unsettle. Therefore, before the match got under way, he menacingly approached his opponent and said in a threatening manner, 'I don't care about reputations, they mean nothing to me. Any bother from you and I'll boot you over the stand.'

After he had unceremoniously smashed Milburn off the pitch with a crunching tackle, Edwards then opened the scoring in the second half. However, against the run of play Newcastle struck back, and the game eventually ended all square. But Edwards had accomplished his mission. He had kept a clearly terrified Milburn quiet. With the match at an end, Edwards approached his shell-shocked opponent and smiled broadly. Shaking the perplexed Milburn by the hand he said, 'Thanks for the game, chief,' before winking and walking away.

Despite being only 19 years of age, Edwards incredibly made his 100th league appearance against Manchester City on 22 September 1956. He celebrated in style as United won the derby 2–0. City captain

Don Revie was blown away by United's wing-halves and told the press, 'There is not a better pair of wing-halves in the country than Edwards and Colman.' *The Times'* football correspondent also showered him with plaudits. 'Edwards is truly a young giant. He covered all of the field in defence, dominating everyone in the air. Some 30-yard passes whistled out to Pegg and once with a prodigious nod he turned the ball back to Wood from outside the penalty area. Yet for all his size he can stroke the most delicate pass even when going at full tilt.'

Disappointingly, a toe injury saw Edwards miss out on Manchester United's first-ever European game, against Anderlecht in Brussels. In his absence, his mates were still able to record a 2-0 win and now looked favourites to progress to the next round.

Desperate to return to the fray, Edwards was back in the team for the midweek second leg, which was to be played at Maine Road, as Old Trafford had not yet installed floodlights. On the night no one from the Football League turned up to offer their support. They were not missed. Roared on by an excited crowd, United were irresistible. Dennis Viollet scored four times, Tommy Taylor bagged a hat-trick, Billy Whelan notched a brace, while Johnny Berry also got on the scoresheet. In total United had scored an astounding ten goals! It remains United's biggest-ever victory.

Edwards had been involved in the build-up to most of the goals and his ability to switch the play, knock it long and short, putting spin on the ball when necessary, had been a lesson in the art of passing. Far from bask in the glory of his towering display, though, he had to leave the ground immediately after the game, catch a bus to the train station and then travel to his base in Shrewsbury so that he could play in a cup game for his depot the next day.

Busby believed that this display from his Babes had come close to capturing all of his ideals of how the game should be played. 'It was the greatest thrill in a lifetime of soccer,' Busby happily reminisced. 'It was the finest display of teamwork I have ever seen from any team, club or international. It was as near perfect football as anyone could wish to see.'

Even the Anderlecht players could do nothing but hold their hands up and admit they had been beaten by a perfect performance. Hippolyte van den Bosch played for the Belgians and he has since admitted that 'this was the best English team I've ever seen. I honestly think that the team we played in 1957 had more talent than the Rooneys and Ronaldos of today.'

Days after the Anderlecht demolition, Edwards helped mastermind a 2-1 win over Arsenal at Highbury. Despite playing a game almost every other day since the season began, he still looked remarkably fresh. Alf Clarke of the *Manchester Evening Chronicle* picked up on his incredible ability to maintain such high standards and his tremendous appetite for the game, 'Edwards the courageous, doing two men's work. You would not think that this was his fourth game in a week, judging by his brilliance today.'

Turning out for club, country as well as for the army and his depot saw Edwards play in over 95 matches this season. Bearing in mind that this was when he was also on National Service, so had little time to rest, coupled with the fact that the pitches would become bogs in the winter, sapping the energy from the players' legs in the process, then this feat makes a mockery of players today who complain about playing too many games.

Something that helped Edwards get around the heavy pitches was his choice of footwear. Slowly but surely the old-fashioned hobnailed, ankle-high boots had started to disappear from the British game and were now being replaced by a lightweight, continental-style boot that he adored.

The old boots had once been suited to the outdated 'kick and rush' style of play in England, as they were designed to help players kick the heavy ball as far as possible and were also perfect for 'hacking'. Yet following Hungary's historic win in 1953, the game had gradually started to change. There was now a greater emphasis on ball control and technique rather than lumping the ball all over the pitch. This change in approach led to some players starting to reconsider their choice of boots.

Blackpool and England winger Stanley Matthews was in fact ahead of his time as he had first started to wear continental-style boots as far back as 1950. After playing for England in Brazil in the 1950 World Cup, he had marvelled at the lightweight soft leather boots that the Brazilians wore, which almost seemed to allow them to float around the pitch. He also noticed that the absence of toe protection enabled them to bend the football with incredible precision. Suitably impressed, he snapped up a pair in Rio and on his return to England he took them to the Cooperative Wholesale Society (CWS) shoe factory in Yorkshire for further examination.

The CWS had never before seen such a boot. Eager to find out more, they pulled it apart so as to understand how it was assembled. They soon learned that the boots were made of soft kangaroo leather, had screw-in studs, rather than ones that were nailed in, and weighed just a few ounces. Spotting an opportunity, they offered to supply Matthews with a similar pair for him to play in and also started to sell Stanley Matthews-endorsed football boots to the masses. Matthews made himself a small fortune with this endorsement, as CWS sold half a million of them throughout the 1950s and he earned himself sixpence a pair.

At the start of the decade, fledgling German sportswear company Adidas had also started to manufacture lightweight boots, but they did not become widely known until after the 1954 World Cup. At that tournament the company's owner, Adi Dassler, had managed to pull off a coup by persuading the West German national team to wear them throughout the competition in Switzerland. The West German players were not paid a penny to wear the boots, they wore them simply because they thought they were the best. Who could blame them? They were the lightest on the market, had no toecaps and, best of all, they were comfortable. Another benefit was that they also looked great as they boasted the distinctive three stripes company logo of Adidas running down the side.

The 1954 World Cup was the moment that turned Adidas into an international company, as it has been said that these new-style boots helped the West Germans triumph over the favourites, Hungary, in the final. Faced with a downpour on the day of the match, which left surface water on the pitch, Adi Dassler decided to screw longer studs into his easily adaptable Adidas boot. The Hungarians, on the other hand, were too focused on the game to worry about a minor thing such as footwear so they wore their normal boots, which had fixed, nailed-in, short studs. This was to prove costly. Despite being overwhelming favourites, having already beaten the West Germans 8-3 earlier in the competition, they struggled in the rain while their opponents were able to keep their balance and glide through the mud. Incredibly, this helped West Germany cause a major upset as they recorded a 3-2 win.

The Adidas boots were swiftly heralded by the German press as 'wonder boots' and Adi Dassler was christened 'the shoemaker of a nation'. Even the British newspapers caught wind of these revolutionary boots, with one publication running a story on them under the headline 'What a Dassler!', declaring that they were 'only half the weight of the orthodox British football boot'.

As interest grew, Adidas started to infiltrate the British market and supplied some of the players at Manchester United with them, such as Kenny Morgans and Duncan Edwards. The latter was so impressed with them that he said 'the modern boot is a vast improvement on the old thick leather type that encased the foot and ankle as if in steel. The present boots allow you to feel the ball through leather, and thus make for better ball control.' It was, however, a worrying thought for Duncan's opponents. He had performed well enough in the old-style boots, but now the Adidas boots promised to allow him to control the ball better than ever before, as well as make him lighter and quicker.

But Edwards wouldn't get a chance to wear his new boots in United's next game, against Charlton, as he was away on England duty in Northern Ireland. This gave reserve left-half Wilf McGuinness an opportunity in the team and he grabbed it with both hands, helping

United to saunter to another victory. The game also saw Busby give Bobby Charlton his debut and he did not disappoint as he struck with two trademark thunderbolts. As had been predicted, Charlton would prove to be another gem in a squad already brimming with talent.

United's young guns were in fact so dominant against Charlton that journalist Bill Fryer proclaimed, 'It's no use. We'll have to make this league championship a handicap . . . United scratch, the rest six points start. At least it would make a race of it.'

More than the result, it was the display of McGuinness that had thrilled Busby. Finally, he had another left-half who he could rely on. This now meant that he could afford to experiment with Edwards in a forward role without weakening his defence. In time, he might even be able to pair Charlton and Edwards together in an attack that would provide power, movement and magic.

Unfortunately, England were unable to match United's peerless performance as they put in a muted display against Northern Ireland. The game ended in a 1-1 draw, a reasonable result, but England showed none of the class and poise that they had so expertly demonstrated against Brazil and West Germany. Brilliant one match, mediocre the next – it was impossible to tell whether this England team were world champions in the making or just also-rans.

With United still unbeaten in the league, they went into their next European encounter, against Borussia Dortmund, feeling invincible. Following the dominant nature of their display against Anderlecht, some sports writers felt that United should be able to win every game against European opposition at a canter. Perhaps some of the United players also felt the same as, although they shot into a three-goal lead, they sloppily allowed Dortmund to get back into the match with two poorly defended goals. Edwards and Colman came in for some particularly harsh criticism, as Frank Taylor of the *News Chronicle* said that they had both played in a 'cocky manner'.

Criticism was again rife when United met Everton at Old Trafford just a few days later. Already chasing the game, Edwards had to leave the field to receive treatment for a twisted ankle. When he eventually returned to the fray he was hobbling badly and if substitutes had been allowed there is no doubt that he would have been replaced. Shortly after returning, he was uncharacteristically caught in possession, which led to Everton increasing their lead. Sensing that Edwards was unable to run, the Merseysiders took full advantage by targeting him at every opportunity. Everton went on to score two more goals, and recorded a shock 5-2 result at the home of the champions. United's unbeaten start to the season had been unceremoniously destroyed and Edwards was left to nurse a badly bruised ankle.

Never one to miss a game through injury, Edwards characteristically declared himself fit for United's next match, the Charity Shield against local rivals and FA Cup holders Manchester City. Throughout his short career he had played in virtually every position for United, apart from in goal, but this game would provide him with the opportunity to prove his worth between the sticks.

Having always enjoyed himself when diving around in training, he happily offered to replace Ray Wood when he was forced to leave the game in the 37th minute through injury. Although his time in goal was shortlived, as he was replaced by reserve goalkeeper David Gaskell at half time (who in the process became the first-ever 'official' United substitute and the club's youngest-ever player), Edwards did manage to keep a clean sheet, which helped United win the game 1-0.

After a draw at Blackpool, Edwards returned to his usual left-half position in a league encounter with Wolves, but his ankle was still causing him problems. Against Bolton he went over on it again and needed yet more vigorous treatment on the sidelines. Despite being in agony, he returned to the match but was limping so badly that Busby decided to stick him up-front out of harm's way. With Edwards unable to do much, the Trotters went on to win 2-0, and his mood was not improved when he was forced to sit out the next game.

After a week of physio, and with the aid of heavy strapping, Edwards declared himself fit for the second leg against Dortmund.

The German press eagerly awaited the return of 'Boom Boom' and this hype helped to swell the crowd, not only with German fans but also with over 7,000 British servicemen who had travelled across Germany to get to the game.

The football on display would sadly turn out to be a disappointment as the game was played in freezing temperatures, which meant that the pitch was frozen solid. This was certainly not a playing surface that helped Edwards' swollen ankle and the elements played a part in subduing his rampaging runs. Playing apprehensively, he had a quiet match, but no one from either team contributed much, as it was a feat in itself just managing to stay upright. In such conditions, Dortmund rarely threatened tying the scores and this meant that United saw out the game and were through to the quarter-finals.

Rarely has a footballer been able to hit a ball as hard as Duncan Edwards and although his long-range shooting usually left most fans and critics looking on in awe, it didn't always meet with everyone's approval. In a game against Luton, which United won 3-1, one newspaper carried the headline, 'Does England Need Duncan Edwards' Rocket Specials?' The hyper-critical report went on to say, 'Yesterday he seemed to be trying to show the selectors that he's the guy to get goals. He turned out at inside-left and within four minutes rocketed one into the net. Not only that, he continued firing these rockets throughout the afternoon. Shoot when you see the whites of their eyes is a good way of going about scoring goals. But not, Duncan, when your colleagues are in a better position.'

In spite of the criticism, the England selectors who had been in the crowd were so impressed with Edwards' display that they opted to play him up-front in their World Cup qualifying fixture against Denmark. The game was played at Molineux, rather than Wembley, and this gave him the opportunity to play for his national team in his home town.

Knowing that the people of Dudley had turned up to watch him, Edwards did not disappoint as he delivered perhaps his best England display. Continuing his good goalscoring form, he struck twice, with one of his blasts described as 'like some rocket setting off for Mars'. He also smashed a free kick that hit the woodwork so hard that Henry Rose of the *Daily Express* reported that it 'almost uprooted the goal-post'. Although he was at fault for one of Denmark's goals, no one minded as his home-town fans rapturously applauded him every time he got on the ball. To the people of Dudley he was now referred to as 'Our Dunc', despite the fact that he played for Manchester United.

Over the course of the next few games, Busby opted to play Edwards in his usual left-half position, but when Tommy Taylor was injured he then asked him to deputise at centre-forward against Portsmouth. His subsequent display had the newspaper writers salivating. United won the game 3-1 and Edwards had terrorised the Portsmouth defence every time he got on the ball. He scored one goal, which Henry Rose described as a 'torpedo', and created several more chances for himself where he was unlucky not to score.

An enthusiastic match report, written by the *Manchester Evening Chronicle*'s Alf Clarke, read, 'The game gave United the opportunity of trying out an experiment everyone wanted to see – the playing of the versatile Duncan Edwards at centre-forward. The fact that Edwards scored once and made another goal, made the experiment eminently worthwhile. It could quite easily have been sensationally successful if the ball had run just a little more kindly for Edwards in front of goal. Five times this burly youngster, who packs one of the fiercest drives in soccer in his boots, had Portsmouth in dire trouble and because he is Duncan Edwards he was expected to score. Each time he failed, which doesn't prove anything, except that Edwards is human.'

After his endeavours on the South Coast, Edwards returned to his normal left-half slot for United's next trip, a clash with Athletic Bilbao in Spain in the quarter-final of the European Cup. While he had enjoyed every minute of his European adventure, there was one aspect of it that he found difficult: flying. The plane trip to Bilbao brought on another intense bout of airsickness which fellow passenger, journalist Frank Taylor witnessed:

As we flew out over the angry-looking bay on the last hop to Bilbao, big Duncan sat alone, silent and apprehensive.

'What's the matter, Duncan?' I asked.

'Too hot for me. I shall be air sick,' came the reply of a man who didn't want to talk.

'Get the heater turned off, man, if you feel that bad.'

'No,' he replied. 'The chairman has been feeling the cold. Leave me alone. I'll be all right.'

History records that the heating had actually been turned on full at the request of the chairman, Harold Hardman, who had started to feel ill. Shortly before this, the cabin had been freezing due to Bill Foulkes accidentally turning on the cold air as his foot had fallen on a lever as he slept. Due to the bitter temperature, Hardman contracted pneumonia and upon landing in Spain he had to be rushed to hospital. While Hardman no doubt cursed Foulkes at the time, it would ultimately save his life. After this incident, he vowed never to fly unless he could help it and as such decided not to travel to Belgrade with the team in 1958. This meant, of course, that he avoided becoming a casualty in Munich by a quirk of fate.

However, while the heating comforted the chairman at this time, it continued to make Edwards feel ill. As always, Roger Byrne carried out his captain's duty with aplomb. Sitting next to United's star player, he joked and chatted with him in an effort to take his mind off the heat and the turbulence. To an extent this worked, but upon landing Edwards still felt ill and Frank Taylor did not hold out much hope for him being fit to face the Spaniards:

'Duncan Edwards still looked like a man who had had gastric flu. Sensing a story, I quizzed him: "Do you think you'll be fit to play on Wednesday, Duncan?"

'He was thunderstruck and looked at me as though I was mad. "Miss the match? What do you take me for – a sissy?" And with that he staggered away, still pretty wobbly at the knees.'

Although Edwards did manage to shake off his sickness, and played, it was in fact a miracle that the game went ahead. The pitch, covered in thick snow, made it impossible for the players to keep the ball on the deck. A driving wind also made it difficult for them to resort to long-ball tactics. With the conditions causing mayhem, the first half was an unmitigated disaster as Bilbao led 3-0 at the break. United looked down and out and set to fall victims to an embarrassing score-line. Refusing to be humiliated, a spirited second-half performance saw United give themselves some hope as they pulled three goals back, but it wasn't enough, as they lost the game 5-3. In the circumstances, it could have been far worse.

The miserable mood in the camp wasn't then helped when the plane on which the players were travelling home managed to get stuck in snow on the runway. Busby panicked for a moment. If they couldn't take off then they might not make it back in time to face Sheffield Wednesday on the Saturday. This would of course fall right into Alan Hardaker's hands. Hardaker would take great pleasure in saying 'I told you so' and he would be more than happy to punish United with a points deduction. Such a thing didn't bear thinking about.

Ordering his players, as well as the newspaper reporters, to grab some shovels, they all pitched in to help clear a path in freezing conditions. Understandably, the players were slightly nervous as the plane taxied down the ice-covered runway, but their concerns were ill-founded as the plane soared into the air with no problems. Busby breathed a sigh of relief. It had been a close call but they would make it home in time.

It would be three long weeks before United had the opportunity to turn things around in the second leg against Bilbao. In the meantime they had a number of vital games that they had to win in order to keep up their pursuit of league and cup glory.

The game that Busby feared the team might miss, Sheffield Wednesday away, saw the Babes look heavy-legged after their exploits in Bilbao and this contributed to a shock 2-1 defeat. This was the first season that a United team had to adjust to travelling and playing in Europe during the week and therefore they initially found it hard to keep up their high standards in the league games that immediately followed. Busby, however, quickly learned how best to prepare his team for such a strenuous stretch of games as he gave the players more time off, rather than slogging them to death, and cut the time that training lasted.

When Harry Gregg signed for the club, at the end of 1957, he was surprised at just how little United actually trained. 'When I arrived at Old Trafford I really thought we would be training all the time,' Gregg recalls. 'That suited me down to the ground as I loved to play football but I couldn't understand why Tom Curry kept cutting training so short. It was of course because of all the games the team were playing at the time. Coming from Doncaster I wasn't used to it, though, so I always wanted to stay out and do extra work.'

Despite the loss to Wednesday, it didn't take too long for the Babes to return to winning ways. An FA Cup fourth round game at Wrexham turned out to be the perfect tonic as a refreshed United scored five goals without reply. One newspaper reported that Edwards had given a 'magnificent exhibition of hard constructive play'. The team then warmed up for the second leg against Bilbao with a 4-2 win in the Manchester derby. Edwards got the fourth goal for United, but for once his effort did not need to be a howitzer to beat the great Bert Trautmann in the City goal. On this occasion he scuffed his shot, which perhaps surprised the German goalkeeper, who had steadied himself for a rocket, as he inexplicably let the ball creep over the line.

Since the loss to Bilbao, the British public had been eagerly anticipating the return fixture. Capitalising on the frenzied interest, Manchester United controversially raised the price of tickets, in some cases to £11, more than the weekly wage of some supporters. The directors of Bilbao, keen to record a famous victory, offered their

players a lucrative win bonus of £200 per man. In contrast, the
United players were offered the meagre incentive of £3!

In order to progress, United needed to win the fixture by three
goals, a tall order against such vaunted opponents. On the brink of
half time, United's valiant efforts appeared to be in vain as they had
rarely threatened the Spaniards' goal. Sensing that the game was slipping away, Busby ordered Edwards to push further forward and these
instructions reaped immediate dividends. Within moments a vicious
shot from Edwards rebounded to Viollet, who as usual was in the right
place at the right time, and smashed the ball into the net.

At half time the aggregate score stood at 5-4 to Bilbao, United
needed two more goals if they were going to continue on their
European adventure. Puffing on cigarettes and gulping down cups of
tea, the players listened intently as Busby urged them not to panic:
'Boys, play the game as you know how. Make your passes and do your
running, but, above all, keep your patience. If you can do that, we will
get there.'

As the second half got under way, United started strongly and it
seemed only a matter of time before they would score. Frustratingly,
the officials disallowed two goals for offside, much to Busby's disgust.
A tense atmosphere pervaded over a packed Maine Road. The cigarette smoke and the breath of the enthralled crowd hung in the air as
United desperately strived to find two more goals. But time was fast
running out. With the clock ticking ever closer to full time, Taylor
pulled another one back but was it too little too late?

Cheering themselves hoarse, the crowd urged United on, but it
seemed that as the final whistle approached the all-important goal was
going to evade them. Just as hope seemed to be slipping away, the ball
fell to Johnny Berry in the penalty area. At the vital moment it looked
to have got stuck under his feet, but as the crowd held their breath he
managed to toe-poke the ball towards goal. Bilbao's keeper, who had
not been expecting Berry to be able to get off a shot, was wrong-footed
and could do nothing but watch helplessly as the ball went past him and

over the line. Bedlam ensued in the stands as mission impossible had been achieved in the most dramatic of circumstances. Busby, usually so conservative, could not resist showing his joy as he danced a jig along the touchline while Jimmy Murphy cried tears of joy. United had done it! Next stop, the semi-finals of the European Cup!

Despite being crestfallen, the Bilbao president, Senor Enrico Guzman, was gracious in defeat: 'Manchester United are a brilliant team and played much better than Bilbao. What struck me most was the passion of the crowd. It was very inspiring to United. I thought our wing-halves let us down. The difference was Duncan Edwards. He was sensational.'

After the drama of the Bilbao game, the players could not afford to rest for a moment. The stakes were now too high to take their foot off the gas. A clash with Arsenal at Old Trafford followed and if United wanted to keep up their pursuit of a second consecutive league title then they needed to win. At the time United were still top of the league, but Spurs were threatening to catch them, and any slip-ups in the title race would be hard to overcome at this stage.

Spurs had been banking on their North London rivals doing them a favour, but it was not to be. Proving that Busby's relaxed new train-ing regime after European games was the way forward, United sensationally struck six goals past the Arsenal defence, with Edwards getting himself on the scoresheet.

United's assault on the league was still on course, but their quest to win the FA Cup faced a tough examination from Everton at a frost-covered Old Trafford. The first half was a tentative affair and the second period continued in the same vein. It seemed that just the one goal would secure victory and it finally came in the 67th minute. Johnny Berry, jinking and weaving, carried the ball towards the oppo-sition goal and let fly but his shot was deflected out to the edge of the penalty area. Without breaking his stride, Edwards seized the chance as he buried the ball into the roof of the net for what he would later describe as 'the best goal of my career'. Everton were stunned and unable to mount any serious attempt at an equaliser, so United marched through to the quarter-finals.

This victory saw some bookmakers now offer odds as low as 5-1 that United would sensationally win the FA Cup, league title and European Cup. To win the Double was thought to be impossible, so the thought of winning a Treble was pie in the sky, but United were close and even the bookmakers were starting to twitch.

Just as the fans started to get carried away, United's attempt to win the league took a blow as they lost to Blackpool and could muster only draws against Aston Villa and Wolves. By now Spurs were breathing down United's neck and a dramatic finale to the season seemed to be in store.

Although United had faltered in the league, their progress in the FA Cup continued unabated as they defeated Bournemouth in the next round. An FA Cup final appearance was, for some players, the pinnacle of their career and the United team were now just one win away from it. The tournament was regarded as the best cup competition in the world and the opportunity to play at Wembley filled players and fans with enormous excitement. It was a chance to drive in the team bus down Wembley Way and see thousands of fans carrying flags and scarves, all enjoying the day out and chanting excitedly for their team. The pitch would be perfectly manicured, a luscious shade of green, fit for the best players in the country to conjure up something special. Royalty would be present to give the match their seal of approval, the national anthem would be sung with vigour by fans and players alike, the Union Jack flag would flutter from the iconic twin towers and best of all, there was the 39 steps leading to the royal box, where the victorious captain could triumphantly lift the greatest trophy of all, the FA Cup. This was the stuff that dreams were truly made of.

All that stood in United's way from reaching such an occasion were Birmingham City. Win against the Brummies and a glorious day out at Wembley awaited them. Losing didn't bear thinking about. On the day the result was never in doubt as United were superior in all areas of the pitch. Goals from Berry and Charlton saw them prevail and the United bandwagon was still very much on course to win an historic Treble. Wembley and glory awaited them.

With things going to plan in the FA Cup, progress was not as smooth in the league, as Bolton beat the champions 2-0 in their next game. The *Guardian* published a particularly harsh assessment of Edwards' efforts, stating: 'Edwards was labouring heavily at centre-forward, though straining to pull his weight like a willing dray horse.' It was no wonder that he was tiring, as by this stage in the season he had already played close to 80 games. But if United were to have any chance of retaining the title, they had to hope that this was a rare off day for their talismanic star.

When a Manchester United team is looking to win a game, and a player is looking to find his form, the last place on earth they want to play is at a hostile Elland Road. Yet a trip to Leeds was unfortunately next up and the Yorkshiremen were desperate to put one over on their Lancashire rivals. Once again, it looked as if United were going to flounder in the league, as with minutes remaining the score remained locked at 1-1. Another draw would be disastrous for their title challenge. Had they run out of steam?

In the closing seconds, United won a corner which led to Busby frantically racing out of his dugout to tell the taker, Berry, to look for Edwards. Seeing the ball lofted towards the penalty spot, Edwards rushed towards it with his strong legs thumping across the mud. Brushing aside his markers, he leapt high above them and met the ball powerfully with his head. As he fell to the floor, he looked up to see that his crashing header seemed to be going directly towards the goalkeeper. But then suddenly, out of nowhere, the outstretched boot of Charlton deflected the ball past the wrong-footed keeper and into the net. Celebrating ecstatically, the two friends raced off with their arms around each other towards the rapturous United fans. Miraculously, United had won and the title was now theirs to lose.

International duty offered Edwards a brief respite from the tireless pursuit of honours, as he was named in the team to face Scotland at Wembley. As always, the atmosphere was intense, with the Scottish and English fans baying for each others' blood. Edwards loved nothing more than putting one over on the Scots, so he particularly enjoyed his goal, which saw him rifle the ball from 25 yards into the corner of the net. It was his third international goal of the season and helped his country to yet another win over their old foes.

Edwards' stupendous exploits for club and country had seen him universally lauded by critics. It was therefore of no great surprise that he was named as the *Manchester Evening Chronicle*'s Footballer of the Year, narrowly beating Preston North End's Tom Finney to the award. The editor of the newspaper said of the accolade going to Edwards, 'Winning the *Evening Chronicle* Player of the Year Trophy is a well-deserved honour for the Manchester and England left-half, who at the age of twenty is one of soccer's most dynamic figures.'

With little chance to enjoy such recognition, Edwards jetted off to Spain for the first leg of the semi-final of the European Cup. The might of European Cup holders Real Madrid awaited him in the intimidating Bernabeu Stadium. Ever since the draw had been made, the United players had been eager to test their wits against the greatest team in Europe. This was exactly the type of contest Busby had envisaged when he had agreed to enter the tournament.

Raring to see just what was in store for his United young guns, Busby had travelled to Nice to watch Madrid play the second leg of their quarter-final tie. On the night Madrid were irresistible, coasting to a resounding 6–2 win. Busby was in awe of the football on display and was concerned at how his team could contain the Spanish masters, in particular Alfredo di Stefano. 'Until that game I thought Alex James and Peter Doherty were the two best inside-forwards I had ever seen,' Busby confided. 'But now I have seen Alfredo the Great ... he's in a class of his own.'

Di Stefano was the conductor of Madrid's sumptuous symphony. Wearing the number nine shirt he played in the 'hole' where he found time and space to devastating effect. His play was almost poetic. Waltzing through defences with consummate ease, he resembled all that was good and pure in the beautiful game. At this time, he was regarded by fans and players alike as the best footballer on the planet. To many he was an unsurpassable genius.

However, it wasn't just di Stefano that Busby was worried about; Madrid boasted world-class players in virtually every position. The club's president, Santiago Bernabeu, had been on an unprecedented shopping spree in recent years where money was no object. Unlike British clubs, who were bound by the rules of the Ministry of Labour forbidding the hiring of players from outside of the British Isles, Madrid were free to scour the globe for the very best. Players were naturally keen to move to a club that offered a huge salary, as well as top-class facilities, so Madrid found it easy to recruit world-class foreign imports such as the exquisite Argentinean inside-forward, Hector Rial, and the French right-wing schemer, Raymond Kopa. This was Madrid's first, and perhaps best, group of 'Galacticos'.

Having witnessed Madrid in full flight, Busby was worried. On his return to Manchester, he refused to discuss his fears as he did not want to unsettle his players. Instead, he constantly reminded them that if they played to their full potential, and gave 100 per cent, then they could do no more. Secretly, he hoped that his boys would do this and Madrid would have a rare off day. That was the only way he could see them emerging victorious. But what if his boys were below par and Madrid played at their very best? The result didn't bear thinking about.

Edwards was certainly up for the challenge, but even he was nervous when, upon landing in Spain, the team were besieged by Madrid supporters in the airport. Although no harm came to any of the United players, they were understandably uneasy at such a swarm of people surrounding them with little or no police protection.

Interest in the game back in the UK was just as fervent. The *Sports Outlook* programme on Granada TV devoted its entire show to previewing the match, as did BBC's *Sportsview*. The BBC also decided to broadcast the last half-hour of the contest on the radio, as well as agreeing to show 25 minutes of highlights the following night. Such in-depth coverage was usually confined to the FA Cup final or international games. It was evidence that the European Cup had captured the imagination of the British public.

Stepping into the Bernabeu Stadium, most of them for the first time, the players looked on in wonder. Used to playing in their ramshackle home at Old Trafford, they didn't realise that football stadiums could be so luxurious. The majestic white bowl of the Bernabeu wrapped around the luscious pitch, and soared high into the sky, while underneath the stands was a dentist's room, doctor's surgery, a chapel and even a mortuary. No expense had been spared to ensure that Madrid's home was as awe-inspiring as the football that graced it.

Throngs of noisy supporters poured into the stadium to help provide a spine-tingling atmosphere for what promised to be a pageant of Europe's finest players. Over 125,000 supporters, burning with passion, filled the air with noise as they greeted their team with an enormous roar. Taken aback by the ferocity of their greeting, the United players seemed to be a little overcome by their surroundings and this allowed Madrid to race into a two-goal lead. Taylor got a goal back, but victory was assured for Madrid when Mateos scored a third late on.

Edwards said of his team's poor display, 'We simply did not get going until Real Madrid went 2-0 in front and by then it was a little too late.' In fact, if it had not been for Edwards' defensive heroics the scoreline could have been much worse. Henry Rose of the *Daily Express* heralded his performance, 'Salute Duncan Edwards who, if he made no impact in attack, performed noble deeds of daring in defence.'

Although Edwards had been one of the few United players to emerge with their reputation still intact, he had been overshadowed on this occasion by Madrid's star, Alfredo di Stefano. Di Stefano had completely dominated the game with his extraordinary movement and imaginative passing. It seemed as though the ball was constantly at his feet and he rarely wasted possession. With the United players desperately trying their best to contain him, they had allowed one of Madrid's other jewels, the lightning quick Gento, plenty of space to raid down the left wing and cause havoc. When they then tried to counter Gento, this had left Kopa and Rial with space to pull the strings. It seemed impossible to put a lid on this team fizzing with talent, but the players were not too downhearted. After all, they were far from out of the competition and, as they had proven in the last round, they were capable of mounting a comeback. But if they were now going to reach the final they really would have to deliver the performance of a lifetime.

There was scant time to reflect before the second leg, as United were now on the home straight with a second successive league title in their sights. The next three games saw United in irresistible form as they beat Luton, then Burnley, before winning the championship at Old Trafford with a memorable performance against Sunderland. Billy Whelan followed up his hat-trick against Burnley with a brace against the Wearsiders, with Edwards and Taylor also scoring in the 4-0 triumph.

A year earlier, Edwards and the United players had celebrated winning the title enthusiastically. This time around they marked their triumph with nothing more than a few drinks in the players' bar before retiring to bed. Looming large in all of their minds was a date with Madrid.

Having recently had floodlights installed, Old Trafford was the venue for the visit of the glamour boys of Europe. It was hoped that the lights, which shone down from the pylons placed in the four corners of the stadium, would inspire United to victory. Unfortunately, United's stars were either too pumped up or they let the crowd's nerves overcome them, as they started the game miserably. Di Stefano again proved to be their downfall as he set up goals for Kopa and

Gento to put Madrid four goals clear on aggregate. United, with their pride hurt, finally came fighting back, with strikes from Taylor and Charlton. Besieging the Madrid goal, they tried against the odds to achieve another miraculous comeback. At times it seemed that such a feat was possible, especially with Edwards causing havoc every time that he stormed forward.

Such was Edwards' determination to get back into the game that he was involved in an incident with Madrid's right-back, Manuel Torres. As United threatened to score again, Torres fell to the floor theatrically feigning injury in an attempt to stop their momentum. Enraged by such dramatics, Edwards ran 50 yards, grabbed the Spaniard under his arms, and dragged him off the pitch so that the game could continue. 'Some of the crowd loved it, some of them thought he'd gone too far,' said a fan at the match. 'Edwards just shrugged and swaggered back into the game. He'd got things moving again.'

Despite Edwards' best efforts, he could not drag his team level by himself and this meant that United's pioneering adventure came to an abrupt end. Although there was a sullen atmosphere in the dressing room after the game, Busby was proud of his players. In their first year in European competition they had reached the semi-final stage and had enjoyed some outstanding victories. He was certain that following such an experience, and given the young talent at his disposal, his team could go all the way the following season.

Colman, always one who looked on the brighter side of life, was said to have chirpily announced in the showers afterwards, 'Well, boys, we've had a hell of a ride. There's always next year.' And that was a thought that his team-mates heartily agreed with. There would be next year, and they were already looking forward to having another crack at a competition they had all swiftly taken to their hearts.

A small consolation to Edwards was that his exploits in Europe that season had seen him come third in the European Footballer of the Year awards. Unsurprisingly, di Stefano won the award but he was in his prime, at 31 years of age and playing in his second European Cup competition. Surely with a few more years under his belt, and a bit more experience in Europe, Edwards would one day make the award his own.

While the players were disappointed at being defeated by Madrid, they still had a day out at Wembley to look forward to. Up for grabs was not only the chance to win the FA Cup, but also the accolade of becoming the first team in the 20th century to win the Double. By coincidence their opponents would be Aston Villa, who had actually been the last team to do the Double in 1897. Edwards was desperate to make up for the disappointment of Madrid, and to deliver a worthwhile consolation prize to the hordes of United fans who travelled down to Wembley, singing on their way the new 'Manchester United Calypso' song:

> 'If ever they're playing in your town,
> You must get to the football ground;
> Take a lesson and come and see,
> Football taught by Matt Busby,
> Manchester, Manchester United;
> A bunch of bouncing Busby Babes,
> They deserve to be knighted ...'

Busby had drilled his team fanatically beforehand and everything seemed in place for United to end the season in style. Yet just six minutes into the match his plans were in tatters. Villa forward Peter McParland charged Ray Wood in the United goal and in the process shattered his cheekbone. For a moment the red mist descended over Edwards. Seeing that Wood was badly injured, he strode towards McParland threatening to do him some serious damage. Somehow, he managed to calm himself, and instead of resorting to physical violence, he unleashed a torrent of verbal abuse, while McParland proclaimed his innocence.

Body-charging a goalkeeper, a tactic which unbelievably was legal, was par for the course during the 1950s. Edwards did not, however, approve. A savage assault on a goalkeeper jarred with his view of how football should be played and he failed to see how it served to improve a match. There was also the issue that, with there being no substitutes, an outfield player would have to deputise in goal. Edwards' view was that if a keeper was injured then that team should be able to call upon a replacement from the bench as 'football was intended to be played between two teams of eleven men, of whom the goalkeeper is generally an irreplaceable specialist'. Once again, he was ahead of his time. It would not be until the 1965–66 season when substitutes would be permitted by the Football League. Even then only one was allowed.

For the time being, Wood was out of the game and, through no fault of their own, United were down to ten men. Jackie Blanchflower volunteered to go in goal until Wood heroically returned, but United's gameplan had gone out of the window. Clutching his hand to his face, Wood looked concussed on his return, as he played on the wing in obvious discomfort.

As luck would have it, McParland went on to score two goals for Villa. Struggling bravely on with ten men, then with a befuddled Wood on the wing, United had spent most of the match defending their goal. As the game crept towards its finale, Busby decided to go for broke. Asking Wood to go back in goal, he pushed Edwards up in attack, hoping that his golden boy would once again defeat the odds.

Refusing to accept defeat, Edwards raced around the field, desperate to make an impact. He hurriedly took throw-ins and free-kicks, and bombarded the Villa team with an unrelenting series of attacking assaults. His tireless endeavours were finally rewarded when, with just minutes remaining, he raced across to take a corner. Picking out the head of Taylor, United pulled one back right at the death. Quickly grabbing the ball from the net, Edwards ushered his team-mates back to the halfway line so that the game could re-start as quickly as possible. There would, however, be little time for any last-minute heroics as moments later the sound of the final whistle shrilled around the stadium. The game was over. Busby's Double dream had slipped away.

After the match, Edwards revealed that the loss was 'the most heart-breaking defeat I ever figured in'. Along with his manager and team-mates, he had dreamed of winning the Double and had never considered for one moment that they would not achieve this historic feat. But there were no tears shed. Yes, the loss hurt, but in his usual optimistic manner he said that everyone in that 'defeated side was quite confident that this was only a temporary set-back that had merely delayed the arrival of the Cup at Old Trafford'.

Obviously disappointed, Busby addressed his crestfallen young charges after the game. The United team listened intently as their boss stood on a chair and reminded them that they were still young, and had plenty of time to achieve all of their hopes and dreams. Bobby Charlton can recall feeling excited and enthused as his boss 'raised a glass to the future of Manchester United', and called for them to win every trophy that was up for grabs the following season.

United may have 'never had it so good', but already they were looking forward to the next campaign. With experience in Europe, and another title under their belt, anything was now possible for the Busby Babes.

11

DESTINY

With Edwards' star in the ascendancy, he was besieged with endorsement offers from companies who were desperate for him to put his name to their product. Earning just £17 per week, he was obviously happy to listen to those who could help him earn a little extra on the side, particularly as he had set his sights on buying a brand-new two-door, black Morris Minor 1000, with red leather interior. All this would set him back the grand sum of £382, and this would only be for the basics; a heater and de-mister would be extra.

One of the first products that Edwards put his name to was Dextrosol glucose tablets. The adverts proclaimed 'Extra Energy Makes the Difference', and were emblazoned with a picture of Edwards in action. Thousands of youths rushed to buy the sugar tablets in an attempt to emulate their idol who told them, 'Playing in top gear until the final whistle can really take it out of you. That's why I find "Dextrosol" Glucose Tablets so handy. They're a natural source of energy you can rely on, anytime, anywhere.'

Although the money he received for the endorsement went into his car fund, there was something else he needed to save it for: retirement. Football may have been the be-all and end-all to Edwards, but he was also bright enough to know that he had to maximise his income in what was a short career. He once told journalist Frank Taylor, 'It's nice to be cheered but you can't live forever on cheers. It's what you have in the bank when you have finished with the game that cheers a footballer most of all. People forget very easily and I don't want to become like some of the old-timers wearing tattered caps and cadging free tickets outside the grounds.'

On their football salaries alone, no footballer could expect to retire on the money that they made in the UK in the 1950s. When their time in the game eventually came to an end, most desperately tried to stay involved in football in some capacity as it was all that they knew. But not everyone was so lucky. With a lot of players not having any qualifications, they needed a contingency plan to ensure that they did not end up on the breadline. For most, the dream became to save enough money to open a newsagent's or a pub.

For a lot of ex-pros, this was as good as they could hope for, but in the late 1950s another option reared its head. Cash-rich Italian clubs had no wage limit and started to offer the stars of the English game the opportunity to increase their earnings by more than 2000 per cent. John Charles and Gerry Hitchens were just two of the names who followed this highly lucrative path abroad. Who could blame them? Not only were the wages far superior, but so were the signing-on fees. The Football League limited English clubs to being able to offer just £10 to a new signing. In contrast, Juventus paid Charles £10,000 when he signed for them.

On the back of a magnificent season, speculation had started to swirl around Manchester that Edwards was also being lined up by an Italian club. Having just added writing a weekly column in the 'Saturday Pink' edition of the *Manchester Evening Chronicle* to the list of 'products' that carried his name, he attempted to head off these rumours:

'In common with Tommy Taylor and most of the other star footballers in this country, my name has been linked with Italian football. Right now I should like to say that there has been no official approach to me, and, if there were, I should refer it immediately to the United manager, Matt Busby. I would regard such a situation as club business, and, after they had made up their minds, I might be in a position to consider it.'

This was hardly an outright denial that he would be interested in such a move if it were to materialise. In all honesty, he would have been mad not to. While some fans believe that players during this era showed more loyalty to their clubs than their modern-day counter-parts, it is important to consider that they were not allowed to move unless their clubs granted them a transfer. There was no such thing as player power forcing a move. Even when a player's contract came to an end, they still could not move on unless their club agreed to it. Furthermore, as the only financial benefit to moving was the £10 signing-on fee – less than a week's wages – there was no real incentive to press for a move to another club, other than pure footballing reasons.

A good example of this concerns Sir Tom Finney, who is often praised for his loyalty due to spending his entire career at Preston North End. However, if the rules had been different, Finney may have left Preston as early as 1952 when Italian club Palermo offered him £10,000 to sign as well as £130 a month, a huge win bonus, a villa on the Mediterranean and a car. At Preston, he was making peanuts in comparison, earning just £14 a week during the season, £12 in the summer and bonuses of £2 for a win and £1 for a draw. Finney's head was obviously turned.

At a meeting with Preston's chairman, Finney informed him of this generous offer and asked if the club would sanction the move. 'What's ten thousand quid to thee, Tom?' came the response. 'Nay lad, tha'll play for us or tha'll play for nobody!' Finney took the refusal on the chin, he had no option. He knew that he was bound to Preston for life until they had no use for him. A footballer's contract was one that effectively tied a player to his club indefinitely.

This situation was finally rectified in 1963, when George Eastham took Newcastle United to court, but with Edwards' views on earning money being very clear, if an Italian club had made an approach for him, would he have become a football mercenary? It is hard to say. He loved playing for the club he supported, he was adored by the fans, he was winning trophies and he had made some great friends in Manchester. But as he said himself, 'It's what you have in the bank when you have finished with the game that cheers a footballer most of all.' If we take him at his word, then perhaps he would have gone to Italy if a move had been sanctioned.

Edwards was, however, irreplaceable and there is little doubt that United would have staunchly resisted any offers for him, especially as his displays in the forthcoming season would see him earn newspaper write-ups such as: 'United beat Burnley because of Duncan Edwards. He reached peak form and was the complete footballer – the pillar which held up United – well worth £60,000, whether Italian lira or pounds sterling. Powerful in defence with his amazing facility of turning defence into attack. He spoon-fed his colleagues and inspired them.'

Before Edwards could reach such heights for his club, he had a number of vital World Cup qualifying matches to play for England in the summer of 1957. Putting all of the transfer speculation to one side, he and his England team-mates hit top gear as they beat the Republic of Ireland 5-1 and followed this up with a 4-1 victory over Denmark. Although England then drew 1-1 with Ireland in Dublin, they had already shown that they could be formidable opposition in next summer's World Cup.

Once his stint with the senior England side was finished, there were still more games to be played, as the England Under-23s called upon Edwards' services for their game against Romania. Putting his tiredness to one side, he was inspirational in the 1-0 win. Setting up Johnny Haynes for the England goal, he had swept a breathtaking 50-yard pass to his feet. Bucharest was another city that had fallen under the spell of the most exciting young footballer in Europe.

England manager Walter Winterbottom was pleased with Edwards' performance but also frustrated at the same time. 'There was a stage where he dribbled up to the edge of the penalty area and he could have scored himself, but he wanted to play in his Manchester United team-mate David Pegg instead, so he passed the ball to him. This was how generous in spirit he was, but we had to correct him from doing this kind of thing. We told him, when you go on a dribble, Duncan, for heaven's sake go all the way. This subsequently became a feature in future England matches as when Duncan set off with the ball his team mates would shout, "All the way, Duncan."'

With Winterbottom's advice fresh in his mind, he signed off his summer in style by scoring both of England Under-23s' goals against Czechoslovakia. The two goals were carbon copies of each other. On each occasion he drove into the Czech half, swatting challenges away with ease, before burying the ball into the corner of the net. For each goal Edwards was spurred on by the cry of 'All the way, Dunc. All the way!'

On Edwards' return to England, he no longer had to concern himself with National Service as on 6 June 1957 Lance Corporal Edwards had been officially demobilised from the army. The *Daily Express* said of this: 'At 2 o'clock yesterday, he stopped being a 9/- [45p] a day "Lance Jack" and became once again the full-time soccer star said to be worth £50,000 in the European Common Market – Soccer Branch.' At long last, Edwards could now put behind him the exhausting schedule that had seen him play so much over the last two years.

Suddenly, with increased free time at his disposal, Edwards found his relationship with Molly grew more serious. He had hoped that he could whisk her off to the Isle of Man for a romantic getaway, but after booking the trip he found that Molly was unable to take any time off work. Stepping into the breach came his good friend David Pegg, who happily agreed to a break from Manchester. Although Edwards had hoped to be spending his holiday relaxing with his girlfriend, he instead had to put up with Pegg's relentless search of partying, women and woeful Frank Sinatra impressions. Pegg no doubt wished his sidekick Tommy Taylor was with them, as he could always be relied upon to join in the fun.

On their last day on the island, the ever-chatty Pegg, with his carefully slicked-back hair and puppy-dog eyes, struck up a conversation with fellow holidaymaker Patricia Bradley. Accompanying Bradley for a walk along the front, Pegg tried in vain to persuade her that he and Edwards were in fact footballers from Manchester United. She was unconvinced, and instead took great delight in joining in with Edwards in mocking Pegg's flowery shirt, which they said was a blouse he had borrowed from his mother. Never one to back down, Pegg proceeded to tie the shirt up to his midriff and minced down the promenade doing an uncanny impersonation of his mother, a joke which saw Edwards and Bradley howl with laughter.

While Pegg was happy to be the butt of the jokes, Bradley recalls that Edwards was very shy, he only really spoke when spoken to. On the rare occasion when he did open his mouth, it would usually be to mention how much he missed his girlfriend back home. Despite Pegg's tomfoolery and Edwards' shyness, Bradley found the two boys to be good company, even though she wasn't sure if their claim to be star footballers was in fact true. A few weeks later, her doubts were, however, cast aside. On a trip to the cinema she sat open-mouthed as a clip of the football was shown on the Pathé news. There, staring back at her, was the lovesick boy from the Isle of Man and his friend in the flowery shirt.

Happy to be reunited with Molly back in Manchester, talk between the two began to focus on marriage and buying a house. They didn't want to rush things but spoke of their desire to tie the knot once Edwards had got another long, hard season out of the way. He was so shy he hated the thought of having a big wedding ceremony and tried to persuade Molly to have a quiet affair, with just a few close family and friends present instead. She wasn't so sure, but Edwards consoled himself that he had at least another 12 months to persuade her to change her mind.

As he was so shy, it is very unlikely that, if he were playing today, he would have sold the rights to his wedding to celebrity magazines like *Hello!*. However, if they had offered to pay him £1 million, as they reportedly did for Wayne Rooney's wedding, then perhaps he would have overcome his doubts.

In the meantime, Edwards began to save half a crown (12½p) a week from his wages, which he kept in a jar in his bedroom. With a bit of luck he hoped that he would be able to save enough for a wedding, a honeymoon in Blackpool, and a bungalow. The bungalow was his dream. Finally, he and Molly would be able to live together. As long as he could play football, and be with Molly, he couldn't ask for any more.

Molly and Duncan were a popular couple, and as such made plenty of friends. One of Molly's friends, Josephine Stott, even invited the pair to become godparents to her daughter, Julie, that summer. Edwards was delighted to be asked, but after the christening, while everyone else got merry, Stott recalls that he stayed clear of the alcohol: 'Duncan was absolutely teetotal and after the christening, I remember him sitting in the kitchen with me, drinking milk! Duncan was a real gentleman, he was a very private person. You never thought of him as a football superstar – he was just Molly's boyfriend.'

Settling back in Manchester, after his stint in the army, Edwards began to focus on what promised to be a very exciting season. Although United had just missed out on winning an unprecedented three trophies the previous season, the Babes were now another year older, and looking all the better for it. The 1957-58 season would surely be theirs for the taking.

Busby, excited at what lay in store for his Babes, told the press of his ambition for the season ahead: 'We must have a chance for all three. But my big aim is to make it a hat-trick of league titles, just like the great Arsenal side did in the 1930s, and the Huddersfield

Town team did in the 1920s.' It was a bold statement but it was certainly realistic.

Warming up for the new campaign, United set off on a pre-season tour of Germany, an event that was rapturously received by the German fans. They had not forgotten 'Boom Boom', and his profile in the country had grown due to the German newspaper plastering his legendary exploits for club and country all over their sports pages.

Journalist Frank Taylor accompanied United to Germany, and not only was he taken aback by the euphoric reception waiting for Edwards, but also by his acute shyness:

As our plane touched down in Tempelhof Airport, there was a wild surge of soccer fans, sports writers and cameraman chanting: 'BOOM BOOM. Where is BOOM BOOM Edwards?'

I was coming out of the plane directly behind Duncan. He shied away at the reception.

'Go on. You go first, Frank,' he said. 'Pretend you are me.'

'Don't be daft, Duncan,' I replied. 'They are looking for a sleek athlete. That rules me out.'

Duncan stared at my roly-poly figure. 'Maybe you have something there.' And with that he heaved himself through the hatch and down the steps to the tarmac.

As soon as the crowd spotted him, they darted forward. 'BOOM BOOM ... This way please ... smile ... a picture, please.'

Edwards tried to brush aside this filmstar-style reception as flashlight bulbs popped in his face. 'Get the whole team. Manchester United are a team. You want the other chaps too.'

As Duncan tried to hide his face, Roger Byrne, smirking all over his face at the big fellow's discomfort, said: 'Go on, Boom Boom. Smile. Watch the birdie.'

After the madness of their pre-season tour, United issued a chilling statement of intent to the rest of the league on the opening day of the season. Brushing Leicester City aside 3-0 at Filbert Street, Billy Whelan was at his scintillating best. Making good use of Edwards' sparkling array of passes, he proceeded to score a sensational hat-trick. Whelan may have dominated the headlines, but Edwards' contribution did not go unnoticed by reporter Alf Clarke: 'The accuracy with which Duncan Edwards sprayed his passes, both long and short, was almost uncanny.'

Everton and Manchester City were next to suffer at the hands of United as they took their goals-scored tally to ten, with just one goal against. During the City game, Edwards scored his first goal of the season in typically explosive fashion. According to the *Daily Herald*'s George Follows, he 'took a pass from Billy Whelan and from 25 yards drove the ball just inside the post past Trautmann in the City goal'.

The cascade of goals continued in the next few games as United exerted their superiority over their opponents. Leeds United were crushed 5-0, Blackpool shipped four, as did Arsenal. Reporters were now running out of superlatives to describe Edwards' form. Archie Ledbrooke of the *Daily Mirror* wrote, 'Duncan Edwards was at his majestic best and therefore nearly the best player in the world. One minute he was clearing off his goal line, the next he was running through half the Blackpool side in a solo dash that owed as much to artistry as it did to sheer strength.'

Even in Europe, United beat top Irish side Shamrock Rovers 6-0. Edwards would, however, miss the next few games as he again fell victim to the flu. His understudy and good friend Wilf McGuinness deputised in his absence, and helped United to beat Shamrock in the second leg and then to dispose of Aston Villa 4-1.

Edwards' illness unfortunately coincided with his 21st birthday celebrations, which meant that rather than paint the town red, he 'celebrated' in bed, with Molly mopping his brow. He was so ill that the cake Molly had made for him was eagerly eaten by some of the Babes who had turned up at Gorse Avenue in the hope that they could drag their team-mate out for a session. Eddie Colman, David

Pegg, Tommy Taylor and Gordon Clayton never needed an excuse for a party, so as Edwards lay in bed they happily went out for the night to celebrate in his honour. In all likelihood, Edwards was glad to have missed out as, rather than sit by himself and watch Taylor and Pegg chat up anything that moved, he got to spend the time with Molly.

Although he was ill, the advent of his 21st birthday saw Edwards boost his spirits by treating himself. Having dreamed of owning a car, he decided to take the plunge and finally bought the Morris Minor 1000 he had been eyeing up for so long. So proud was he with his first car that he could be seen out in the streets polishing its sleek black exterior most afternoons. If he was lucky, he could sometimes manage to persuade one of his young admirers on Gorse Avenue to grab a rag and chip in. Now that he had wheels, this added a whole new element to the time Molly and he spent together. Whenever they had some spare time, they would set off on an adventure, never knowing where they were heading, but just enjoying being young and carefree. They would, however, have to do without motorways as the first one in the UK, the Preston bypass, would not open until December 1958.

Finally fit again, Edwards made his return against Nottingham Forest and he looked as if he had never been away. United won the game 2-1 and he reigned supreme. The *Daily Express* called him 'that hunk of excellence' who is the 'most effective one-man performer in British football'. Another paper said, 'That extra edge was the tremendous performance of Duncan Edwards, the young giant left-half. He kept popping up like a hero of a film serial to save his side from disaster.' Even the normally conservative reports from *The Times* could not fail but to heap praise on the star of British football, 'Yet one man stood out above all others. He was Duncan Edwards, now more than usual guarding the backward areas around Blanchflower. His was a massive performance.'

Although Edwards had just returned to the team, he would miss the next United game as he was called up to play for England against Wales at Ninian Park. Ironically, the manager of Wales was Manchester United's very own Jimmy Murphy, and he was given the thankless task of devising some tactics to stop his protégé.

In his book *Matt, United and Me*, Murphy revealed what he had said to his team before the game: 'I had gone through our tactics to play England. I dealt with all aspects, until Reg Davies, the very talented Newcastle United and Welsh inside-forward, who was a very good player for one so small and frail, piped up: "You have mentioned everyone Jimmy, but what about Duncan Edwards?" "You just keep out of his bloody way, son," I replied.'

It seems that the Welsh team took Murphy at his word as Edwards strolled around the field unchallenged, helping his country to a satisfying 4-0 win. Such was his dominance that when taking a throw he even had time to engage in a spot of banter with his coach. 'Are there no early trains back to Manchester, Jim? You're wasting my time here,' Edwards shouted at a sour-faced Murphy. Never one to back down from some verbal jousting, Murphy jokingly replied, 'I'll see you later and tell you where you are going wrong.' Yet even the grumpy Murphy had to acknowledge that his protégé had not put a foot out of place. Manchester United's finest destroyed the Welsh that day and *The Times* stated that he did it all at 'walking pace'.

No matter how well Edwards was playing, he could not help England avoid a humiliating defeat at Wembley to Northern Ireland. Though he scored in the 3-2 loss, a soon-to-be Manchester United colleague kept England at bay on several occasions. Showing just why he was being talked of as the best goalkeeper in the world, Doncaster Rovers' Harry Gregg was in inspired form as he had made a series of show-stopping acrobatic saves. On another day, and with another keeper, the result may have been very different. Busby could not fail but to take note of Gregg's match-winning performance.

In a season that promised so much, this result was just a small setback as Edwards continued to perform at the peak of his powers. 'For

United the real hero was once again Duncan Edwards,' said *The Times*, after his starring role in defeating Dukla Prague 3-0 in the European Cup. 'From the first minute to the last, he was wonderful. There was no other word for him. He was an express train in full cry, always under control, always influencing affairs, always a danger whenever in possession. It was a snorting shot of his from some 25 yards out that brought the Czechoslovakian goalkeeper full length to a great save that probably gave United the first signal to go about their duty.'

A tactical masterstroke, and Edwards' versatility, saw United narrowly win their next league game. Newcastle United had been leading 1-0 at half time, and had comfortably repelled everything that the United attack had thrown at them. Deciding to mix things up, Busby subsequently ordered inside-forward Billy Whelan and Edwards to switch roles. As the second half got under way, the Newcastle defence were immediately put on the back foot, unable to cope with the change. Although United dominated the half, it took until the final minutes for Edwards to put his decisive stamp on proceedings. Expertly controlling a through ball from Tommy Taylor, he then swiftly sidestepped the advancing goalkeeper before slotting the ball into an empty net for the equaliser. With the bit between their teeth, United threw everything they had at Newcastle, with all of the forwards, as well as the wing-halves, pouring forward in search of the winner. Just as it looked as though their efforts would be in vain, they were rewarded for their sense of adventure as Taylor scored in the final minute of the match.

Taylor and Edwards were a match-winning combination and they linked up together shortly afterwards when England played France. Desperate to make amends for their poor showing against Northern Ireland, England were irresistible against the French. Taylor helped himself to two goals while a debutant by the name of Bobby Robson completed the scoring by adding another two.

England's future manager said the following about playing alongside Manchester United's left-half: 'Duncan was most likeable in the short period of time I had an opportunity to know him. What I shall always remember about Duncan, however, was that he was very boyish in his ways. That is not surprising. He would have only been twenty-one – he played like a man – almost a demon. Two wonderful accurate feet and his running with the ball and bringing the ball through the mid-field was an awe-inspiring sight. He was exceptionally quick for such a big lad and really took some stopping and tackling. When he tackled it was like being hit by a Sherman tank. What was beyond dispute was that Duncan Edwards, at the age of twenty-one, was the finest young player in the country.'

Such was Edwards' stellar reputation that teams now began to try to mark him out of games. Spurs were one of the first teams to do this and successfully managed to frustrate his shock-and-awe bombarding runs, as they sensationally beat Manchester United 4–3 at Old Trafford. It had been a bad day at the office for both club and player, especially just before their crucial second-leg European Cup tie away to Dukla Prague.

These defensive tactics caught on as Prague also deployed man-to-man marking on Edwards. Clearly frustrated, he attempted to shake off his markers by moving into different areas of the field, but he found that he always seemed to have two men following him. With his influence diminished, he was again unable to get into the game and United were poorer for this.

Prague, who camped in United's half for most of the match, tried everything that they could muster in an attempt to pull back the three-goal deficit. Busby and Murphy roared their disapproval at their team's inability to get into the game, especially when the Czechs, who had enjoyed the lion's share of possession, managed to score. In the face of further attacks, United's defence managed to hold firm and while this saw them squeeze through to the next round, neither Busby nor the small travelling contingent of United fans were impressed with the uninspiring display.

A trip to St Andrews a few days later saw United again fail to win or to deliver the significant improvement that Busby had demanded.

Birmingham City were in the lower echelons of the table, but United's confidence was for once at a low ebb and consequently the game finished in a 3-3 draw. With United stuck in a rut, Chelsea were next to take advantage of their fragile self-belief as they beat the champions at Old Trafford.

From looking invincible, United were now vulnerable and had fallen from the top of the table. Although they were through to the quarter-final stage of the European Cup, they desperately needed to get back to winning ways fast if they were to accomplish Busby's dream of a third straight title win.

Sensing that his tiring team were in need of a boost, Busby paid a world-record amount for a goalkeeper (£23,500) and welcomed Northern Ireland's Harry Gregg to Old Trafford. Busby recognised that Gregg had a number of qualities that could shake up his team. Not only was he a fine goalkeeper but he was also an excellent leader and this is perhaps what persuaded Busby, more than anything else, to splash out such an extravagant sum. The going was getting tough and Gregg was tougher than most.

Gregg went straight into the team, alongside fellow debutant Kenny Morgans, for the game against Leicester City. His debut was an immediate success, as not only did he keep a clean sheet but United won for the first time in four games, thrashing Leicester 4-0. Organising his defence in his strong Northern Irish accent, Gregg had commanded his box ferociously. Mark Jones and Roger Byrne had both taken a battering as Gregg claimed every cross by roughly barging his own players out of the way. They soon learned that the six-yard area was Gregg's domain and left him to it.

Continuing their upsurge in form, two games against Luton, on Christmas Day and Boxing Day, saw United beat their opponents 3-0 in the first game, with Edwards scoring a penalty, and then emerge with a valuable point at Kenilworth Road the next day. Just before New Year's Eve, United then played out another draw, this time against Manchester City at Maine Road. Entering the New

Year they were still in touch with the title-chasing pack and were once more beginning to show flashes of their best form.

Over the years, United had fallen victim to lower league opposition in the FA Cup, but they made no such mistake this time around, as in the first fixture of 1958 they beat Workington 3-1, thanks to a Dennis Viollet hat-trick. Workington had attempted some gamesmanship beforehand by leaving the match ball to soak in a bucket of water overnight, thus making it as heavy as a bowling ball. Nevertheless, this had little effect on Edwards' passing game as he was still able to switch the play with his thunderous cross-field passes which frequently stretched the Workington defence.

United's struggles to win away from home in the league were, however, becoming a concern, as was Edwards' form, which had also dipped. United had followed up their FA Cup victory by drawing against Leeds United at Elland Road, when he was frustrated to find that he was again being man-marked. He was now beginning to realise that he might have to adapt his game if he was going to be able to shake off the attentions of his man-markers, who now followed him in almost every match that he played.

This was an unprecedented situation, as man-to-man marking did not become a common strategy until the 1960s, when Italian teams used it to great effect in their *catenaccio* formation. Edwards was therefore one of the first players who had to learn how to counter such tactics, as they had very rarely been used in the British game before this. It was a testament to his ability that he was one of the very few players at this time who opposition managers felt compelled to stop at all costs by adopting this ploy. Although it may have been a compliment, he still found it incredibly frustrating.

In mid-January the United fans swarmed to Old Trafford in preparation for the first leg of their European Cup quarter-final tie with Red Star Belgrade. Once more Edwards was subjected to tight man-marking, and on the rare occasions he did manage to evade his markers, he was unceremoniously brought down. The *Manchester*

Evening Chronicle said of this tactic, 'Rugby league fans would have quarrelled at the punishment that Duncan Edwards took as he waded through.' However, such was his strength that at one point he picked up the ball in his own half, surged past three men, before switching the play with a raking 50-yard cross-field ball to Albert Scanlon. Due to so many Red Star players taking an interest in Edwards, an unmarked Scanlon found himself in acres of space and he therefore had plenty of time to pick out Bobby Charlton to open the scoring.

Despite going a goal down, the Yugoslavian team were undeterred as they continued to storm forward. At one point their skilful inside-forward Dragoslav Sekularac threatened to dominate proceedings before Edwards got to grips with him. Steaming into the small Yugoslav, the crowd winced as he flew into the air, flipped upside down, and landed on his head. As Sekularac lay sprawled on the turf Edwards jogged innocently away. His job was done. Unsurprisingly, little was seen of Sekularac after this, and United managed to win 2-1.

Lancashire neighbours Bolton Wanderers were United's next opponents at Old Trafford, and it was very much a family affair, with Edwards again coming face to face with his cousin, Dennis Stevens. Edwards' family all made sure that they were at the game and beforehand the two cousins caught up in the tunnel and laughed about old times.

Perhaps Edwards was feeling charitable, as early on he passed the ball straight to Stevens, who galloped away to set up a Bolton goal. No doubt feeling slightly embarrassed, he proceeded to kick his mickey-taking cousin out of the game with a horror tackle. Stevens said that the lunge was 'over the top of the ball' and that it 'crocked me'.

Edwards was certainly no angel when he was on the football field. As Harry Gregg has said, 'If he couldn't go past you then he would go through you. If he was playing now he would definitely need to calm down some of his tackles. He would be banned for life today as it's virtually a non-contact sport.' The hard edge to his game was natural, but he was also encouraged by Murphy's mantra, 'When you tackle, do it fucking properly, take the ball and take the man with it. Let him know you're there. Don't go pussy-footing around. Get into him!' Whether it was family, friend, or even a team-mate in training, Edwards showed no mercy. His motto was much like Murphy's: 'Win at all costs'.

With Stevens limping heavily, United were rampant. Charlton scored a hat-trick, Viollet notched twice, Scanlon once and a late Edwards penalty completed a 7-2 rout. If they could keep up their momentum, and league leaders Wolves faltered, then a Treble could still be within United's sights, especially after another Charlton double saw them beat Ipswich in the fourth round of the FA Cup.

Glory with Manchester United wasn't the only thing on Edwards' mind. That summer England would be taking part in the 1958 World Cup in Sweden. Despite going down to the likes of Northern Ireland, results against world champions West Germany and the star-studded Brazilian team had proved that England, on their day, were among the best sides in the world and deserved to be going into the tournament touted as one of the favourites.

Later in his life, Walter Winterbottom confided that he had been confident that Edwards and his Manchester United colleagues would provide their winning mentality to his squad: 'Along with his team-mates Roger Byrne and Tommy Taylor, this Busby Babe confidence transferred itself to the England team. We felt for sure that we were going to win the World Cup.' His confidence was also shared by an expectant nation who truly believed that soon England would earn their rightful place as world champions.

As the season entered February, United faced two potentially tricky fixtures that they had to win if they were to remain championship contenders. First up was an away trip to Arsenal, followed by a home match against Wolverhampton Wanderers, who were sat pretty at the top of the table.

Winning in London was imperative, but the trip to the capital also allowed Edwards to take care of some business. A few months earlier he had been asked to write a football instruction manual for children entitled *Tackle Soccer This Way*. He was thrilled to be asked to share his knowledge and experience on the game and he had diligently written the book himself on his Remington portable typewriter. Molly had helped her fiancé with his grammar and punctuation, and by February 1958 the book was ready to be handed over to publishers Stanley Paul. Upon arrival at his London hotel, Edwards was met by William Luscombe, who was there to pick up the manuscript. Luscombe was pleased with Edwards' efforts and told the young author that the book should be in the shops within the next few months.

Once business was taken care of, Edwards turned his mind to the upcoming clash with Arsenal. The game that followed was one of British football's most entertaining matches. All who saw it were in thrall of the brilliance of the Busby Babes.

Before the match, Highbury rocked to the sound of the number one single at the time, Elvis Presley's 'Jailhouse Rock'. Thousands of fans, who were squashed into the stands, sang along as they looked forward to watching the Babes of Manchester United put on a show. Edwards didn't leave them short-changed. After only ten minutes he opened the scoring with a trademark bullet from distance that left Arsenal goalkeeper Jack Kelsey grasping at thin air.

Taylor and Charlton went on to add two more goals, and at the break United were 3-0 up and cruising. Everyone was playing at the top of their game, no one more so than Albert Scanlon, who was giving Arsenal's full-backs a torrid time. United's first-half display had been one of the most complete league performances that the Babes had ever given. Resolute at the back, creative and dynamic in mid-field, and magical up-front, there seemed to be no room for improvement.

Perhaps their dominance became their downfall, as in the second half they carelessly took their foot off the pedal. In just five second-half minutes, Arsenal improbably scored three goals to level the scores.

The Highbury crowd were enraptured as both teams went toe to toe, desperately trying to deliver a knockout blow. United had no option but to try to win the game, as they knew that at this stage of the season a draw would not be enough if they were to overhaul Wolves' lead at the top of the table. Roger Byrne, the inspirational captain, led by example as he threw himself into challenges and urged his colleagues on. Thrillingly, Viollet put United back into the lead and then minutes later Taylor scored from a seemingly impossible angle to provide a two-goal cushion. Arsenal were not, however, content to sit down and die and they struck back instantly with a goal from Welsh international Derek Tapscott.

Despite Arsenal's tremendous efforts, United stood up to the test and won the battle. Their team may have been defeated, but the generous Highbury faithful acknowledged that they had just witnessed a performance of peerless quality. Cheering the Babes off the pitch they showed their appreciation for a game that would forever be ingrained in their memories.

The journalists at the game were also unanimous in their praise. 'The thermometer was doing a war dance,' said a reporter from *The Times*. 'There was no breath left in anyone. The players came off arm in arm. They knew they had fashioned something of which to be proud.'

Dennis Evans, the Arsenal full-back, was also proud to have taken part in such a magnificent match, despite losing. 'Everyone was cheering. Not because of Arsenal, not because of United, but because of the game itself. No one left until five minutes after the game. They just stood cheering.'

Jack Kelsey was equally generous in his praise for United's display and, in particular, for Edwards: 'They just kept coming at us, and the score could easily have been 10-7. It was the kind of game, even one which was played in ankle-deep mud, which would pack grounds all over the country at any time. It was the finest match that I ever played in, and in Duncan Edwards, Manchester United had a player with all the promise in the world. Even in the conditions that day, his strength stood out. He was a colossus.'

A 15-year-old Terry Venables, who would of course go on to manage England, was lucky to be in the crowd that day. He grew up as a Tottenham fan, but he was so keen to see the great Duncan Edwards that he begged his father to take him to their bitter rivals' ground. He remembers:

When I was growing up, there was no televised football to speak of, and if you wanted to see a particular player or team, it meant going to one of their matches. It was February 1958 and United had just caused a stir by beating Bolton 7-2, and everyone was talking about Duncan Edwards. So I persuaded my dad to come with me to Highbury to see United play Arsenal. It was an unusual trip for two committed Spurs fans, and a day I will never forget. It took Duncan Edwards less than ten minutes to show us what the fuss was about. Jack Kelsey, a legend at Highbury, was in goal for Arsenal but, good as he was, he was beaten all the way when Duncan opened the scoring with a cracking shot. That was my moment. We had travelled in to see him and, with the late-comers still arriving, he had me turning to my dad with a 'Did you see that?' look. Edwards had taken a pass from Viollet and strode forward like an unstoppable giant before shooting past Kelsey from 25 yards. There were eight more goals in a fantastic match, but Duncan's, and his overall performance, are all I really remember. Afterwards, I just couldn't get it out of my head how good United were. Duncan was marvellous. Everything he did comes back to me as if it was yesterday. Such strength, such poise. We are talking about a long time ago, but I can still see him, and that tremendous power of his, even now.

After such a supreme performance, the journey back to Manchester was full of laughter and leg-pulling. Edwards, in particular, was on the receiving end of some good-natured banter. 'Coming back on the train from that last Arsenal game the lads were taking the mickey out of him without mercy,' remembers Gregg. 'There had been talk and gossip going on about Billy Wright [England's captain] moving from centre-half and captain, and all the lads were ribbing Duncan about taking over, calling him the blue-eyed boy and everything. I remember Duncan was so embarrassed. He was blushing and saying: "Mark [Jones] is a far better centre-half than me. He should be in."'

In spite of his modesty, Edwards was now in his pomp. With his team-mates teasing him about how he might become England captain, the 1958 World Cup around the corner, and United challenging for trophies on three fronts, everything pointed towards a dazzling future. Immortality beckoned.

12

SWANSONG

Sandwiched between United's memorable game at Highbury and their top-of-the-table clash with Wolves was the small matter of the away leg against Red Star Belgrade. Leading by just a solitary goal after the first leg at Old Trafford, United knew that they were in for a tough test. While many were already excited by the prospect of United and Wolves going head-to-head, Edwards was keen to ensure that focus remained on the Belgrade game. He sensibly told the press, 'Let's get this Red Star side out of the European Cup first, and then we'll deal with Wolves.'

United's dominance in their previous European away adventures, and their recent display against Arsenal, had now provided the team with a steely self-belief and determination. Playing in unknown locations such as Belgrade no longer held any fear for this United team. They were now well aware that they were more than a match for most European opposition.

Although Edwards always looked forward to a football match, as we have seen he was never keen on flying, or the exotic food that was served abroad. As Yugoslavia was in the Eastern Bloc, the United players had all been warned that the food was likely to be unpalatable and that they should bring their own. Heeding this advice, Edwards packed some biscuits, sweets and fruit into his bag, while the likes of Eddie Colman even went so far as to bring his own teabags and sugar with him. However, the players need not have worried about food. After the club's miserable experiences in Prague, where the fare served up had been atrocious, Matt Busby had ordered that the club take with them huge hampers of tinned meat, soup and fresh fruit.

Upon arrival in the bitter cold of Belgrade, the players were whisked to their hotel by bus. Sat in the back, Colman was his usual bubbly self, talking enthusiastically of the pneumatic charms of Marilyn Monroe, while David Pegg waxed lyrical over Frank Sinatra's latest number. In contrast, Edwards sat quietly as he took in the sights and sounds of the impoverished Yugoslav capital, with beggars, street stalls, tanks and soldiers bombarding his senses.

Driving through the tired and depressing streets left Bill Foulkes feeling sorry for the people of Belgrade. 'The overall atmosphere was one of poverty,' Foulkes recalled. 'The faces of the people on the streets seemed to be pinched with hardship. Clearly, life was anything but easy.'

Kenny Morgans was also shocked by the poor quality of life that the Yugoslavs endured: 'I bought some dark green suede shoes before we went to Belgrade. People on the streets kept stopping me to have a look at them. They'd never seen suede before. Most of them didn't even own a pair of shoes, they wore pieces of tyre tied to their feet with rags. You should have seen the shops. There was nothing in them! Life was terrible for these people. I couldn't believe it.'

Bracing themselves for another abominable hotel, the players were pleasantly surprised when they checked in. Walking up the marble stairs and into the luxuriously furnished lobby, it was clear that their accommodation was unlike the pitiful buildings that surrounded it. The staircase was decorated with ornate gold fixtures, the furniture was made of solid oak and the staff were dressed immaculately. To all intents and purposes, it could have been a top-class hotel in London.

After quickly throwing their bags into their spacious rooms, the players then made their way to a nearby training pitch where they went through a pre-match workout in order to stretch their legs. Despite the pitch being described by Foulkes as a 'swamp recently drained', the United players happily splish-sploshed across it in front of a small crowd. Roger Byrne was given a late fitness test and, after a quick sprint, he gave the thumbs up to Tom Curry. This was bad luck for reserve Geoff Bent, who had travelled just in case Byrne did not make it. The atmosphere among the squad was jovial and calm and there was no doubt that the players' minds were firmly on the job at hand.

Following their hour-long workout, the players then trooped off to take in the stadium. A light dusting of snow had settled on the pitch but it seemed in good condition. The players were satisfied that it would suit their high-tempo passing game.

After a surprisingly decent meal in the hotel's restaurant, the players retired to bed for an early night. When they awoke and ventured down to breakfast the next morning, the hotel lobby was already packed with Yugoslav autograph-hunters. Edwards' signature was in high demand and due to his shy nature he made a concerted effort to avoid all of the fuss by keeping his head down.

Finally, after all the travel and anticipation, the players boarded the bus and made their way to the stadium. Edwards was pleased that it had not snowed again during the night. The pitch, he thought, would be perfect. On their way, the team passed thousands of friendly Belgrade fans who were also going to the game. On sight of the United players, some supporters started chanting 'Busby Babes, Busby Babes, Busby Babes.' Edwards smiled and gave them the thumbs up, which only saw the chanting get louder.

In the bowels of the stadium, Busby, dressed in a thick overcoat and trilby hat, calmed his players' nerves with some last words of encouragement. 'There are no terrors out there for you boys now,' he told his team, who listened intently. 'You know this team: they are good but not good enough to beat you. We've beaten them once. Now let's do it again. Enjoy the game, express yourselves. Don't forget your own strengths, always play to them. You should know that you have nothing to fear.'

Jimmy Murphy was not on hand to offer any profanity-littered, last-minute advice, as he had stayed behind to coach the Wales team. There was, however, no shortage of words from captain Byrne, who rallied his colleagues as they strode purposefully into the bitter Belgrade air. As the Babes marched out onto the field, they were greeted by an almighty din. Over 55,000 fans filled the stadium, with another 10,000 locked outside. The reputation of the young Manchester United team had travelled far and wide across Europe.

In the frosty weather, the Babes lined up together for the photographers before kick-off. Edwards jumped up and down, bringing his knees to his chest, and rubbed his hands together, gearing himself up for action. It was freezing. Every time he took a breath it looked as though he was breathing out smoke. Snow was piled high on the side of the pitch and the temperature was below zero. Despite this, neither Edwards nor any of his team-mates wore long-sleeved shirts or gloves.

United were keen to get the game won early and they therefore started in rip-roaring fashion. After just two minutes, Dennis Viollet struck to put United in front. Bobby Charlton, in devastating form, then popped up with another two goals to add to his ever-growing goalscoring tally. Within half an hour, United had moved into a 3-0 lead and were now 5-1 ahead on aggregate. The Yugoslavs, obviously frustrated, started to lash out and Morgans was on the receiving end of a particularly nasty challenge, which sliced open his thigh.

Edwards' influence was limited in the opening stages of the game as he again went over on his troublesome ankle. Rubbing his injured limb profusely, it took him some time to run the injury off. Yet when he was finally moving again at full tilt, he provided a moment that the fans of Belgrade would talk about for decades to come. Lining up a shot on the edge of the penalty area, he caught the ball so venomously that he managed to burst it. As the burst pig's bladder bounced haphazardly towards goal, players on both sides stood and watched in awe. No one had ever seen the likes of it before.

Just as had been the case at Highbury a few days earlier, United led 3-0 at the interval and had once again delivered a performance to rank among their best. History, however, repeated itself as United failed to produce the same brand of sparkling, high-intensity football in the second half. Sensing that their opponents were happy to sit back, thinking that the game had been won, Belgrade piled on the pressure straight from kick-off. Within minutes of the restart they had scored. Smelling blood, the Yugoslavs went for broke and shortly afterwards they struck again, this time via a disputed penalty.

The tension in the stadium became unbearable, Belgrade were now within two goals of catching United's seemingly impregnable lead. Fans began to spill onto the running track surrounding the pitch, which served to create an increasingly intimidating atmosphere. With such fervent support behind them, Belgrade swamped United and in the dying stages they amazingly equalised to make the score 3-3. United had blown a second three-goal lead in the space of just a few days. Thankfully this was to prove to be the last act in a riveting game. The Babes had done it, just. They were through to the semi-final stage of the competition for a second successive year by the skin of their teeth.

Leaving the field to a mixture of boos and cheers, Edwards let out a sigh of relief. His ankle was still throbbing but he was ecstatic that he would have the opportunity to hopefully avenge United's defeat against the mighty Real Madrid. Huddling around a heater in the dressing room, the players tried to thaw, as the ever cheerful Colman cried out, 'Bring on the Wolves.' The season was well and truly on track.

After the game, the Yugoslavs laid on a slap-up banquet in United's honour where good food and fine wine was served. Happily tucking into the feast, the euphoric United players fancied letting their hair down before they had to focus on the upcoming Wolves game. After a quiet word in the boss's ear, Byrne managed to obtain Busby's blessing for the United stars to hit the town to celebrate. Off they all went into the Belgrade night to enjoy a cabaret act, including jugglers and dancers, and an ocean of celebratory beers where the players made a toast to the future.

Once the cabaret act was at an end, Colman and company continued the partying at the home of a British embassy official. Feeling shattered, Edwards and Charlton had already returned to the hotel in order to prepare for their flight back to the UK the next day. Sitting on their beds, the two friends happily munched their way through the bag of food that Edwards had brought with him as they went over the game. They both agreed this United team could quite conceivably win the European Cup. They were better than the previous year, and while they respected Madrid they no longer feared them.

Waking up early the next morning, some of the United players were suffering from pounding heads. Nursing hangovers, they eventually assembled themselves outside their hotel so that the bus could take them to the airport. A few players lit up cigarettes to warm themselves and for once even Colman was quiet, as he tried to stop himself from being sick. Edwards, always eager to be liked, had once tried smoking to fit in with his mates, but after choking on the smoke, he decided that it was not for him.

Busby had no time to feel sympathy for his worse-for-wear players. He needed them to board the bus and swiftly get through customs in Belgrade airport if they were to make it back to England without breaking Football League rules. There was no way that Busby was going to allow Alan Hardaker the satisfaction of landing United with a heavy fine and points deduction. In any event, he also needed to get his players home quickly so that they had adequate time to prepare for their title clash with Wolves.

Once Busby had finally ushered all of his players onto the 'Elizabethan' British European Airways plane, he relaxed. The journey home would involve a short refuelling stop in Munich before they would arrive in Manchester later that afternoon. If everything went to plan, then their arrival would be plenty of time before Hardaker's deadline.

The plane ferrying the players home was named 'Zulu Uniform' and had once been used by Queen Elizabeth to travel across Europe. It was comfortable and spacious, with seats facing back and front, providing more than enough room for the players to put up their tired legs or to rest their pounding heads. No one particularly enjoyed flying, but as far as the players were concerned, this was as good as it got.

The players on the plane were Geoff Bent, Johnny Berry, Jackie Blanchflower, Bobby Charlton, Eddie Colman, Duncan Edwards, Bill Foulkes, Harry Gregg, Mark Jones, Kenny Morgans, David Pegg, Albert Scanlon, Tommy Taylor, Dennis Viollet, Billy Whelan and Ray Wood. Although Jimmy Murphy had not travelled, Walter Crickmer, the club secretary, manager Matt Busby and his two assistants, Tom Curry and Bert Whalley, were all on board.

As well as the players and officials, the cream of the British press were also on the flight. Many of them had followed Edwards' short but glorious career since his days as an England youth international. He knew them all by first name and was quite happy to talk freely with them about football and life in general. One of his favourite journalists was the former England goalkeeper Frank Swift, who wrote for the *News of the World*. Over the years, Swift had written many complimentary articles on Edwards and he was someone who the young star respected immensely. Busby was also quite happy for his players to talk freely with Swift, as they were close friends and he knew that he would not take any liberties.

As the plane taxied down the runway, some of the players were already playing cards, while others took the opportunity to try to sleep off their hangovers. Once they were in the air, Gregg stretched across three chairs and fell into a contented sleep, having cleaned up at cards the night before. He was not willing, just yet, to give his mates an opportunity to win back their money. Busby and Whalley dozed on each other's shoulders, while Curry sat behind them, puffing away reflectively on his pipe. Swift bellowed down the plane for all the press boys to join him in the tail. He had heard that in World War II many tail gunners' lives had been saved because they were at the back of the plane and therefore on every flight he insisted on a seat in the rear. Frank Taylor, Henry Rose and the other members of the press gathered around Swift as he then mercilessly ripped shreds out of them all, much to the United players' amusement.

With cards, snoozing and banter in full flow, the fasten seatbelt sign on the bulkhead became illuminated and the clipped voice of stewardess Margaret Bellis was heard over the intercom. 'In a few minutes we shall be landing in Munich. Extinguish your cigarettes. No more smoking please, and fasten your safety belts. We have time only for light refreshment in Munich, but we will be serving a proper meal after we take off for Manchester.' If the announcement didn't wake the sleeping players, the bumpy landing on the snow-covered runway certainly did.

Once the plane was at a standstill, Edwards hurriedly put on his big Crombie overcoat and walked briskly to the exit. Without exception, he was always the first to get off. As the door opened, a freezing wind battered his face. Poking his head outside he turned back and shouted to his team-mates, 'Get your snow shoes on, lads. Short studs are no use in this stuff.'

Crunching across the tarmac, the players battled against a howling wind as they made their way to the airport terminal, where they hoped to grab a quick cup of tea to warm up. Some of the players commented that the conditions were so bad that they may not be able to take off again, but the stewardess told them not to worry. This was music to Edwards' ears. He was not only looking forward to the in-flight meal, which would be served once they were back in the air, but also to seeing his beloved Molly back in Manchester.

Colman was quick to order several cups of tea for his shivering mates and he amazingly wiggled his way through the press boys while juggling a few mugs in his hand. As he swivelled past one table, portly journalist Eric Thompson shouted to him, 'Watch it Eddie, you nearly sent the table the wrong way with that body swerve.' The United players laughed as Colman cheekily replied, 'It's a good job I didn't have to swerve past you, Eric. I'd still be going.'

Huddled deep into an armchair, Edwards gulped down his tea but he was disturbed by an open door, which was letting in the cold air. 'Shut that door, Rog,' he shouted at the culprit, skipper Byrne. 'It's bloody freezing in here.' Without any hesitation, Pegg and Colman immediately went into a rendition of 'Baby It's Cold Outside'. Paying them little attention, Berry drank his steaming cup of tea so quickly he burned the roof of his mouth. He knew he had to slug it down swiftly as there wasn't much time before they had to re-board and he was eager to buy some mechanical toys that he had seen in the airport shop for his children.

Struggling to be heard over the banter of the players and the press, Curry shouted, 'That's it, lads. Everyone back on board. Quick as you can!' Curry stood by the doorway, shielding himself from the freezing wind, and counted everyone as they went past to ensure that no one was left behind. As the plane's engines restarted, and the players made themselves comfortable, there was a brief wait as they realised that they were missing someone. Finally, Alf Clarke of the *Manchester Evening Chronicle* rushed on board. Clarke had been on the phone to his newspaper relaying the latest United news back home so that it could make the late edition. The players and press boys thought that Clarke must have some breaking news, so they all started shouting, 'Scoop, Scoop.' Clarke grinned mischievously, sat down in his chair, and fastened his seatbelt in preparation for take-off.

Sat in their seats, the players idly chatted away as the plane set off down the runway, gradually gaining speed. Snow and slush whipped past the windows and it seemed only a matter of seconds before they would leave the ground, but then suddenly there was a shudder as the plane came to an abrupt stop. Confused chatter filled the air as the aircraft returned to the terminal. The time was 14.31.

In the cockpit, Captain James Thain blamed a fluctuation of boost pressure for the aborted take-off and asked the control tower if they could try again. Just minutes later, the captain asked the passengers to fasten their seatbelts and to prepare for another take-off attempt. Leg-pulling and cards were already back in full flow and no one felt that anything was amiss. With the plane gathering speed on the runway, the pilots noted that there was an uneven note being emitted by the engines, and that the needles on the boost indicators were still fluctuating. Once again the brakes were applied and the plane came to a stop. The time was now 14.35.

For the first time there were a few grumblings of discontent, which led to Swift, who was egged on by his colleagues, striding down to the cockpit to find out what was going on. Having been told that there was a minor technical difficulty, the passengers were asked to depart the plane and wait in the terminal for a further announcement.

'There was no point of concern until after the second aborted take-off,' remembers Bobby Charlton. 'Then the mood dipped, not in any dramatic way but quite perceptibly; certainly conversation became less chirpy and the card players were less absorbed by their game.'

Edwards and Charlton discussed the potential issues with Frank Taylor as they again squelched their way across the slush on the tarmac. The temperature was dropping rapidly and Edwards expressed his concern that ice was gathering on the wings. Taylor told him not to worry, as he was sure they would be de-iced before they set off again, but still Edwards was nervous.

Back once again in the terminal, the press gang attempted to lighten up the tense atmosphere with a few high jinks. Thompson, a small but chubby man, tried on Swift's massive overcoat and shuffled around pretending to be a grizzly bear. In turn, Swift tried to squeeze his huge frame into Thompson's coat, but was unable to do so, much to the laughter of a few of the players. Due to the delay, the atmosphere was a lot quieter than when they had last been in the terminal. Everyone was noticeably on edge and the journalists were desperate to get going as they all had to attend a press ball that night. Busby kept looking anxiously at his watch. He knew that if they didn't set off soon then the Football League would have a field day.

At one point a rumour swept through the party that the flight had been cancelled and that they would have to wait until the next day to return to Manchester. On hearing this news, Edwards rushed to the telephone bank and sent his landlady a telegram which read, 'Flights cancelled. Flying Tomorrow – Duncan.'

As the players huddled into the corner and discussed potential accommodation and, more importantly, food arrangements, an announcement broke out over the tannoy: 'Could the Manchester United party please re-board.' Curry was up in a flash: 'Come on then, lads. Quickly. Back on board,' he urged. Maybe they would get back in time after all.

While no one suggested that they shouldn't attempt to fly, the atmosphere was certainly an uneasy one. Having heard Swift's story that it was safer in the back, some decided to swap seats and head to the tail. Edwards and Colman were two of those who listened to Swift's advice. Conversation was muted as the plane again sat on the runway in preparation for a third take-off attempt. The time was now 14.59.

Captain Thain controlled the throttles while his colleague, Captain Ken Rayment, opened them to 28 inches, with the brakes on. With the engines steady, Captain Rayment released the brakes, lurching the plane forward. Slowly releasing the throttles until the levers were fully open, Captain Thain tapped his colleague's hand – the sign to go for full power.

The passengers were getting increasingly fraught with nerves as the plane set off down the runway. The card school consisting of Foulkes, Morgans, Pegg and Scanlon had long since stopped. Edwards, sitting next to Colman, hoped that his normally chirpy friend would say something to break the ice, but for once he was silent. Byrne sat stony-faced, forever acting the captain, trying not to show any sign of nerves, but as someone laughed nervously Berry snapped, 'I don't know what you are laughing at, we're all going to be killed.' The fiercely religious Whelan replied, 'If this is the end, then I'm ready for it.'

Gregg was also feeling far from confident, and while the plane built up speed on the runway, he curled up in a crash position. 'I thought I was going to die,' he remembers. 'I braced myself and waited for the end.'

In the cockpit, Captain Thain looked at the air-speed indicator and saw that it registered 117 knots. Watching intently, he waited for it to increase so that he could shout 'V2', the sign that the aircraft had built up enough speed to take off. As he waited in readiness, his heart dropped as he saw that the speed indicator had started to fall dramatically. The plane was running out of runway and it had not built enough speed to take off. It was also now too late to stop. 'Christ, we won't make it,' shouted Captain Rayment in panic, as he saw the end of the runway in sight.

The first sign the players had that something had gone drastically wrong was as the plane crashed through a perimeter fence, which sent a jolt through the carriage. As passengers started to scream, luggage was thrown from the overhead bins, sending duty-free alcohol and perfume smashing onto the floor. Moments later, the plane hurtled into the side of an empty house which ripped the steel shell in two, spinning the back half of the vessel around like a ball in a roulette wheel. Such was the impact that some passenger seats were ripped away from the plane and tossed out of the aircraft, with their occupants still sat in them.

Still speeding forward, the front half of the plane slammed into the surrounding woodland, which crumpled the port side of the cockpit like a piece of paper. The momentum of this clash saw the starboard side of the fuselage rip away and thunder into a wooden hut. On impact there was a tremendous explosion, sending fire shooting into the air. By sheer bad luck, the hut had contained a truck full of fuel. Where there had once been the laughter and chatter of young men in their prime, there was now an unearthly silence. Pockets of flames, resembling numerous funeral pyres, lit up the bleak dark sky and illuminated the tragic scene. The majestic Elizabethan plane, fit for royalty, was now just a mangled tangle of shredded metal. The time was 15.04.

Everywhere there was carnage. Broken bodies and parts of the crippled vessel were scattered across the snow. Bill Foulkes came around, still strapped into his seat, in the shell of the plane. After regaining his senses, he lunged towards a gaping hole in the side of the debris. As he sprinted away, fearing that it may go up in flames, he briefly looked over his shoulder. 'I could not believe the sight that met my eyes,' he tearfully remembered. 'The aircraft was cut in half; it was just a mass of jagged metal. Much worse, bodies were strewn from it in a neat line, and they were in slush and water where the snow had melted. The tail end of the plane appeared to have hit a house or a lorry or both. It was perched on high, looming over them, with burning bushes and drums scattered everywhere. The Union Jack was blazing away on the tail, and that part of the plane was caught up with the truck. The sound of burning was terrible.'

Harry Gregg, who had waited for death, also came round in the darkness. 'I felt something trickling down my forehead and in my nose. I put my hand to my face and felt the warmth of blood,' he remembers. 'I began to crawl towards the hole in the aircraft. The first person I saw was Bert Whalley, lying in the snow, eyes wide open. He was dead. I thought, my God, I'm the only one alive, but then the captain appeared with a little fire extinguisher and bellowed, "Run, you silly bugger, she's going to blow."' Despite this warning, Gregg bravely continued to search the crash site for any more survivors and heroically rushed back into the plane to rescue a screaming baby.

Sirens wailing in the distance served to wake Bobby Charlton from his unconscious state. He was on the slush-covered ground still strapped into his seat. Dennis Viollet lay next to him, murmuring in distress. Charlton unstrapped himself from his chair and tended to Viollet before looking for other survivors. Anxiously he looked for Eddie Colman, David Pegg and of course Duncan Edwards, but couldn't find them. Panic gripped him: what if his best friends were dead?

As the survivors desperately tried to help their injured colleagues, they were forced to witness some heartbreaking scenes. Their friends lay dead or maimed all around them. Some were barely recognisable from the titanic figures they had cut just 24 hours before in Belgrade. Someone told Charlton that Roger Byrne hadn't made it. The captain of the team was dead. He felt sick.

Finding a stricken Matt Busby in terrible pain, lying in the snow, Charlton took off his coat and put it under him so as to keep him warm. Gregg and Foulkes rubbed his shivering hands, but no one felt that their manager would make it. His foot was facing the wrong way, clearly broken, while his laboured breathing and cries of pain led them to believe that these could be his final moments.

Within minutes of the paramedics and fire engines arriving on the scene, Charlton, Foulkes and Gregg were persuaded, against their will, to hop onto a truck so that it could take them to hospital. Amazingly, Foulkes and Gregg had emerged virtually unscathed, while Charlton was just suffering from concussion. Sitting stunned in the back of the truck, none of them knew if Edwards had survived the crash.

Munich's Rechts der Isar Hospital was a hive of activity as it braced itself to treat the survivors. Appeals were immediately made for blood donors, while trolleys and stretchers were at the ready to hurriedly shepherd those most in need to operating theatres. Survivors were gradually being found amid the wreckage, but they didn't outnumber the dead whose number had now reached 22.

Charlton, drifting in and out of consciousness, would not know the true extent of the casualties until the following morning. He woke in his hospital bed hoping that it had all been a bad dream, but the sight of a fellow patient reading a newspaper, which was dominated by the story of the crash, brought it all back to him. Who had died, who had been injured, what had happened?

Suddenly snapping awake, Charlton pleaded with the German patient to let him know the full extent of the crash. Slowly but surely, an extensive list of the dead was read out. The tragic roll call included Roger Byrne, the fearless captain of the team; Tommy Taylor, England centre-forward always full of mischief; Billy Whelan, the great hope of Irish football; Mark Jones, the father figure of the Babes and one of the finest defenders in the country; and Geoff Bent, the reserve who had been on the trip only due to Byrne's injury concerns. Coaches Bert Whalley and Tom Curry, among the nicest and most gentle men in football, had also not made it. The majority of the press gang, who were some of the finest sports writers this country has ever produced, such as Alf Clarke, Don Davies, George Follows, Tom Jackson, Archie Ledbrooke, Henry Rose, Frank Swift and Eric Thompson, were also dead. Charlton stared ahead in deep shock as the German then confirmed his worst fear. His two close friends, David Pegg and Eddie 'Snakehips' Colman, had also perished.

'How could it possibly be?' Charlton later said. 'It was as though my life was being taken away piece by piece. I had invited David Pegg to my home for a North Eastern New Year, had spent so many hours in Eddie's house in Salford, where the talk was mostly of football and soldiering; I had shared digs with Billy Whelan, and most Saturdays I would have a few beers at the Bridge Inn in Sale with Tommy Taylor, who would wait for me if I had been away with the reserves.

'It was impossible to grasp that those days were gone, that I would never see Eddie swaggering into the ground again, humming some Sinatra tune, walking on the balls of his feet – or have Mark Jones, the kindest of pros, touching my sleeve after a game and giving me some encouraging word. A game never seemed to pass without that tough Yorkshireman taking the chance to say something like, "Well done, son", or "That was a lovely touch.'"

Amid the stomach-churning sickness, Charlton realised that Edwards' name was not among the dead. Could it be that this small mercy would be granted? Had Duncan Edwards been spared?

13

FIGHT FOR LIFE

As news of the tragedy broke, much of the world came to a grief-fuelled, stunned shock. It scarcely seemed possible that so many lives had been cut short in their prime. Crowds in Manchester flocked around newspaper stands, while others cried in the streets. A small group of fans had even gathered at Ringway airport to welcome the victorious team home, only to be told that the flight had not made it.

Wilf McGuinness, who had been left in Manchester due to injury, has never forgotten the circumstances of how he found out the news of the crash:

> Joe, a sales rep with the *News Chronicle* and a close friend, had done me a big favour by ferrying me to see an orthopaedic specialist in central Manchester. After the appointment, we were on our way back to the car when we clocked the feverish activity around the news-stand. Joe wondered why there was so much interest in the late edition and it was only then that I caught the words the young paper boy was shouting: 'United in plane crash.' At first I couldn't believe my ears, couldn't take in the potential enormity of the situation, but then I caught sight of a placard which revealed I had not misheard the cry.

We bought a paper and, because it mentioned a crash on the runway, I immediately felt a measure of relief flood through me. My instant reaction was that the damage couldn't be that extensive if the aircraft hadn't even left the tarmac. But Joe was more cautious. 'I'm afraid this sounds serious,' he told me, and we went to the *News Chronicle* office to find further information.

As soon as we arrived, it was clear that we were talking about a catastrophic accident. People were rushing around the office at top speed, and the Reuters news agency wire machine was spewing out yards of paper carrying the latest facts and speculation as the true position began to emerge. Amid all this frantic activity, Joe sat me down in a relatively quiet corner and brought over some copy from the wire. It revealed the horrifying news that there had been numerous fatalities, although no victims had yet been named.

Molly Leach had been cycling to work when she heard the cry 'United players in plane crash' from a young boy selling newspapers. She quickly stopped, grabbed a paper, and desperately scoured it for news on Duncan. There was none. With tears streaming down her cheeks, she cycled furiously to her friend Josephine's house in nearby Sale so that she could ring Gordon Clayton to see if he knew any more. Neither Clayton nor anyone else from Manchester United had further news at this stage. Sat distraught in the living room, Molly anxiously listened to the radio and TV for updates. What had happened to Duncan? What would she do if he hadn't survived?

A similar scene was played out in Dudley, as Annie and Gladstone Edwards huddled around their radio for any sign of news that their only son had survived. Annie was hysterical, she had already lost one daughter and the thought that Duncan, her Duncan, could also be taken away from her was too much to bear.

Finally, after what seemed like hours of nailbiting tension, news broke over the wireless of those who had survived the crash. The

names of Matt Busby, Bobby Charlton, Dennis Viollet, Albert
Scanlon, Harry Gregg and Bill Foulkes were solemnly read out, and
then finally Duncan Edwards. Annie and Gladstone unashamedly
wept with joy: their son was alive. At this stage they were still not sure
what condition he was in, but he was alive!

On hearing the news, Molly cried on her friend's shoulder. Her
fiancé had made it! With barely any time to pack a few clothes, she
was on the next plane to Munich, along with Sandy Busby, Jean
Busby [Matt's wife] and Jimmy Murphy. Molly kept praying and
thanking God for sparing her beloved 'Big Dunc'.

It wasn't just Molly and Duncan's parents who had prayed that he
would be found alive, some felt that the very future of English football depended on his survival. Walter Winterbottom, who was one of
Edwards' biggest fans, breathed a sigh of relief when he heard that his
young star had survived. 'I heard the news that Duncan hadn't been
killed and my heart leapt because here was the player who counted a
great deal more than anyone else in the England side.'

Back in the Rechts der Isar Hospital, doctors and nurses worked
around the clock, in a dramatic effort to keep Duncan Edwards'
crushed body alive. He had been admitted with broken ribs, a collapsed lung, broken pelvis, multiple fractures of the right thigh and
severely damaged kidneys. From the neck up, he didn't have a mark
on him, but the injuries to his legs meant that there was a chance he
might never walk again, let alone kick a ball. It was, however, the
damage to his kidneys that was causing the most concern and his life
was still far from safe.

On arrival he was listed as 'mortally injured', meaning that the doctors did not feel he would be able to survive his injuries. Most people
with similar injuries would have died at the crash site, but as always
Edwards put up a brave fight. Doctors hoped that his incredible fighting spirit and strength would allow him to beat the slender odds.

Frantic with worry, Molly arrived in the hospital the day after
the crash. Dashing down the corridor towards the intensive care

unit, mascara smeared her pale cheeks. On seeing his battered body, she let out a sob and held his hand tightly. He was in a coma and breathing heavily, but it appeared that everything was going to be all right.

At home, the nation was gripped by the golden boy of British football's fight for life. Vigils were being held in churches throughout the country and every football club flew their flag at half-mast. It seemed that everyone was pinning their hopes that at the very least English football's brightest star would be saved.

Twice a day, Professor Maurer, the man charged with saving Edwards, issued a statement on his condition. On hearing his voice on the radio, Manchester would come to a stop. Everyone prayed he would bring some good news. Some days the news seemed positive, other days it appeared hopeless. No one knew for sure whether he would make it.

One thing was for sure, no one was better qualified to save Edwards than Maurer. Having served as a medic in the Second World War, he had dealt with all manner of catastrophic injuries and he was therefore used to working under intense pressure. The battle of Dunkirk was perhaps his toughest assignment, but his tireless efforts saw him save the lives of both British and German soldiers. For this heroic feat he was awarded the Iron Cross. Maurer was meticulous when dealing with patients; he never left anything to chance. Such was his extraordinary attention to detail that he even appointed electricians to man all of the hospital lifts, in case one broke down while it was taking a patient to one of his operating theatres.

Maurer did everything that he could to save Edwards, and almost a week after the crash his efforts appeared to be working as the big man fragilely opened his eyes. When he awoke he was confused and agitated, not quite sure of what had happened. No one dared tell him the full extent of the disaster, as the doctors were worried that the shock could kill him. Amid all of the confusion, he was upset that he had lost a gold watch that had been given to him after the Real Madrid game a year earlier. He wore the watch everywhere he went and begged the nurses to find it for him. Incredibly, the watch had been found in the wreckage, and it was soon put back on his wrist, which saw him calm down.

Matt Busby had joined Edwards in the intensive care unit and he also clung desperately to life. Suffering from a crushed chest, severe lung damage and a shattered foot, the prognosis was bleak. At one point he was even given the last rites by a Catholic priest. Although he kept defying the doctor's pessimistic predictions, there wasn't much hope that Busby would pull through.

After an emotional journey, Murphy arrived at the hospital to visit his beloved boss and the surviving United players. Murphy was desperate to talk to Busby about what exactly had happened, but the doctors had warned him that his condition was so fragile that any talk of the crash could be too much for him to bear.

Walking across the corridor in shock after seeing the grey, drawn face of Busby lying under an oxygen tent, Murphy's spirits were lifted when he saw that Edwards was awake. 'What time is kick-off on Saturday, Jim?' Edwards painfully muttered to his mentor. 'Three o'clock, the usual time, son,' Murphy said, fighting back the tears. 'Get stuck in,' was Edwards' simple reply. Despite the tragedy and intense pain, Duncan Edwards' mind was still on the vital championship-decider with Wolves. In fact, the game had been postponed due to the crash, but Murphy daren't tell him this.

As Murphy tried to entertain Edwards with some of his football tales, the young lad, who he had lovingly nurtured into one of the world's best footballers, fell into a deep sleep. Gazing at the broken body of the boy he believed would one day conquer the world, the normally cheerful Welshman wept. Finally managing to drag himself away from Edwards' bedside, he let out all of the emotions he had been building up and broke down in a stairwell outside.

Kept in for observation for just under a week, Bobby Charlton was eventually told that he could go home, where he would join up with

Bill Foulkes and Harry Gregg. Charlton had been overjoyed to hear that his good friend Edwards had survived, and before departing he made sure that he paid him a visit. 'I went in to see him as I was coming away, and he gave me a bollocking!' Charlton wistfully recalled. '"Where have you been?" he demanded. "I've been down-stairs," I told him. And then he rambled . . .' Having to leave behind his severely injured pal brought tears to Charlton's eyes as he left the ward, unsure of when he would see the smiling face of Duncan Edwards again.

Before Bill Foulkes had started the painful journey back to Manchester a few days earlier, he asked one of the doctors, 'Is Duncan going to pull through?' 'He's fifty-fifty,' the doctor replied. Foulkes was happy with this. He thought to himself that if Edwards had an even chance then he would be okay.

However, on 11 February, Edwards' condition took a turn for the worse. A report informed a gripped nation, 'Early today doctors at the Isar hospital reported his condition as unchanged. But this afternoon doctors were alarmed at the unusually high percentage of nitrogen in the player's blood. Edwards had six times more nitrogen in his blood than is normal in a human.'

On hearing this, Gladstone and Annie were on the next plane bound for Munich. Their journey to be at their son's side was all over the news: 'Duncan Edwards' parents and a family friend, Mr I.P. Woodley, are making a dramatic dash to his bedside. Early this afternoon they left Dudley on a three-hour race against time by road for London airport, hoping to catch the 5.15 Viscount to Munich. Police along the route were alerted by BEA and asked to facilitate the passengers of the car.'

Reports of Edwards' brave fight were by now becoming increasingly gloomy, 'Doctors early today said Edwards was "in very acute danger and getting worse". But they added: "He is still young and therefore has more chances."' Only one thing could now save Edwards, an artificial kidney to help filter the nitrogen out of his bloodstream. Unfortunately, the closest one to the Munich hospital was over 210 miles away. So began a dramatic rush to bring it to him, as the doctors prayed that Edwards could hold on until they had the machine.

Finally, on 12 February, stories in the press broke that the vital machine had arrived in the nick of time: 'As soon as the kidney arrived, it was put in a lift and taken to the fourth floor for immediate connection to Edwards. The kidney is the doctors' last chance to save Edwards, who was critically injured last week. Dr George Lang said the machine would be left running with Edwards' blood circulating through it for about six hours. Then the blood would be allowed to return to the normal circulating system. The purpose of the apparatus was to take the strain off Edwards' injured kidneys. The artificial kidney was called for when Dr George Maurer found a further deterioration in Edwards' condition, which has been critical from the start. The United and England half-back was said to be near to death this morning after the nitrogen content of his blood rose to 500 promile during the night. Doctors said a 45 promile content is normal.'

Within 24 hours, Edwards seemed to be on the verge of a dramatic recovery as the machine worked wonders. At one point he even woke and asked the doctors in a strained, whispered voice, 'Where am I?' As had been hoped, the nitrogen in his blood started to drop, and the doctors were so pleased with his progress that they even allowed him to drink a little milk. The nation breathed a sigh of relief; surely he would now go from strength to strength.

With the news having proclaimed that their son was close to death, Annie and Gladstone were overwhelmed with joy when they saw him. He had a little colour in his face and looked to be on the mend. Annie could not contain herself as she kept kissing his forehead and whispering to him that everything was going to be all right. Edwards may have been the lionheart of England and Manchester United, but he was still just a boy at 21 years of age and his spirits were boosted at having his mum there to look after him.

Sitting in bed all day was, however, beginning to agitate the restless Edwards, as he felt that his injuries weren't as bad as were being described. 'Get me out of here, Mum,' he told Annie. 'I've got better things to do besides lying around in here.'

'I'll get you out, son,' Annie tearfully replied. 'Besides you better hurry up and get better as you have your car to look after back home.'

'Keep it on the road, Mum,' said Edwards, 'for when I get better.'

But once more, just as Edwards seemed to be improving, he went downhill. The nitrogen began to rise again in his body, and as a result he suffered from increasing periods of unconsciousness. Molly, Annie and Gladstone kept a vigil as the doctors told them that they were amazed at his courage. Anyone else would be dead by now, but he would not give in.

Suddenly, on 15 February, Edwards' fight seemed to be coming to an end. He was suffering from severe haemorrhages, which the medical staff could not stop. Again there was a frenzy of speculation in the newspapers as to whether this would be the end of the road for 'Big Dunc':

Police radio cars raced to the homes of Munich blood donors early today when Manchester United star Duncan Edwards began to have severe haemorrhages. Prof Maurer explained later that the use of the artificial kidney had reduced the ability of Edwards' blood to clot. Shortly after midnight Edwards began to bleed internally. Prof Maurer was awakened at 2am. Donors were reached through police radio patrol cars and taken to the hospital. After several transfusions, Edwards' bleeding was brought to a halt. Dr Graham Taylor of BEA saw Edwards today. Afterwards he said Edwards' condition was unchanged and he remained dangerously ill. It was too early to say whether the artificial kidney, which was used for seven hours yesterday, would have to be used again.

Dr Taylor said that surgeons and doctors of the hospital had commented that Edwards had a strong will to live. They really admire his fighting spirit a lot. He has plenty of pluck, that boy, apart from his splendid former physical condition, and the doctors feel that these are helping him to pull through. Dr Taylor said that Edwards was conscious all the time, but was very restless. He added, 'I told him this morning to keep quiet and to not talk more than necessary. He said that he understood.'

Again Edwards dug deep and refused to give in. The next few days gave hope to his family, team-mates and fans as once more he seemed on the verge of a miraculous recovery. His breathing became stronger and he seemed to be more alert. On 17 February, the doctors even commented that his damaged kidney seemed to be starting to work again. Molly and his parents breathed a sigh of relief; they had braced themselves for the end but now he seemed to have turned the corner.

After spending another restful night, with no further complications, the doctors also began to believe that maybe, just maybe, this remarkable boy had seen off the worst. There seemed to be no doubt about it: he was on the mend.

Yet the next day his condition plummeted. 'Doctors gave grim news about the condition of Duncan Edwards,' the pessimistic reports read. 'He has taken a turn for the worse and is showing signs of distress. The bulletin said he was weaker, following further treatment with the artificial kidney. He has been given direct person-to-person blood transfusions. Use of the artificial kidney has developed into a vicious circle, which is gradually sapping his strength. A BEA doctor said: "Edwards' condition is about the worst it has been since kidney treatment was started last week."'

With their son clinging to life, Annie and Gladstone spent their time praying in the hospital's chapel. The chaplain was on hand to offer words of comfort, but Annie would not accept that her Duncan was going to die, she was sure that he would bounce back. He always did.

Hopes were raised when at one point there seemed to be a very slight improvement in his condition. Kenny Morgans, who had been the last survivor to be pulled out of the crash, had heard that Edwards was a little better and had demanded to see his team-mate. Taken to intensive care in a wheelchair, Morgans entered the ward only to see that Edwards was asleep. He looked peaceful so he didn't want to disturb him. Returning back to his bed he told the other surviving players that 'Big Dunc' looked okay. Maybe the worst was over.

But it was not to be. In the early hours of 21 February 1958, Duncan Edwards' brave fight for life came to an end as he quietly passed away in his sleep. He had fought his last fight. At just 21 years of age, the great hope of English football, who was going to some day captain his country to the World Cup, was dead.

As the news flashed across radio and television sets that morning, the nation could scarcely believe what it was hearing: 'Team-mates of Manchester United's plucky young footballer Duncan Edwards wept in the Rechts der Isar Hospital here today when they were told that soccer's "wonder boy" had lost his 15-day fight for life. The lion-hearted Edwards died peacefully in his sleep, with no pain, at 2.15am today, after a desperate last-minute battle to save him. About midnight doctors noticed that his circulation was failing. Injections caused a temporary improvement but his strength ebbed away. Nurses at his bedside, well used to suffering and sudden death, broke down and wept as the flame for life for which they had fought so hard flickered out.'

Scenes of indescribable grief were seen as Gladstone, Annie and Molly were told that the boy who they had loved so much had passed away. Gladstone stood in shock, not speaking, not moving, his eyes glazed over, unable to process the information. His reaction was in direct contrast to Annie, who collapsed into a ball on the floor and wailed. She had been convinced that her Duncan was going to make it. Duncan was all that had ever mattered to her and now he was gone, how could she go on? Molly, who had dreamed of buying a home with her fiancé and raising a family with him, was inconsolable. Tears overwhelmed her pretty face and she needed attention from the doctors as she started to scream incoherently and suffered from a panic attack.

When the three of them visited the hospital mortuary to have one last moment with Duncan, Molly and Annie were so hysterical that they needed to be sedated. Their screams of anguish echoed through the hospital corridors.

Later that morning, Professor Maurer was faced with having to confirm the news to those survivors he felt were strong enough to be told. Ray Wood, Kenny Morgans, Dennis Viollet and Albert Scanlon were gently informed that their friend, team-mate and talisman had played his last game.

Frank Taylor, the only sports journalist to survive the crash, was also told the news that morning, as he lay in his hospital bed next to Jackie Blanchflower. 'I'm afraid I have some bad news for you both,' Dr Graham Taylor of BEA told them. 'I know you'll understand but Duncan couldn't quite make it. He died early this morning. I know you won't tell Matt Busby this sad news. He is too ill to be told yet.'

'My heart sank in numbing despair,' Taylor sadly remembered:

It was inconceivable. Never again would we see that sudden spurt of Edwards, all muscle and strength, as he came running out of the players' tunnel; those wild boyish leaps of sheer exuberance as he ran on to the pitch. Why, it seemed he could never wait for the whistle to blow and the game to get started. Never again to see that matchless physique crashing into thrilling action; a giant of the football world while little more than a boy.

'O God, help his family,' I whispered.

Yet when the tears were dried, one of Duncan's nearest and dearest friends told me: 'Maybe it was better this way.' The doctors said, had he lived, he might have to spend the rest of his life in a wheelchair. Duncan couldn't have stood that. Now I can remember him as he was – the greatest thing that has happened in British football for years.

There were many tears that day in Munich, and far beyond, for a boy who had taken the world of sport by storm; who epitomised the power and zest and all that's best in British sport. A worthy young sports idol for the youth of the nation. Duncan Edwards was unforgettable. So long, Dunc. It was great while it lasted.

Busby was deemed to be in too fragile a state to know of any of the casualties, but a few days later he learned of the tragic news by accident. Slowly recovering in bed, he was keen to find out how his golden boy was holding up. He knew that he had been hurt in the crash, but was under the assumption that he was on the mend. As a Franciscan friar passed his bedside, Busby enquired, 'How is Duncan Edwards today?' The friar was caught unawares; he had thought that Busby had known that Edwards had perished. After taking a moment to compose himself, he softly told him, 'My son, I must tell you the truth, Duncan Edwards is dead.'

Nothing more needed to be said. The friar slowly walked away from Busby's bedside to leave him with his thoughts. That night, when Jean Busby visited her husband, she was met by his plea for the truth. He wrote of their heartbreaking conversation in his autobiography, *Soccer at the Top*:

My wife, Jean, was at my bedside. When I asked what had happened, she changed the subject. 'Don't worry,' she would say. 'Don't talk. I'm supposed to do the talking.' Finally I could stand it no longer. I said: 'Jean, I want to know. I want to know the worst. For my peace of mind.' So began a new torture, for Jean and for me. I would name a name and without saying a word she would nod or shake her head. When even now I think about her feelings at that time, let alone mine, in those dreadful moments of telling me about those poor kids, and those other friends, I could weep, and I am not by nature a weeping man. This new torture, this constant mental torture, knocked me back and I was as near the brink as ever. I was spared, but even if I survived how could I face the loved ones of the lads who were not spared? Was I to blame? Was I to blame? Why can't I die?'

Bobby Charlton, who by this time was recuperating at home in Ashington, took the news harder than most. Walking down to breakfast he was greeted by the sight of his ashen-faced mother, who struggled to tell her son that his best friend was dead. Charlton's world collapsed at hearing the news. He shook with grief at the thought that never again would he grace the same field as his pal or stay up late into the night discussing football with him. 'He was fantastic and I loved him,' Charlton has tearfully confided.

Mrs Dorman, Edwards' landlady, felt as though she had lost her own son. 'He has left hundreds of friends and thousands of happy memories. He was a quiet, reserved boy who any mother would have been proud of. He had never liked flying, and always seemed to go quiet a couple of days before any trips, and always insisted that the safest place to sit was at the back of the plane. Duncan will be missed by the children of Gorse Park Junior School. He was in his element when he and Tommy Taylor had snowball fights with the boys during the winter. He also used to love his new car, which he bought after his twenty-first birthday. He used to spend hours cleaning it.'

Footballers from around the country were left in mourning. Future England World Cup-winning captain Bobby Moore was only a youngster at West Ham at the time but he was deeply affected by the news, 'I cried when I heard. I was visiting Malcolm Allison and Noel Cantwell and we all sat there crying, two grown men and me.'

Edwards' death wasn't just being grieved by friends, family and fans of Manchester United, the whole of England also mourned. There was no doubt that the tragedy had now drastically reduced England's chances of winning their first World Cup that summer. Walter Winterbottom knew in his heart that without the likes of Tommy Taylor, Roger Byrne and especially Duncan Edwards that victory would now be impossible. He told the press, 'I have great sadness in realising not only the loss to England and Manchester United, but it is also a huge loss to football. He was a magnificent boy, a lovely lad, always smiling. He played with tremendous joy and his spirit stimulated the whole England team. It was in the character and spirit of Duncan Edwards that I saw the true revival of British football.'

Even Manchester City fans were distraught at his death. Colin Shindler, an ardent City fan, wrote about how he reacted to the news in his book, *Manchester United Ruined My Life*. When asked by his schoolteacher to write a diary on the disaster, Shindler has confessed that 'the day Duncan Edwards died I could scarcely write for tears', as his passing felt as if 'it was a death in the immediate family'.

Edwards' favourite magazine, *Charles Buchan's Football Monthly*, had been published the week of his death, and its front cover was adorned with a photo of the United star that had been taken just days before the crash. In it Edwards stared out at the readers with a broad grin adorning his clean-cut, handsome face. He is crouched over, tying his bootlaces, in preparation for another match. For all the world he looks a supreme athlete with years ahead of him to set yet more records and achieve new miracles. Inside the magazine the publishers hurriedly added the following note:

Every reader of *Football Monthly* will join the staff of our magazine in expressing deepest sympathy to the relatives of the Manchester United men who died in the tragic air crash on their way home from Belgrade. This edition was produced some days before the accident occurred. We hope that our front cover will be taken as a tribute and a reminder of happier days.

To our fine friends who died it can truly be said:

'In their death they were not divided: they were swifter than eagles, they were stronger than lions.'

Poignantly, as Edwards' body was flown home, and his coffin was being carried off the plane, Manchester United were already back in action. Some 66,124 fans packed Old Trafford for the league game against Nottingham Forest, all wanting desperately to be with each other during this time of incredible sadness. Representatives from Red Star Belgrade attended the game, as did members of the families of those players who had died. Before the match the Dean of Manchester conducted an inter-denominational service on the pitch in tribute to Edwards and his team-mates.

Two weeks after the disaster, those in Manchester had only just grasped the enormity of what had happened, but now Edwards' death deepened their grief. No one could believe that he was gone. How could it be that they would never again see his marauding runs and cannon-ball shot? Or his match-saving tackles, unerring passes to all corners of Old Trafford and his incredible love for the game that saw him play every match with a smile? Some opted never to return to Old Trafford, their romance with the game of football had been brutally snatched from them.

The unhappy occasion of Edwards' funeral took place on 26 February 1958. Matching the sombre mood of the crowds in Dudley, who had turned up in their droves to pay their respects to their fallen son, the weather was cold and bitter. A solemn silence hung in the freezing air. Dudley's streets were full of mourners who all wanted to witness 'Our Dunc's' tragic homecoming. They all wanted to give their hero the send-off that he so richly deserved.

Driving the two miles towards St Francis's Church, where the funeral service would be held, the cortege passed many of the streets and parks where he had spent his youth playing football, dreaming of one day becoming the best footballer in the country. His dream had come true, but it had ultimately ended in tragedy.

His pallbearers were supposed to have been his United team-mates Gordon Clayton and Bobby English, along with Billy Wright, Ray Barlow, Don Howe and Ronnie Clayton. However, a snowstorm delayed the arrival of Gordon Clayton and English, so Peter McParland and Pat Saward were asked to step into the breach at the last moment. McParland was of course the man who had broken Ray Wood's jaw in the 1957 FA Cup final and who Edwards had come close to punching. Neither man could have foreseen that less than a year later this tragic course of events would come to pass.

'It was a very sad occasion,' Don Howe has recalled. 'I've never seen anything like it. We were walking down the aisle with the coffin on our shoulders and everybody was standing up. All the seats were taken, and anywhere you wanted to stand you couldn't get in. It was absolutely jam-packed. It was the same outside: there were people everywhere. Following the hearse through the crowds afterwards, it really was awesome. Everybody had their heads down and it was all very respectful. He was a hero in a place like Dudley, of course.'

Inside the small church, Reverend A.D.Catterall delivered the service in front of over 300 friends and family. Annie, Gladstone and Molly sat side by side, weeping in the front row. Mr and Mrs Dorman were also there to pay their respects, as were officials from Manchester United and other football clubs. The reverend told the tearful congregation, 'We are proud that the great Duncan Edwards was one of our sons. He goes to join the immortal company of Steve Bloomer and Alex James. Talent and even genius we shall see again, but there will only ever be one Duncan Edwards.'

With the service at an end, the hearse carrying Edwards' body began its journey to his final resting place, Queens Cross Cemetery. Mayhem broke out when the hearse drove through the gates, as hundreds of people desperately tried to get a better view of his coffin. Stretching for over 30 yards in each direction, his grave was already covered with wreaths that had been sent by most of the football clubs in the Football League. One of the most prominent wreaths was made of roses and shaped in the number six, the number which he had worn with such pride for club and country.

To Annie, Gladstone and Molly this didn't seem possible. They were oblivious to the bitter wind rushing through the graveyard. Their minds were entirely focused on why this had happened to somebody like Duncan? A boy who lived for football, who wouldn't hurt a fly, hardly touched a drop of alcohol, didn't smoke and cared for all of his friends and family deeply. Why did God have to take him?

14

LIFE AFTER DUNCAN

Duncan Edwards' death was a tragedy without comparison in the sporting world, but life somehow had to go on. Staggeringly, shortly after the crash, Bobby Charlton, Bill Foulkes and Harry Gregg were back in action for Manchester United. With so many of their colleagues either dead or injured, the team, made up of reserve and youth team players plus a few new recruits, was in desperate need of some class and experience. Jimmy Murphy, who admirably took on responsibility while the boss, Matt Busby, remained in serious condition in hospital, begged the survivors to play. His plea pinged at their conscience. They were, he said, now all playing for the memory of those who had lost their lives in Munich.

The team may have been decimated, but they were still in contention for three major honours, and the players did everything that they could to win at least one trophy to commemorate their fallen comrades. It seemed an impossible mission, but they performed admirably in the circumstances. Although they were narrowly knocked out of the European Cup in the semi-finals by AC Milan, and plummeted down the league table after only one win out of 14, the team enjoyed a remarkable run in the FA Cup, which Charlton described as 'riding a tide of emotion'.

Ultimately, they ended up back at Wembley, where they would play Bolton Wanderers, the club Edwards had turned down in favour of signing for United. In the Bolton side that day was Edwards' cousin, Dennis Stevens. It was an unhappy reminder that what should have been a happy, family celebration had been marred by tragedy. Having fought against incredible odds to reach the final, it seemed to be United's destiny to win the Cup. They were cheered on by most football supporters in the UK, who willed them to do it for their departed friends. But this wasn't a Hollywood film. The tears and the pain made that quite clear. Although Busby had returned to the sidelines for the first time since Belgrade, the United players just fell short at the final hurdle as they lost the game 2-0.

A tide of emotion may have allowed United to reach the final, but over the next few years they gradually fell out of contention for major trophies. Busby was left with the monumental task of rebuilding one of the greatest club sides that had ever graced British football. Unsurprisingly this would take time, as the likes of Duncan Edwards were irreplaceable.

Munich may have instantly killed many of United's stars, but the careers of some of its survivors were also stopped in their tracks. Such was the severity of their injuries, Johnny Berry and Jackie Blanchflower never played professional football again, while Kenny Morgans struggled to regain his pre-Munich form and eventually left Manchester United to join Swansea.

The grieving process was a long and hard one, but in time Charlton blossomed into one of the world's greatest footballers, and the youth system, so brilliantly looked after by Murphy, produced another world-class star in the shape of George Best. Denis Law, one of the best strikers in British football, was also signed from Torino in 1962 and soon became the darling of the Stretford End. Against the odds, Busby had again built a team that threatened to dominate the domestic and European game.

The holy trinity of Best, Law and Charlton inspired United to league titles in 1965 and 1967 and this also heralded the return of the club to the European Cup. Europe had of course been Busby's great obsession and he vowed that he would do everything in his power to win the trophy in tribute to his fallen Babes.

Finally, in 1968, that fervent wish, that burning ambition of his, became a reality, as Manchester United defeated Benfica at Wembley in the European Cup final. On a night of high emotion, Munich survivor Bobby Charlton fittingly scored twice. At the end of the game Charlton and Busby found each other, amid the mêlée, and embraced. Nothing needed to be said; they both understood who this victory was for.

While it took United a decade to recover from their loss, it was a disaster that also devastated the England football team. Edwards had made the left-half position his own, and had shone in displays against Brazil and West Germany. Surely the 1958 World Cup in Sweden would have seen him announce his arrival on the world stage. England had been touted as one of the favourites, but with the loss of Roger Byrne, Tommy Taylor and Edwards, all vital players, they were always going to face an uphill task to win the trophy. Tommy Banks, Derek Kevan and Bill Slater were their respective replacements.

Before the tournament, England played Yugoslavia in a friendly, but shorn of their United stars they humiliatingly lost 5-0. For the first time, Billy Wright realised that Munich had destroyed their dreams of winning the World Cup. 'This was the match when it really dawned on us just how much we had gone back since the Munich air crash,' Wright said regretfully. 'We were disjointed and totally lacking any sort of team pattern. If anything, the final scoreline flattered us. It did severe damage to our confidence with the World Cup finals so close. We were very subdued in the dressing room afterwards and all Walter Winterbottom could bring himself to say was, "Well, at least we've got the bad game out of our system. Now let's focus on doing much, much better in the World Cup."'

In the circumstances, England did show plenty of pluck and spirit as they drew 0–0 with eventual winners Brazil, before being knocked out of the tournament by the Soviet Union. Bill Nicholson, manager of Tottenham Hotspur and assistant to Winterbottom, admitted afterwards that replacing Edwards and the other Babes had proved to be an impossible task. 'We'd lost some terrific players, not only Duncan Edwards, Roger Byrne and Tommy Taylor, but also David Pegg and Eddie Colman ... From being in a position to win the World Cup, we had to think again,' said Nicholson ruefully. 'Duncan had it all. The range of his ability was exceptional and he had tremendous enthusiasm for the game. I think if Edwards had lived, Byrne and Taylor, too, because they were both outstanding in their positions, England would have gone close in Sweden. It was a hell of a job [replacing them] because there were not that many international-class players around, and one or two who looked up to it weren't ready.'

One of those who wasn't quite ready to make an impact in 1958 was Charlton, but he would soon become a major player for his country. Four years later, in Chile, a virtuoso Charlton helped take England to the quarter-final stages, but Brazil, inspired by Garrincha, ultimately ended their tournament. Finally, in 1966, England and Bobby Charlton did win the World Cup, under the stewardship of Alf Ramsey. On what should have been one of the greatest days of his life, Charlton still could not help thinking that Edwards should have been celebrating on the Wembley pitch with him.

Bobby Moore of West Ham United famously lifted the Jules Rimet trophy at Wembley Stadium, and has been heralded as one of the greatest footballers of all time. Yet if Edwards had lived, would Moore have been in the team, let alone its captain? We will never truly know the answer but some, such as Terry Venables, feel that it is beyond doubt that Edwards would have taken Moore's position. 'Perhaps Bobby would have got in the team in another position, because he was a great player too, but you would never have picked Moore in front of Edwards. Duncan had the edge everywhere.'

England international Colin Harvey also believes that Moore

may have been unable to get in the side. 'For me Duncan would have developed into a dynamic second centre-back and Bobby Moore would have had problems staying in the England side – if he'd ever got in. I think Duncan, and not Bobby, would have played alongside Jackie Charlton. It's sad, isn't it, that we never saw his full potential.'

Wilf McGuinness speculates that while Ramsey would have found room for Moore, it would have been another World Cup winner who may have missed out. 'If he had lived he would have dropped back to centre-half and he would have been the greatest centre-half you've ever seen. He would have been a commanding defender who could bring the ball out of defence. Bobby Moore would have played in sixty-six, but he wouldn't have been captain and I don't think we would have heard of Jack Charlton.'

Edwards was of course England's youngest international in the 20th century until Michael Owen made his debut in 1998. If he had lived and avoided serious injury, there is little doubt that he could have accumulated a record number of England caps. He was so dedicated to keeping fit and looking after himself that he could have still been playing for his country well into his 30s, just like his idol Stanley Matthews. As he was so versatile, he could also have switched positions with ease, to ensure a place in the team once the power in his legs had started to wane. 'He was England's youngest player,' Matt Busby said in his autobiography, which was published in 1973, 'and I have little doubt he would have lived to be the oldest. Duncan Edwards was then, and has always remained to me, incomparable. His death after the Munich crash in 1958 when he was only 21, but with 18 caps already, was as far as football is concerned the biggest single tragedy that has happened to England and Manchester United. I believe he would have been playing for England still.'

One can only speculate just how different the fortunes of Manchester United and England might have been if Edwards had lived. There can be little doubt that both club and country would have been in contention for every major honour. England may have won another World Cup and Manchester United another European trophy.

Edwards' old army pal, Blackpool legend Jimmy Armfield, certainly believes that this would have been the case, 'There is no doubt in my mind that with Byrne, Edwards and Taylor in the team we would have won the World Cup in Sweden in 1958 and in South America four years later. England could have had a hat-trick of World Cup wins.'

It was not, however, just Manchester United and England who were never again quite the same. As could only be expected after such a tragedy, Annie and Gladstone Edwards were broken by the loss of their only son. Until their dying days, both were haunted and scarred by Munich.

After the crash, Gladstone quit his job at the ironworks and began working at the cemetery where his young son was buried. He said of this, 'People think I came to this job because he's here. But that wasn't the reason. I had to change my work, and I've always liked flowers and gardening. I felt I wanted to be out of doors.' Anyone who saw Gladstone spend the majority of his days tending to Duncan's grave knew, however, that there was only one reason for his change of career, a desperate need to be near his son. Over the years, Gladstone speculated just how different things might have been if Edwards had instead decided to sign for Wolves, rather than Manchester United. It was a thought that tormented him until his dying day.

Back at the family house in Elm Road, Annie made the living room into a shrine dedicated to her beloved Duncan. On the back wall was a glass display cabinet that contained all of his England caps, each lovingly filled with tissue so that they would keep their shape. Photographs on the top of the cabinet captured her son as a carefree spirit in the prime of his life. The first photo was of him posing in his army uniform, the second was of him and Molly smiling broadly, while the third showed him standing proudly in his Manchester United kit. Emblazoned across the opposite wall was a huge portrait of Edwards in action, next to it was a framed £5 note, the last gift he ever gave his mother.

Until her death in 2003, Annie Edwards would only ever really come to life when she could reminisce about her son. Even in her later years, with her health failing, she was only too happy to invite journalists and fans into her home, make them a cup of tea, and talk about Edwards. In a DVD dedicated to Edwards, which was filmed shortly before her death, you can see in her face pure joy as she speaks of him growing up, but on the subject of Munich her excited chatter slows, tears fill her eyes, and at times she appears lost for words. Until her last breath, Annie Edwards prayed that it had all just been a bad dream. She hoped that she would wake up to the sound of him bouncing through the door, shouting out in his booming voice, 'Mum, I'm home, put the kettle on will ya.'

To help ease her pain, she speculated that perhaps he had been taken from her to fulfil a higher purpose, 'We don't know what's beyond, do we? Maybe he was taken to do greater things elsewhere. Who knows? Nobody knows, do they? I always think that!'

Molly Leach, the love of Duncan's life, and the girl he planned to marry, was also unable to get over her loss. Her friend Josephine Stott said, 'Molly came back from Germany dressed all in black. I'd never seen such a change in a person. At the time Molly was only 22 and I never thought she'd get over it. They had all their lives to look forward to and the plane crash took that all away.' In order to escape the bad memories of Manchester, she moved to Weston-super-Mare to live with her brother. Despite vowing to never get involved with another man, she eventually married a semi-professional footballer, and gave birth to two daughters. Until her dying day she was, however, too traumatised to speak about the love she lost on a Munich runway and claimed that she no longer believed in God.

Numerous tributes have been erected in Edwards' honour since his death. The first was in August 1961, when two stained-glass windows were dedicated to him at St Francis's Church in Dudley. The windows show Edwards in his Manchester United shirt, bent down on one knee, with the words 'God is with us for our Captain' running across his chest. All of the survivors of the Munich air crash were present for the dedication where Busby told the tearful congregation, 'These windows should keep the name of Duncan Edwards alive for ever, and shine as a monument and an example to the youth of Dudley.'

Other tributes to Edwards over the years have included the Duncan Edwards Social Club, which is attached to the town football club, as well as a display of his trophies and shirts at the Dudley Leisure Centre. In 1999, a statue of Edwards, designed by Malcolm Sier, was also erected in Dudley town centre. The statue captures him in all his glory, playing for England, and looking every inch a titan in his prime.

Sir Bobby Charlton and Annie Edwards were both in attendance when the statue was unveiled before a horde of fans. Over the years, Sir Bobby has been keen to attend any tributes to his friend to ensure that he is not forgotten. At the unveiling of the statue he told the watching crowd, 'I find that I think about Duncan a lot. I have seen all the players who in their time have been labelled the best in the world – Puskas, Di Stefano, Gento, Didi, John Charles and the rest – and not one of them has been as good as Big Duncan. There was no other player in the world like him then and there has been nobody to equal him since. This man was incomparable.'

Keen to dismiss the notion that Edwards has only been so revered due to his tragic and dramatic demise, Sir Bobby warned, 'Sometimes I fear there is a danger that people will think that we who knew him and saw him in action boost him because he is dead. Sentiment can throw a man's judgement out of perspective. Yet it is not the case with him. Whatever praise one likes to heap on Duncan, it is no more than he deserved. He was out on his own at left-half and a first division player in every other position. There was no one else to start with him. I am not a person to dramatise things or dispense fulsome praise. It is not in my make-up. A man is a good player or he is not. A few are great, and they deserve respect. But Duncan Edwards was the greatest. I see him in my mind's eye and I wonder that anyone should have so much talent. He was simply the greatest footballer of them all.'

This is certainly something that Jimmy Murphy, Edwards' biggest admirer, agreed with. To Murphy, he was the boy who had it all, there were no weaknesses in his game or in his character, and he felt robbed of the opportunity to see him blossom into the greatest player the world had ever seen. In time he would nurture the likes of George Best into the first team, but Murphy always insisted that no one could ever compare to Edwards. He once sadly reminisced, 'If I shut my eyes now I can see him; the pants hitched up, the wild leaps of boyish enthusiasm as he came running out of the tunnel, the tremendous power of his tackling, always fair but fearsome, his immense power on the ball ... When I used to hear Muhammad Ali proclaim to the world that he was the greatest, I would always smile. The greatest of them all was a footballer named Duncan Edwards.'

So was Duncan Edwards really the greatest footballer who ever lived?

To answer this question one should consider whether there has ever been a footballer who has played in just about every outfield position and at the same time has excelled in all of them? Could Best, Pelé, Maradona, Ronaldo, Messi or Rooney play for both club and country in defence, midfield or attack and still shine? It is doubtful. All of these players are world-class in their respective positions, but anywhere else on the field and they would probably just be making up the numbers.

Ronaldo and Messi are currently lauded as the two best players in the world, but it is hard to imagine them being talked about as world-class defenders as well as attackers. Wayne Rooney is certainly one modern-day player who has the all-round ability and determination to play in most positions, but though he has played in midfield, could one imagine him playing for England as centre-back ahead of John Terry or Rio Ferdinand?

Some of the game's greatest talent-spotters, such as Terry Venables, Sir Matt Busby, Sir Bobby Robson and Jimmy Murphy, have all argued that Edwards could have played in the 1966 England side at centre-back ahead of Bobby Moore, or in attack ahead of Roger Hunt. This is the greatest England side of all time, packed full of players who had glorious careers, yet it is said by people of impeccable football pedigree that Edwards could have conceivably taken any of their places had he lived. Is there any player today who could play for England all over the pitch ahead of the current incumbent? In fact, is there any player in the world at the moment that would be able to do this? In my opinion, there is not.

Duncan Edwards had a unique combination of physicality, pace, bravery, intelligence and immense skill. Most top footballers have a lot of these attributes, but few possess all of them. Even if they do, they rarely excel in most of these areas, as Edwards did. Such a melting pot of talent saw Sir Matt Busby say that he was a 'one-man team', while Bill Foulkes described him as 'the perfect player'. I cannot think of one player from my lifetime that has ticked all of these boxes so emphatically. Duncan Edwards' gift truly was a rare one.

Rarer still is to have all of these attributes and still remain level-headed and grounded. Most geniuses seem to have a dark side to their character, which usually manifests itself off the pitch, as seen with Diego Maradona, George Best and Paul Gascoigne. Though Edwards died at an early age, there were certainly no signs that he would ever have developed such a problem. In fact, the only addiction he did have was towards football and his fiancée Molly. There seemed to be nothing in his make-up that would have allowed him to self-destruct.

He was of course just 21 years of age when he died. It is usually between the ages of 18 and 21 that most young footballers get themselves into a spot of trouble, but Edwards had a clean slate. There were no tales of dogging, roasting, falling out of nightclubs, fighting or arguments with his team-mates or manager. Of course, times were different then, the media interest not as fierce as it is today, but even if it were it appears that it is very unlikely that they would have been able to dig up any dirt on Edwards.

Hearing all of this talk about Edwards may make many think that we are talking about a saint. That is not the case. I have shown how Edwards did not think twice about going over the top of the ball in a game against Bolton where he crocked his cousin Dennis Stevens. On the football pitch sometimes his passion boiled over and this resulted in many football fans up and down the country choosing to heckle him every time he touched the ball. If he were playing today, there is little doubt that he would need to rein in this side of his game or he could become the player the opposition crowd love to hate and to whom the referee shows a card on a regular basis.

But during the 1950s these sorts of challenges were commonplace. Though the referee may have given the culprit a talking-to, it usually had to be a horrific tackle for the player to receive their marching orders. Would Edwards have been able to keep his enthusiasm in check if he were playing today? We will never know. Perhaps he would have been the equivalent of Wayne Rooney, who despite numerous brushes with the authorities for some of his on-field conduct has not been able to entirely mend his ways. Maybe the football chatrooms and phone-in radio shows would be full of debate regarding why Duncan Edwards can't control himself on the pitch. Some would suggest that if we did take away this part of his game, he would not be half the player that he is, while others would want his body dragged across hot coals.

Indeed, there is also evidence that if a top Italian club had sought his services, he may have been tempted by the pursuit of money rather than striving for glory with the club he supported. No doubt the supporters of today would have a field day, calling him a 'mercenary', 'greedy' and a 'money grabber'. However, this was of course during the era when a footballer could earn no more than £17 a week, so we should not judge him too harshly for perhaps considering a transfer that could have set him up for life. These days, most

Premier League footballers could comfortably retire on what they earn; Edwards would not have had such a luxury if he had lived and stayed at Manchester United.

Despite these minor issues, off the football pitch you will not find anyone who has a bad word to say about him. It has been over 50 years since he perished, yet not one single story has emerged that has suggested that there were any skeletons in the closet or that he upset anybody in any way. According to everyone I spoke to, Duncan Edwards was just a simple boy who loved his family and loved his football.

When I consider all of these factors, and take on board the valued opinions of the likes of Sir Bobby Charlton, Sir Matt Busby, Sir Tom Finney, Sir Bobby Robson, Don Revie, Jimmy Murphy and Terry Venables, then I have to admit that my godfather was right: Duncan Edwards truly was the greatest footballer who ever lived.

Will we ever see his like again? It is doubtful. But at least for a brief moment in time we were lucky to have him as one of our own: an English lionheart who was the terror of the continent, who earned the love and respect of everyone who had the privilege to see him in action and who above all was a thoroughly decent hero of whom we can be proud.

Rest in peace 'Big Dunc'. Your feats will echo in eternity.

CAREER STATISTICS

Manchester United

	Lge	Gls	FAC	Gls	Eur	Gls	Tot	Gls
1952–53	1	–	–	–	–	–	1	–
1953–54	24	–	1	–	–	–	25	–
1954–55	33	6	3	–	–	–	36	6
1955–56	33	3	–	–	–	–	33	3
1956–57	34	5	6	1	7	–	47	6
1957–58	26	6	2	–	5	–	33	6
Totals	151	20	12	1	12	–	175	21

Edwards also appeared in the Charity Shield games of October 1956 and October 1957.

Edwards made his senior United debut on 4 April 1953 against Cardiff City at Old Trafford; United lost the game 4-1.

In his 177 games for United, Edwards played 157 times at left-half (No 6), 15 times at inside-left (No 10), 4 times at centre-forward (No 9) and once at inside-right (No 8).

England Schoolboy Under-15 Internationals

	Apps	Goals
1949–50	1*	–
1950–51	4*	–
1951–52	4	–
Total	9	–

*One match in 1949–50, one in 1950–51 was as an Under-14 team
as Northern Ireland's school leaving age had not been raised at the time.

England Under-23 Internationals

	Apps	Goals
1953–54	1	–
1954–55	2	3
1955–56	1	–
1956–57	2	2
Total	6	5

England B Internationals

	Apps	Goals
1953–54	2	–
1954–55	1	–
1955–56	1	–
Total	4	–

England Internationals

	Apps	Goals
1954–55	4	–
1955–56	5	1
1956–57	6	3
1957–58	3	1
Total	18	5

List of England Internationals

Date	Opposition	Venue	Result	Position	Goals
2/4/1955	Scotland	Wembley	7-2	Left-half	
15/5/1955	France	Paris	0-1	Left-half	
18/5/1955	Spain	Madrid	1-1	Left-half	
22/5/1955	Portugal	Oporto	1-3	Left-half	
14/4/1956	Scotland	Hampden Park	1-1	Left-half	
9/5/1956	Brazil	Wembley	4-2	Left-half	
16/5/1956	Sweden	Stockholm	0-0	Left-half	
20/5/1956	Finland	Helsinki	5-1	Left-half	
26/5/1656	W Germany	Berlin	3-1	Left-half	One
6/10/1956	N Ireland	Belfast	1-1	Left-half	
5/12/1956	Denmark	Molineux	5-2	Inside-left	Two
6/4/1957	Scotland	Wembley	2-1	Left-half	One
8/5/1957	Rep of Ireland	Wembley	5-1	Left-half	
15/5/1957	Denmark	Copenhagen	4-1	Left-half	
19/5/1957	Rep of Ireland	Dalymount Park	1-1	Left-half	
19/10/1957	Wales	Ninian Park	4-0	Left-half	
6/11/1957	N Ireland	Wembley	2-3	Left-half	One
27/11/1957	France	Wembley	4-0	Left-half	

ACKNOWLEDGEMENTS

Researching and writing a book such as this is always a considerable challenge. Without plenty of support along the way, the process could have been a lot harder. There are therefore many people who I must thank from the bottom of my heart for giving me their help without expecting anything in return.

Firstly, as with all of my books, this wouldn't have been possible without the encouragement of my mother and father as well as my brother Alex. I really couldn't have done it without you!

A writer's life can be a lonely one at times, so I am very grateful to my girlfriend, Charlotte Watkins, aunt and uncle Anita and Roy Kenny, cousin Neil Wilkie and godfather Barry Hobson for always being there to give me a smile, kind word or a kick up the backside when I needed it most.

Reading through several drafts is always a chore, but it was made much easier thanks to Julia Macleur, a paragon of patience, who put up with all of my printing requests with a smile. Thanks, Jules. You're a star!

Something everyone looks for at an early age is a teacher who gives them support and inspiration. I was lucky to have such a teacher in Mr Roy Hopwood. There is no doubt that without his help I would not have set out to become a writer and, disastrously, this would have meant that I would not be able to watch hundreds of hours of football all in the name of 'research', something which doesn't bear thinking about.

This book would have been a lot poorer without the contribution of Wilf McGuinness, Harry Gregg, Kenny Morgans, Don Howe, Dave and Pat Sharrock, Richard Foulser and Patricia Bradley. Whether it was happily offering to speak to me on the phone or inviting me into their homes, they have all been incredibly generous with their time and have provided me with a real insight into Duncan Edwards, the footballer as well as the man. I hope that I have done their friend and team-mate justice.

Every writer needs a good agent, and I am lucky to have one in Darley Anderson. As a lifelong United fan, he showed a real interest in my manuscript right from the start, and has provided me with support and great advice. Without his help then it is unlikely that this book would be in the shops today.

At Simon & Schuster I am very grateful to Ian Chapman and Rhea Halford for their enthusiasm for this book as well as for all of their help. It has been a pleasure working with a team who love football as much as I do.

Finally, I must give an enormous amount of credit to my editor, Ian Marshall, who not only helped to add some of his polish to my rough manuscript, but his incredible knowledge of all things connected to Manchester United has really added value to this book. Thanks also to the various publishers who have given permission to quote from their books.

It's certainly been a fun, exhausting, challenging, emotional experience, but I got there in the end. I hope you all enjoy the final result.

James Leighton
Cardiff, November 2011

BIBLIOGRAPHY

While I have undertaken numerous interviews and have consulted many websites in the process of researching this book the following is a list of publications that helped to provide me with some excellent background information:

A Strange Kind of Glory, Sir Matt Busby and Manchester United, Eamon Dunphy (Aurum Press, 2007)

Best and Edwards, Football, Fame and Oblivion, Gordon Burn (Faber and Faber, 2006)

Bill Foulkes, United in Triumph and Tragedy, Bill Foulkes with Ivan Ponting (Know the Score, 2008)

The Black Country, Edward Chitham (Amberley Publishing, 1972)

The Boy Wonders, Wayne Rooney, Duncan Edwards and the Changing Face of Football, Colin Malam (Highdown, 2006)

Charles Buchan's Football Monthly, Manchester United Gift Book (Malavan Media, 2007)

The Day a Team Died, The Classic Eye-Witness Account of Munich 1958, Frank Taylor OBE (Souvenir Press, 1983)

Duncan Edwards, A Biography, Iain McCartney and Roy Cavanagh (Temple Nostalgia, 1998)

Duncan Edwards, The Full Report, Iain McCartney (Britespot Publishing Solutions, 2001)

Duncan Edwards, Derek Dougan, Hugh Jamieson and Frank Taylor OBE (The Duncan Edwards Sport Medicine Centre Appeal, 1988)

The Football Man, People and Passions in Soccer, Arthur Hopcraft (Collins, 1958)

Harry's Game, The Autobiography, Harry Gregg (Mainstream, 2002)

The Lost Babes, Manchester United and the Forgotten Victims of Munich, Jeff Connor (Harper Sport, 2006)

Manchester United Man and Babe, by Wilf McGuinness (Know the Score, 2008)

Manchester United Ruined my Life, Colin Shindler (Headline Book Publishing, 1998)

Manchester United, The Biography, Jim White (Sphere, 2008)

Matt Busby, Soccer at The Top, Matt Busby (Weidenfeld and Nicholson, 1973)

My Manchester United Years, The Autobiography, Sir Bobby Charlton (Headline Publishing Group, 2007)

Old Trafford, 100 Years at the Home of Manchester United, The Official Story, Ian Marshall (Simon & Schuster, 2010)

Pitch Invasion, Adidas, Puma and the Making of Modern Sport, Barbara Smit (Penguin Books, 2007)

The Restless Generation, How Rock Music Changed the Face of 1950s Britain, Pete Frame (Rogan House, 2007)

Right Back to the Beginning, The Autobiography, Jimmy Armfield (Headline Book Publishing, 2004)

Soccer in the Fifties, Geoffrey Green (Ian Allan, 1974)

Tackle Soccer This Way, Duncan Edwards (New Kelmscott Press, 1958/2009)

The Team That Wouldn't Die, The Story of the Busby Babes, John Roberts (Aurum Press, 2008)

INDEX

References to cities and countries are to football teams